WITC
& WAR

EFFECTS OF THE EVIL EYE

From Frontispiece to a book by Christian Frommand
in 1674

WITCHES
& WARLOCKS

PHILIP W. SERGEANT

INTRODUCTION BY ARTHUR MACHEN

SENATE

Witches and Warlocks

First published in 1936 by Hutchinson & Company (Publishers) Ltd, London.

This edition first published in 1996 by Senate, an imprint of Random House UK Ltd, Random House, 20 Vauxhall Bridge Road, London SW1V 2SA

Copyright © Philip W. Sergeant 1936

All rights reserved. This publication may not be reproduced, stored in a retrieval system or transmitted, in any form or by any means, electronic, mechanical, photocopying or otherwise, without the prior written permission of the publishers.

ISBN 1 85958 484 5

Printed and bound in Guernsey by The Guernsey Press Co. Ltd

INTRODUCTION

By Arthur Machen

A FEW weeks ago, some serious and responsible personage writing to the paper about delusions past and present, dwelt with especial fervour on the witchcraft prosecutions of the Seventeenth Century. He was horrified at the iniquity of such proceedings, at the wickedness of executing these poor women for crimes which, as he said, they could not possibly have committed.

He meant, I take it, that there was no such thing as witchcraft, that there never had been such a thing, that in the nature of things there never could be any such thing. He meant that when the Seventeenth Century accused people of witchcraft it might just as well have accused them of breeding Wyverns and Gorgons.

Very well. But I would remark, in the frequent phrase of an old Yorkshire friend of mine : " A don't know about that."

Let me go again to the newspaper, and to the issue of this very day of writing. Here I read :

" A nerve specialist told a representative of the *Daily Telegraph* yesterday that an unusual number of people were going to him for treatment, and there was a big demand for tonics. . . .

" ' My experience is ' (said the doctor) ' that busy people do not need tonics. They are demanded by people with a good deal of leisure, and no satisfactory way of filling it. I have told some of my patients that a visit to a cinema would probably do them more good than a bottle of medicine.' "

One can imagine the symptoms of the sort of patient that the consulting physician had in mind. They are very distinctly physical. The sufferer feels that his joints have turned to a weak jelly. His head is heavy, as if a weight rested on it. It aches a little. There is a lack of appetite, a general and a most depressing *malaise*, a sense of utter unfitness. So the unfortunate individual consults Harley Street, in the expectation of being given certain vegetable or mineral substances—quinine, perhaps, or iron, or strychnine—which will remove these distressing physical symptoms, and make him as fit as a fiddle.

And the doctor says : "Go to the pictures." Or, in other words : "There's nothing really the matter with your joints, or your head, or your stomach. The trouble is in your mind. Apply a mental remedy and your physical ailments will disappear."

The mind, that is, has dominion over the body. But the essence of this alleged offence of witchcraft is that certain persons were said to have the power of exercising, and did exercise, an injurious and sometimes fatal mental dominion over the bodies of others. And I suppose there are still parts of Africa where at this very moment black Ngamba and Nbamba are being told by the witch that their days are numbered. Whereupon, the said Ngamba and Nbamba know that doom is upon them and—it may safely be prophesied—will soon be dead. And it is not necessary to go so far as Africa. I was talking a week or two ago to a Portuguese friend. He was telling me about the methods of witchcraft in his country. One of these, he said, was the concoction of certain foul matters made slab and thick with pitch. A portion of this abomination was placed at night on the doorstep of the person attacked by the witch, as a sign that he was " overlooked." And quite recently, my friend proceeded, a wealthy business man of Lisbon, setting forth for his office in the morning, saw the black horror on the step before him as he opened the door. I think the poor man was stout and middle-aged ; but he leapt into the air, as if he contended for the High Jump at the Olympic Games. The story went no farther ; but it seems to me probable that this Lisbon merchant had little appetite for lunch that day, and that his dinner disagreed with him. And, for all I know, the consequences of this mental shock may have had yet more serious results.

But I have a better instance than this. The story was
told me about forty years ago by a friend of mine, a solicitor,
a sober man and no dabbler in occult things. The scene
is laid in Drury Lane, between the corn-dealer's and the
chemist's. In those days, it must be remembered, the horse
was still abroad, and I daresay that there were many
stables poked away among the purlieus and dark passages
about the Lane. By consequence, there was a corn-dealer,
who set out his various stores in small bins before his
shop window. And the small and villainous boys of
Drury Lane delighted to rush past this good man's shop,
howling derisively and grabbing handfuls of grain from
the bins as they dashed by. The corn merchant was vexed
and irritated by these outrages. He set an ambush and
caught one of the young ruffians. He threatened the boy
with a terrible punishment, and forthwith dragged him
to the chemist's shop, which, I think I remember as being
at the entrance of Broad Court, leading into Bow Street.
Here, holding the criminal tightly the while, he whispered
a few words in the ear of his friend the chemist. He gave
the boy, already white with terror, an awful glance and
went busily to work—or seemed to go to work—with his
dreadful Latin bottles on the shelves. Holding a vessel
inscribed with unknown characters in his hand, he
appeared to the lad to measure terror and destruction
into it. He went into the hidden place at the back of the
shop and glass was heard clinking. Then he emerged
with his hieroglyphic vessel filled with a clear, colourless
fluid, and held it to the boy's lips, with the words :
" Drink that you young scoundrel, and you'll remember it
to the last day of your life."
The boy staggered away to his home, more dead than
alive already. The next morning his foaming mother,
accompanied by an officer from Bow Street Police Station,
appeared at the chemist's shop. She charged the chemist
with having administered to her son a dose so vile and
so virulent that he had all but died in the night. She
described the symptoms, which were, indeed, severe. For
a detailed account of them, read in *Don Quixote* of the state
of Sancho Panza, after he had partaken of the Balsam of
Fierabras.

The chemist summoned his young man, and between them they were able to convince the constable that the wretched boy had drunk pure distilled water and nothing else. But it is difficult to distinguish this matter of threat and event from many cases of witchcraft, ancient and modern.

But my last example is, perhaps, the strangest of all. The account of it appeared fifty years ago or more in a textbook of medical psychology, and has often been quoted.

A lady was sitting in her garden on a fine summer morning, watching her little girl playing at the open drawing-room window, inside the room. The child—five or six years old, if I remember—presently stopped her play, and leaned forward to speak to her mother, one of her small hands resting on the sill of the window. At that moment, there was the crack of a breaking cord, and to her horror, the mother saw the heavy window frame flash down like the guillotine blade on her child's hand. She fainted forthwith. In the turmoil of the house that followed, the child was found crying but unharmed. She had been quicker than the descending window, and had drawn back her hand in time. Her mother was still insensible, and the doctor was summoned. He soon brought the patient back to consciousness, and she told him the story of the shock she had suffered. She complained that the fingers of one of her hands were painful. The doctor examined the hand and found the fingers red and swollen. In due course the skin broke, and in the exact though unpleasant language of the surgeon : " purulent sloughing set in." In common English : the poor woman's fingers became dreadful sores, reproducing in her (physically) untouched, uninjured member what would have been the state of her child's hand—if the little girl had allowed the heavy window to fall on it.

Of course, I might urge in addition the phenomenon of the stigmata, which a few years ago was regarded as perhaps a mere lie, perhaps a swindling trick, but most certainly nòt as a plain fact in the natural order. Now the stigmata are accepted by all men of science ; as Mr. Gerald Heard said recently, we know that the mind can raise blisters on the body. Still, it has perhaps not yet filtered down into the general consciousness that a passing thought, the emotion of a moment, can do as much harm, and the same sort of harm to the physical human frame as a coal-hammer or the kitchen poker. And let us note this : in theory, at all events, this stroke of thought or emotion must be capable of almost any degree of intensification. It would not have been incredible, or even improbable, if the story of the young guttersnipe of Drury Lane had ended with his agonising death. And supposing that it had been the head, and not the fingers of the little girl that had been under the falling window : would the mother have escaped so lightly? Probably not. The emotion or thought, " my child's hand is terribly hurt " produced in the mother a hand that was terribly hurt. The emotion or thought, " my child is killed " would, it seems probable, have stricken the mother with death.

So far, we are on solid ground. Given certain circumstances, a certain degree of belief, and a certain sensitive habit, it is clear that mind can alter body, as Mr. Heard puts it. Sometimes the result of this mental process may be a mere blister, sometimes, it seems likely, it may be death. And there are cases amongst those recorded by Mr. Sergeant wherein the witch has intimated by a threatening word or look her potent displeasure to the person who presently finds himself bewitched. In such cases as these, the necessary condition or circumstance is the general belief, shared by learned and ignorant, of the malefic powers of the witch. In the Seventeenth Century, Mr. Sergeant's chief hunting ground, the belief in witchcraft was firm and general. If a woman, whom you held to be a witch, intimated to you that you were under her displeasure and would suffer for it, the high probability was that you did suffer. The Drury Lane boy knew very well that terrible doses sometimes came out of the learned jars and bottles of the chemist at the corner of Broad Court. The lady in the garden knew that a heavy window falling on her child's hand would hurt it most grievously : in all of these cases, old and new, you have that necessary substratum or ground of belief.

So much is firmly established : now we enter on more

dubious ground. The next question is : can one person communicate a thought, an emotion, a message, or an image to another, without the use of the ordinary physical means of communication ? We are agreed, I take it, that the curse, the threat, the scowl, the menacing gesture of the reputed witch would, probably, result in unpleasant consequences for the person cursed, denounced, or menaced ; these consequences ranging from a bad toothache down to death. But could the witch produce the like results without making use of any of the sensible channels of communication ? And, put in other words, that question is : are we to regard the theory of telepathy as established ? To the best of my belief, that question is to be answered in the affirmative. The matter is too ample and intricate to be argued here, but I do think that there is a large body of solid evidence in favour of the existence of telepathy—the faculty of communicating impressions from one mind to another without using the medium of the senses.

And if that proposition is granted, then the whole ground of witchcraft is accepted. We must be prepared to affirm that it is entirely possible for one human being grievously to afflict the mind and body of another human being by the telepathic transmission of mental impressions. And that is witchcraft.

So much for the theory. Here comes Mr. Sergeant with his account of the practice.

AUTHOR'S PREFACE

THIS, it need hardly be said, is not an attempt to write a history of Witchcraft. How many volumes would be required for that, I should not care to guess. Edmund Gurney, in his note upon the subject in *Phantasms of the Living*, admitted to having searched about two hundred and sixty books on it, chiefly of the Sixteenth to Eighteenth Centuries, in addition to the records of witchcraft-trials ; and his end in view was not to write a history, but to look for material for one chapter concerning the evidence as to the alleged phenomena of magic. What amount of reading, then, would be necessary before essaying a history of the whole matter ?

So this is no history. I merely try to glance at some aspects of sorcery, mainly in England, in order to arrive at an idea of what " witches " actually did, what they were supposed to do, and what—the clearest part of the affair— they suffered for it.

A great number of terms will be found scattered throughout the literature of witchcraft, vaguely synonymous with the word witch, but bearing slightly different shades of meaning. It is almost impossible to observe a distinction between them all ; and perhaps the task would not be worth attempting, since there never has been agreement upon the point in the past, and there is no likelihood of it to-day. Some of the terms can be restricted to a particular connotation ; others must be left wide and indefinite.

" Witch " in itself is useful as the general name of the kind of person whom it is desired to describe, without reference necessarily to sex. In Old English, it is true, there were separate forms of the word, masculine and feminine. The latter survived, with a change of spelling, from the original *wicce*, we are told ; but it did not remain entirely feminine, since we read of he-witches (or man-witches) and she-witches. Mainly nowadays people think of witches as women ; but, on the other hand, a witch-doctor commonly implies a man.

" Wizard " is said to be the adjective wise, with the contemptuous termination in -ard, and if so, has no relation with the word witch, though so often used as its masculine counterpart. I have preferred, in the title of this book, to use rather the word " warlock," precisely because of the tinge of contempt in " wizard." " Warlock " is a name that commands respect of a kind, and is essentially masculine, though this might not be inferred from its accepted first meaning of " liar against the truth," or " breaker of oaths." In the Middle English speech, according to Murray, it was applied especially to the Devil, as the arch-liar. It came, largely in Scots, but also in North-country English, to convey the less terrific meaning of sorcerer. It is, at any rate, an imposing word, only applicable to imposing people. In one of the Towneley Mystery Plays Pharao calls Moses " yond warlow with his wand." Faust was a true warlock. So too were, among those who particularly figure in this book, Dr. Dee in a mild, and Edward Kelly in a sinister, sense.

" Conjurer " is a term which has had the odd fate of losing all evil significance, so as to convey now no more than one who practices only the kind of magic that requires inverted commas. It is a Maskelyne word. Once it implied the conjuring-up of spirits by whose aid wonders, seldom with good intent, might be wrought.

" Necromancer " should be limited to the original meaning of one who divines through the agency of the dead, conveniently raised for the purpose of answering questions. This was one of Kelly's pretensions, forbidden to him in his association with Dr. Dee. Necromancy is no necessary part of the equipment of a " sorcerer," or " magician," whose titles need no definition beyond that of practisers of sorcery or magic.

Roughly speaking, I use " witch " as the inclusive name of those who claim or are asserted to be able to bewitch, and " warlock " as the name of the male super-witch.

PHILIP W. SERGEANT

London, 1936.

CONTENTS

LIST OF ILLUSTRATIONS

PART I

CONCERNING WITCHCRAFT

CHAPTER I

FANCY AND FACT

BOSWELL once, in 1772, challenged Dr. Johnson to say what witches " properly meant." " Why, sir," answered Johnson, " they properly mean those who make use of the aid of evil spirits." There was no doubt, suggested Boswell, a general report and belief of their having existed. Not only that, was Johnson's reply, " but you have many voluntary solemn confessions." The Doctor, his biographer notes, did not affirm anything upon a subject which it was the fashion of the times to laugh at as a matter of absurd credulity, but seemed willing as a candid enquirer after truth, however strange and inexplicable, to show that he understood what might be urged for it.

A year later, at Boswell's house in Edinburgh, Johnson was induced to express an opinion on witchcraft that certainly has interest, though we may have the temerity to ask whether he was not, for once, misinterpreting facts, or rather taking for a fact what was not really a fact. The subject being raised at the supper-table, the advocate Crosbie had stated his view that it was the greatest blasphemy to suppose that evil spirits could counteract God and, for instance, raise storms destructive to life. Whether there had been any allusion to the witches of North Berwick in 1590[1] does not appear. It is evident that the judicial punishment of witches had been mentioned, for Johnson bade Crosbie consider that wise and great men had condemned witches to die. But an Act of Parliament put an end to witchcraft, retorted the advocate ; ready no doubt to cite (if he had not already cited) *9 Geo. II*, whereby in future people were only to be prosecuted for " pretending " to exercise witchcraft, in place of the savage

[1] See pp. 258 *ff.*

penalties of *1 Jas. I*, not repealed till then. Johnson
spoke : " No, sir, witchcraft had ceased ; and therefore
an Act of Parliament was passed to prevent persecution of
what was not witchcraft. Why it ceased," he continued,
" we cannot tell, as we cannot tell the reason of many
other things."

Elsewhere, in his *Observations on Macbeth*, Johnson, re-
marking that the frequency of witchcraft was in proportion
to the gross darkness of ignorance, explained that the
Reformation failed to drive it out at once because " the
Reformation did not immediately arrive at its meridian,
and, though the day was gradually increasing upon us,
the goblins of witchcraft still continued to hover in the
twilight."

So apparently we seem justified in assuming as the
Johnsonian view of the matter : (1) that there was reason
for supposing that witchcraft had existed ; and (2) that
by 1736 it had ceased to exist.

The fashion of the times, as Boswell says, was to laugh
at the idea of witchcraft as absurd. There were, however,
still in the Age of Reason, people who clung to the full
belief of their ancestors as to the existence and origin of
witchcraft. There was, for instance, John Wesley, who
would not give up " to all the Deists in Great Britain " its
actuality until he gave up the credit of all history, sacred
and profane, and could state in his *Journal :* " At the
present time I have not only as strong but stronger proofs
of this from eye- and ear-witnesses than I have of murder ;
so that I cannot rationally doubt of one any more than of
the other."

It was not, therefore, only among the unlearned that a
strong belief in the active intervention of devils in human
affairs, typified by witchcraft, continued to exercise its
influence well into the Eighteenth Century. John Wesley
was perhaps an extreme case. He credited the story of the
Sunderland ghost ; and Johnson did not regard him as a
very " stationary man."[1] But he was not an isolated
example of the clinging to old beliefs among the educated
classes, of those who would not have rejected Sir Edward
Coke's definition of a witch, two centuries earlier, as " a

[1] See my *Historic British Ghosts* (Hutchinson & Co., 1936), pp. 43-6.

person who hath conference with the Devil, to take
counsel with him or to do some act."

Granting, however, that there was a great change in the
Eighteenth Century in the attitude of most educated people
towards witchcraft, we cannot find that what " ceased "
was the thing itself, but its supposed source of inspiration.
It was not witchcraft that died, but the Devil. To bring the
latter in now is to embrace a lost cause ; though a few—
? out of devilment—persist in the embracing. We have no
need for the hypothesis.

That does not involve, of course, the disuse of the adjective diabolical, as conveying the extremity of evil. Witchcraft may be stript of its Devil ; but does it still remain as
supremely evil ?

The division has been suggested in the Preface between
what witches actually did and what they were supposed
to do. (The use of the past tense, by the way, must not
be taken as presuming anything as to the continuance,
or the reverse, of the phenomenon.) Now it is plainly
much easier to say what witches were supposed to do than
what they did. Their craft was based on something
concealed from the public eye ; " a crime," said one of
their great persecutors, Henri Boguet, in 1590, " usually
committed at night, and always secretly." Outsiders
were not admitted to the ceremonies, though witch-parents
might take their children to them. There was proselytism,
but it was cautious, the stories of constant urgings to
join notwithstanding. Such stories (which we shall hear
later, especially in the chapter on Salem) are indeed difficult to believe. They seem contrary to the spirit of an
underground organisation, and throw doubt on the theory
of its reality in the particular instances.

But, if we leave aside for the present what the witches
did, it is not difficult to say what they were credited with
doing, and it may be said briefly. They began by making
a compact with the Devil or some agent of his. They
renounced Christianity, and bound themselves to worship
the Devil instead, giving him their " souls." They
received a physical mark from him on some part of the
body, and also a familiar spirit, with whom they might
communicate for the exercise of the new power given

them, *i.e.* to work evil. They were admitted to a society,
usually called a "coven," which was part of a larger
circle. This larger circle had periodical Sabbats (a word
constantly appearing also as Sabbaths), and these were
orgies of blasphemy and license.

There were many other touches in the legend, not
universal, but very common ; such as the signing of the
name of the neophyte in a book, often in his or her own
blood, and a new baptism. Sometimes a new name was
given, and the frequency of an *alias* among the witches may
possibly be connected with this. Among the common
charges was that of partaking at the Sabbat of a mock-
eucharist, administered by the Devil or his minister. In
the orgies was included the act of physical connection with
the Devil, in the form of an *incubus* where she-witches were
concerned, or of a *succubus* where he-witches ; the she-
witches far outnumbering the others.

As to the powers received, they included the gift of
being able to kill or to blast human beings, animals, and
crops, to raise storms, to ride through the air, to foretell
the future, etc.,[1] down to mere trivialities. The great
textbook of the Inquisition, *Malleus Maleficarum,* "The
Hammer of the Witches," devoted much space to the way
in which the evildoers prevented natural generation and
produced impotence ; but it also expatiated on love-
philtres.

Mostly the powers were intended, as has been said, for
the working of harm. But there was also an occasional
case where it was charged that the witch, though obtaining

[1] Apuleius, near the beginning of the *Metamorphosis*, gives a concise
summary of a witch's capacity for evil. When Aristomenes remon-
strates with Socrates for abandoning his wife and home for a *scortum
scorteum,* Meroe the innkeeper (an elderly woman but trim enough,
Socrates protests), he is told to hold his peace lest his unchecked
tongue bring harm upon him. "What do you say ? " enquires the
astonished Aristomenes, " this potent being, this queen among land-
ladies, what manner of a woman is it ? " "A witch," replies Socrates,
"and a godlike, who has the power to bring down Heaven, hang up
the earth, to harden fountains and melt mountains, to call up the
dead, undermine the gods, put out the stars, and cast light on the
depths of Hell ! "

Apuleius, writing in the Second Century A.D., presents a picture
untouched by Christianity, yet not so different from later ideas.

the power from a diabolical source, might work good. It was a matter of contention whether the gift was not equally damnable if the magic was " white," not " black " ; as to an opinion on which the reader may be referred to page 112.[1]

We may take as illustrations of the distinction between black and white witchcraft two stories, both drawn from the Seventeenth Century.

The first is the case of Mary, wife of Henry Smith, a glover of King's Lynn, Norfolk, who was hanged for witchcraft on January 12th, 1616.[2] It was alleged against her that the origin of her fall was this, that she, " possessed with a wrathfull indignation against some of her neighbours, in regard that they made gaine of their buying and selling cheese, which shee (using the same trade) could not doe, or they better than she did, oftentimes cursed them and became incensed with unruly passions, armed with a settled resolution to effect some mischievous projects and designes against them." When she was in this state of mind, the Devil appeared to her one day, " in the shape of a black man," and she made a compact with him.

We shall very frequently hear of a similar beginning of a witch's career ; as also of the succeeding step in it. A next-door neighbour, John Orkton, a sailor, struck her son, whereupon she cursed him and ultimately caused his death. She was accused further of wicked practices against two women and a man, though they did not die therefrom. She was condemned, " and all these, her grievous offences . . . she confessed openly at the place of execution, in the audience of a multitude of people gathered together (as is usual at such times) to be beholders of her

---

[1] I may add here that Boguet, in his *Discours des Sorciers*, expresses his opinion that witches heal only through the power of Satan. Among other proofs of the truth of this, he gives the fact that without a belief that the witch will cure the patient does not recover. He quotes the physician, Auger Ferrier (whose best known work was on a subject remote from witchcraft, *De Lue Hispanica sive Morbo Gallico*, Paris, 1564) as saying : " If it so happen that the sufferer has no faith in the sorcerer, but considers the remedy absurd . . . the sorcerer will accomplish nothing, for there is a spirit present hostile to that of which he is persuaded."

[2] The case is in *State Trials*, II, p. 1049, being derived from a " curious tract " of 1616, by Alexander Roberts, B.D., of King's Lynn.

death ; and made there also profession of her faith and hope of a better life hereafter."

The other story is of a man unnamed, somewhere in Yorkshire in 1653, and comes from John Webster's *Supposed Displaying of Witchcraft* (London, 1677).

This man, apprehended for suspicion of witchcraft, was shown to have effected cures by means of a white powder, which he said he had received from the fairies, and, by his cures, from former extreme poverty to have acquired sufficient means to maintain himself, his wife, and several small children. The judge at his trial asked him how he had come by his powder, when he told the following tale, though we abbreviate it.

One night as he was going home from work, very sad at not knowing how to get meat and drink for his family, he met a fair woman in fine clothes, who asked him why he was so sad. When he told her the reason, she said that if he followed her counsel she would help him to that which would get him a good living. He would consent with all his heart, he replied, if it were not by unlawful ways. She assured him it should not be by such ways, but by doing good and curing sick people. He was to be again at the same spot next night.

Accordingly they met again the next night, when she led him to a little hill. She knocked three times, the hill opened, and they passed in to a fair hall, where was a Queen sitting, with many people about her. The man was presented to the Queen, who bade him welcome, and told his introducer to give him some of the white powder and teach him how to use it. So a little box was given him, full of white powder, of which he was to administer two or three grains to any that were sick, when it would heal them. With his powder he was led by his guide out of the hill.

Was the hall within the hill light or dark ? asked the judge.—Indifferent, as it is with us in the twilight.

How did he get more powder ?—When he wanted it he went to the hill and knocked three times, saying every time, " I am coming, I am coming." Thereon the hill opened, and the woman he had first met conducted him to the Queen, and he was given more powder.

" This," concludes Webster, " was the plain and simple
story (however it may be judged of) that he told before the
judge, the whole court, and the jury, and, there being no
proof but what cures he had done to very many, the jury
did acquit him."

He offered to show any gentleman present the hill,
though we do not hear that the offer was accepted. It is
a pity.

The second story has not the same authentication as the
first ; but we have no reason to suspect that Webster either
invented it or accepted a mere fairy-tale as a record of
statements actually made. The point is that the accused
man used a certain powder to effect cures, said that he had
it from folk who were obviously fairies, and was acquitted.
It may be argued that his tale of how he procured the
powder was not believed. But he was, on his own confession,
a trafficker in magic ; and we shall hear later of the
refusal to make any difference in favour of white as opposed
to black witches.

Lest it should be thought that the difference in date
between 1616 and 1653 accounts for the superior humanity
and common sense shown in the second trial, it may be
pointed out that an era of particularly fierce witch-persecution had set in with the Commonwealth, as will be seen
when we come to the Essex witches. So far from there
being a spread of enlightenment with the Puritans, James I,
for all his hatred of witches, was a very mild opponent
to them when compared with the rulers of the Commonwealth.[1] The Yorkshire white witch of 1653 was lucky in
his judge and jury.

The introduction of the fairies into this second tale is
very interesting ; but we need not delay over that here.
The subject is discussed later.

We have stated, very shortly, what it was supposed that
witches did, and it is natural to go on to ask how people
arrived at the idea of their doings. No one since Dr.
Johnson's time has been able to suggest a better ground for

[1] " The popular ideas of the holocausts of witches in the reign of
James I are anything but historically exact, and, instead of shuddering
at the large numbers who perished, we may well be surprised that the
executions in England were so few." (Rev. Montague Summers,
The Geography of Witchcraft, p. 132.)

the belief than the " many voluntary solemn confessions "
of the witches themselves. Nor, indeed, in the periods of
great witch-persecutions, whether in this country or in any
other, was anyone ever able to produce other evidence that
carries conviction—except in the law of the day.

Reginald Scot, in his *Discoverie of Witchcraft* in 1584,
asked, with reference to the charges against prisoners of
compacts with the Devil : " What credible witness is
there brought at any time of this their corporal, visible,
and incredible bargain ; saving the confession of some
person diseased both in body and mind, wilfully made or
injuriously constrained ? "

" Injuriously constrained "—that is the point. Obviously
confessions so obtained are not voluntary, though they
may be solemn. Miss Margaret Murray, in her *Witch-Cult
in Western Europe*, minimises the extent of the use of torture
to extract confessions from witches, and would put down
the general uniformity of the confessions not to the code of
questions they were forced to answer, but to the fact that
what they confessed were real occurrences. We are
reluctant to differ from so diligent a student of the subject.
Nevertheless, we are compelled by a reading of the records,
or at least of a very large number of them, to say that to us the
term " voluntary confession " does not at all exclude the
employment of torture. The subject will often arise later,
so that it need not be dwelt upon now. It suffices perhaps
to state that we do not limit the word torture to the rack
and similar gross forms of physical maltreatment. Matthew
Hopkins had his methods as well as the Inquisitors ; and
Scot's " injurious constraint " is a good enough expression
to cover both. We would dare venture the opinion that
there were *no voluntary confessions*, except in the cases of
frightened children, or of older persons stricken with
disease—or " penitence."

Still all this, we admit, does not preclude the possibility of
the confessions being of real occurrences, and so, where
credible, we cannot disregard them.

Can we then deduce from their confessions what the
witches actually did ? Perhaps we may say that, accepting
the genuineness of these, we can arrive at an idea of what
they thought they did. But, in spite of the general uni-

A WITCH

From a Seventeenth Century Manuscript

GILLES DE LAVAL, SEIGNEUR DE RAIS

formity that has been commented on by so many writers, with all kinds of varying attitudes of mind towards witchcraft, we cannot pretend that a common creed of the craft is ascertainable. It must be a very slender chain of links that binds together the " common witch " and the avowed " Satanist," who may be taken as the opposite poles in the world of sorcery.

The common witch, of whom so many examples occur in later chapters, is usually an old woman, who, by curses and charms, thinks that she influences in some small degree the forces of nature. She tries to heal or harm, generally to harm, and in certain cases to destroy. She enjoys her prestige, and the fear she inspires. Beyond that, it is difficult to accept that she has *consciously* the notion of a religion different from that of her neighbours. She blasphemes, but not in honour of Satan, nor of any particular old god.

At the other end of the chain we get men like Francis Stewart Hepburn, fifth Earl of Bothwell, or the French Gilles de Laval, Seigneur de Rais, to whom the proceedings of the common witch are trumpery. We may call them Satanists ; but that does not take us much further. And, among women, there is Dame Alice Kyteler ; whose mental development, however, would not seem to have been greater than that of the more dangerous varieties of common witch. But we have, we must remember, only the ecclesiastical version of her case. That is true, too, of Gilles de Rais, the civil evidence being subsidiary ; and those who look upon him as merely a particularly horrible type of " Bluebeard," may be advised to read the extremely able book of Dr. Ludovico Hernandez, *Le Procès Inquisitorial de Gilles de Rais* (Paris, 1921), where the rehabilitation of one who was in many ways a great man is attempted with a considerable measure of success.

The plebeian witch had as instruments of her craft (since it is generally *her*) words, looks, and touches, supplemented by the use of herbs. Boguet is instructive on the subject of the words, looks, and touches. He mentions the testimony of Johann Nider, the Fifteenth-Century Dominican, that he saw[1] a witch who by a single word caused

---

[1] Nider did not say he saw the actual performances of the witches.

people to die suddenly, and another who similarly turned
her neighbour's chin upside down ; and he also speaks of
Françoise Secretain, a witch with whom he came much in
contact, who would strike beasts with her wand, saying :
" I touch thee to kill ! "   As to looks, he believes little
children particularly susceptible to the evil effects of these ;
but he does not agree with the Inquisitor Sprenger that
witches' glances can corrupt their judges. Justice, he says,
coming direct from God, cannot be confounded, and he
had proved in his own person that a judge is immune.

In any case, whether it be of words, looks, or touches, he
will not have that they accomplish the witch's object.
It is always Satan's power that does that, while they are
merely the symbols of the witch's compact with Satan.
It is impossible that God should have endowed man with
such deadly power.

Of the witch as herbalist there is much that might be
said.   But, roughly, it is only necessary to distinguish
between the use of herbs as poison and as magic-workers.
The demonstrable administration of poisonous herbs is
very rare.   In the case of human beings, the passing of a
compound from hand to hand is seldom alleged, except
perhaps of love-philtres.   In the case of animals, " dying
by witchcraft," it is always to be suspected.   Even then
the administration is rarely stated to have been seen.
When it is, one may wonder why there was not immediate
intervention on the part of the owner, followed by summary
retaliation.

The raising of winds, either for the bringing of rain or
for more sinister ends, is another attribute that witches
did not deny.   Rain-bringing might be a purely benevolent
function, a fertility-rite for the good of the crops.   Where
something more is sought, the witch is a worker of evil.
It is noticeable that sudden storms, whirlwinds, were
popularly connected with magic almost everywhere.   In
County Cork, a correspondent[1] wrote the other day, the
name for a whirlwind is still *shiggeea*, that is *sidhe-gaoithe*,
the fairies' wind ; and in Germany there is the *fahrendes
Weib*, the roving lady—who is a witch or an ancient goddess
—and there was, in the long past, *Frau Holde* or *Hulde*,

[1] Miss or Mrs. K. M. Buck, in *The Observer*. I have lost the date.

perhaps Freya in the aspect of the goddess of whirlwinds. (The witches' journey to the Sabbat was known as *Hollen-fahrt*, *Holla* being another form of this name.) A sudden storm seeming unnatural, a magic explanation was put forward ; and the witches did not discourage the belief. At North Berwick, as will be seen, there was a coincidence between incantations and an actual storm.

The foretelling of the future is a branch of witchcraft that is of unmeasurable antiquity, and as a subject demanding volumes to itself defies compression. Almost every witch known to history has claimed the power, though their methods have differed, from those of the Witch of Endor to the modern clairvoyant's in Blank Street. The augurs of Rome, it was said, could not pass one another in the street without a smile ; but fortune-tellers are often very serious, especially the amateurs among them. They may not see the joke, and in truth it is not a good one. It was a worse when Satan was reputed to be your principal.

So far it is not difficult to follow the proceedings of witches. But when we come to the question of an esoteric doctrine underlying the common magical practices the difficulty is immense. It is not scientific to take the whole body of the confessions and build a theory out of them, though this is a plan that has been adopted by the majority of writers, however they may differ in their theories. On the other hand, how are we to differentiate between what we can accept and what we cannot ?

The great test of witchcraft is the question of the Sabbat and of the ceremonies performed at it. Without this the gravamen of the charges against witches is not very heavy ; and the persecutors recognised this by constantly trying to extort admissions from prisoners that they had attended one or more of these meetings. Of course, there were numberless trials involving no mention of it. There were so many other grounds on which condemnation could be secured. Murder, attempt to murder, injury to health of man or beast, damage to property were sufficient. Even general repute of being a witch was nearly good enough to warrant some punishment. But for the gallows there was one sure road save in very exceptional circumstances.

We come then to the Sabbat, the grand gathering of witches on a day fixed beforehand.[1] We may take a summary of the proceedings from Boguet, based on his own examination of a great number of accused persons, as well as on the researches of his predecessors in prosecution.

The proceedings, after the arrival of the witches at the appointed spot, began with what Boguet calls the worship of Satan, who appeared sometimes as a big black man, sometimes as a goat. (This goat-shape is not English, but is particularly common in France.) Candles were offered to him, which when lighted gave a blue flame. Then came the ceremony of the kiss given by the worshippers, of a shameful and degrading character in the case of the majority, though some, the higher witches presumably, kissed on the shoulder. It is inferred by some, though not by Boguet, that the other kiss was bestowed upon a mask or false head worn *a tergo* by the representative of the " Devil."

Dancing followed, usually in a ring, but back to back, so that the dancers might not be recognised, Boguet explains, and in his time masks were worn. Demons in the shape of goats or rams would join in. Sometimes there was dancing in couples, always in great confusion, the dances being those of the fairies, " who bore rule not so long while ago." Most often Satan played the flute for them, but otherwise the witches sang, at haphazard, so that one could not hear another.

After the dancing came promiscuous sexual license, on which we may take Boguet's account as read, beyond noting that the Devil took a full share in it ; and then the feast, of which there were very varying stories. It is different according to locality and the rank of the witches. There might be nothing but water to drink (a feature not

---

[1] Boguet says that he was once of the opinion that the Sabbat was held only on Thursday nights, because all the witches he examined reported so. But later reading showed him that the night might be Monday, Wednesday, Friday, or Sunday, witches going as commanded by Satan. One woman confessed that she had been to the Sabbat at each of the great Christian festivals for seven years, the last two occasions being on Christmas and Easter Eves. " So," says Boguet, " does the Evil One hold his assemblies on holy days, and seduce God's creatures from His Service."

found in the few English descriptions), and some witches complained of cold food ; one that it was " nothing but wind." On the whole, Boguet learnt that all were agreed that the dishes at the Sabbat were tasteless, that the meat was horseflesh, and most that they left the table as hungry as when they sat down. One strict rule was that there must be no salt. Halomaniacs, who cannot taste the natural savour of food and would inflict their salt upon others, will no doubt sympathise with Boguet's saltless witches ; but the rule is strange.

The feast ended, the witches rendered account to Satan of what they had done since the last meeting, those who had caused most death and destruction gaining the most applause, while those who had done little evil were derided, and might even be chastised by Satan himself. At the end he made all repeat their renunciation of the Christian faith and renew their oath of allegiance to himself, and he urged on them to do all the harm they could, in particular to avenge themselves on their enemies—" or ye shall die ! "

" Sometimes " adds Boguet, " they celebrate Mass at the Sabbat, but I cannot without horror describe the manner in which this is done." He then proceeds to describe how a black host is administered and a disgusting liquid used for *asperges*. Finally, " Satan takes on a goat's shape and consumes away in fire, burning to ashes, which are gathered up and kept for use in the hateful and abominable projects of the witches."

Now of all this what is there to be said ? It presents the conventional picture of the " Witches' Sabbath," and it is confirmed by confessional evidence from other countries than those from which Boguet drew his account ; confirmed, that is to say, one detail here, another there, until there is nothing lacking support. So far, therefore, as we admit the evidence, we must accept the general picture. We can only take exception to the colouring given to the picture, which makes it (1) blasphemous, or anti-Christian ; and (2) obscene.

The alleged blasphemy is explicable if we consider that the examinations of the accused took place in Christian countries, were conducted by means of Christian questionings, and were interpreted by Christian commentators. Thus there was the tendency, or rather the desire, to represent witchcraft as a by-product of Christianity, a perversion of it, with a god who, since he was not the Christian God, must be God's enemy, *alias* the Devil. It could on no account be allowed that the deity worshipped by the witches was an older one, having nothing whatever to do with Christianity. The witches themselves, under examination, lent support to their examiners. Brought up in Christian surroundings they adopted the prevailing religion's terminology in common speech ; and it is not to be supposed that they would reveal, save occasionally in extremity of torture, their own sacred names and terms. Some real " Satanism " doubtless had crept in, but it was not a genuine part of the witch-faith.

As to the obscene element in the Sabbat, that is not to be glossed over lightly. But there are two points to be considered. Firstly, the persecuting religion habitually charges the rites of that which it desires to suppress with obscenity. What was alleged against the early Christians in the times of Tiberius, Nero, and other emperors ? Secondly, the conduct of many of the accused was not that of adherents of an obscene cult. Pierre de l'Ancre, a fierce persecutor, in his *Tableau de l'Inconstance des mauvais Anges* (Paris, 1613), tells of one Marie de la Ralde, a very beautiful girl of eighteen, who " deposed that she had a singular pleasure in going to the Sabbat, so that when summoned to one she went as to a wedding ; not so much for the liberty and license with which one must acquaint oneself (though through modesty she said she had neither ever practised it nor seen it practised), but because the Devil held so strongly bound their hearts and their wills that scarcely any other desire could enter." The expression " the Devil " is perhaps due to De l'Ancre himself,[1] or it may have been merely accepted by the accused, who is also represented as saying that " the Devil made them believe that he was the true god, and that the joy that the

[1] Miss Murray issues a warning against renderings of terms in prisoners' evidence ; as when Joan of Arc at her trial spoke of " the King of Heaven " and was made to say " our Lord " (*The Witch-Cult in Western Europe*, p. 271 n.).

witches took in the Sabbat was but the beginning of a much greater glory."

Another girl, aged nineteen, said that the Sabbat was the true Paradise, and that those who went to it found the time at it so short that they could not come away without a wonderful regret, so that it seemed infinitely long until they returned to it. This is hardly the language of an abandoned sensualist.

De l'Ancre expresses astonishment at the joy of witches in " false martyrdom," which no torture could lessen. " You would say that they were going to true martyrdom and to death for love of him [the Devil], as gaily as though they went to a festival of pleasure and of public rejoicing. . . . In their prison they are impatient of nothing so much as that they cannot testify to him how much they suffer and desire to suffer for him."

It is a common feature, as will be seen, for witches to die without contrition, but glorying in their faith. The executioners might look on the attitude in a different light ; as when two women at Northampton, in 1705, " being desired to say their prayers, set up a loud laughter, calling on the Devil to come and help them, in such a blasphemous manner as is not fit to mention . . . and as they lived the Devil's true factors so they resolutely died in his service."

This may not show that the Sabbat, the witches' festival, had not in it the element of the worship of Priapus, god of fertility, to which Richard Payne Knight would reduce witchcraft.' But it shows that there was much more. Who turns martyr for an organ ?

Still, if the priapic element be granted, it certainly excuses or explains the extreme bitterness of the Church against witchcraft, and the monotonous insistence upon the carnal side of the religion. The Inquisitors devoted what might seem a disproportionate part of their attention to it ; but they had, as it seemed to them, a double problem with which to deal. There was the promiscuous incontinence among men and women ; there was also the *concubitus contra naturam cum creatura spirituali*, the unnatural connection with a spiritual being. The Inquisitors had warrant for severity in the Bull *Summis desiderantes affectibus*, of Pope Innocent VIII, in the first year of his pontificate,

1484, which made special mention of "intercourse with demons, *Incubi* and *Succubi*." On this matter the celebrated *Malleus Maleficarum*, five years later than the Bull, certainly did not fail to carry out His Holiness's wishes. Heinrich Krämer and Jacob Sprenger, the two Dominicans who were entrusted with the chief task of inquisition into the evil and of its punishment, put their souls into it and left the *Malleus* as a monument to their rage against the witches, and a treasure for all future workers in the field to draw upon. On this book were based almost all the examinations of witches conducted under Roman Catholicism, and its influence upon the Reformed prosecutors and persecutors is also tremendous. As against witchcraft there was a common front.

A problem that exercised the mind of the authors of the *Malleus* was whether procreation might result from the intercourse of men and women with spirits or demons, and, though they held not, they nevertheless treated the inter-course as the enormity of enormities. A chapter was devoted to the method. The comforting conclusion was reached that *Procreare hominem est actus vivi corporis, sed dæmones sumptis corporibus non dant vitam;* that there could be no procreation.

The connection was alleged to take place not only at the Sabbat, but at individual meetings between the witch and the Devil. Particularly do we find in the later witchcraft cases these individual acts made a prominent charge. It requires the pen of an Inquisitor to write upon the subject; and, that lacking, there is a bar of reticence which creates difficulty. However, it may be said that witches, including elderly women and some most unattractive old hags, could be induced to confess to relations with their devils, spirits, or whatever they might call them, on numerous occasions, and with the Devil himself at the Sabbat.

On this, Henry More, in his *Antidote Against Atheism*, asserts that, "witches confessing so frequently as they do that the Devil lies with them, and withal complaining of his tedious and offensive coldness, it is a shrewd presumption that he doth lie with them indeed, and that it is not a mere dream." But what was easy for Henry More to presume in 1655 is now not a matter of presumption.

The modern theory seems to be that the individual acts were performed with a man in the usual way, though he might be disguised as an animal, or merely masked, when described as in animal form ; and that the " Devil " at the Sabbat was its leader, who performed the act symbolically and artificially—hence the " offensive coldness " which is mentioned time after time in the confessions.

Miss Murray remarks that the witches never admitted in so many words that the Devil of the Sabbats was a man disguised, though their evidence points strongly to the fact. And, as to the reported appearances in animal form, she suggests that any masking was entirely ritual, not intended as a disguise. In their own estimation, and in the belief of fellow-witches, to whom they communicated the change, the witches *became* animals, though to the uninitiated eye they remained unchanged.

If we could get into the mind of the African negro, and his witch-doctor in his mask, etc., we might perhaps discover something analogous to this. But probably we should still not have worked far enough back, being in search of Primitive Man ; and not only is the African not primitive man, but Sir James Frazer[1] seems to think that not even the Australian native is truly primitive, representing indeed a comparatively advanced type in man's development. The primitive survives even in the most advanced man, but it cannot so be stirred up as to be analysed ; and as we cannot analyse it in ourselves we are without a clue whereby to analyse it in others.

A very difficult point in the records of witches' confessions is that they are so often made to confuse their " familiars " with the Devil, in many cases calling them " my devil " ;

[1] Perhaps the name of Sir James Frazer might suggest that there was originally something in witchcraft connected with what he calls the " conceptional theory " of totemism, observed by him among the Central Australian aborigines ; the theory that the physical contact of man and woman is not the cause of procreation, which is due to impregnation by a totem. In the fertility-rite the object is procreation, the so-called " Devil " of the Sabbat representing a spirit. Now the totem is a spirit, though it may be in the *shape* of an animal, a plant, or some natural object.

But obviously if there was anything of totemism in original witchcraft it was so overlaid as to be buried out of sight.

and as the familiar is sometimes an animal, sometimes a being in human form, the confusion may be quite baffling. With all due deference to Miss Murray, it cannot be said that in almost every case the disguised man can be distinguished from the animal-familiar.

Let us take the case—though she does not cite it as one where it is easy to distinguish—of John Winnick, a male witch at Huntingdon in 1646. He had lost a purse containing money, when there appeared to him " a spirit, black and shaggy, and having paws like a bear, but in bulk not fully as big as a coney." This spirit enquired about his trouble, and when told of the loss, said that if he would renounce God and Christ and worship it he should have his purse back. Winnick did as required, and next day found his purse. The bear-spirit, as he now calls it, then brought two other spirits, one like a white cat, the other like a grey coney, which he agreed to worship also, calling them his lords and gods, and allowed to suck his blood.

This story is connected with the Essex witch-persecutions, and is not a separate fable. As she includes it in a section headed " The Domestic Familiar " (*Witch-Cult*, p. 216), Miss Murray would seem to regard the coney-bear as such. But its behaviour is that of a disguised man. In any case, however, we can only regard Winnick as raving. Huntingdon must have had a peculiar atmosphere, for a woman there at the same time had two mice that sucked her blood and persuaded her to take them for her gods.

A puzzle in connection with domestic familiars is why they should have been peculiarly English. They were so, commonly under the name of " imps," and very often in connection with witch-marks, which they were supposed to suck. Bishop Francis Hutchinson wrote in 1718 : " I meet with little mention of *Imps* in any country but ours, where the Law makes the feeding, suckling, or rewarding them to be Felony."

It may be that the keeping of animal pets was more a habit in England than in other countries ; but it can hardly be said that this was productive of " humaner " treatment of the animals, except by their owners. When

it was a case of a witch's pet, the tale is often horrible. One
instance will suffice. We have heard of Mary Smith, the
King's Lynn witch, in 1616. She had a "great cat" that
unfortunately had the habit of frequenting the house of
one of the women she was accused of bewitching ; and
the woman's husband, upon the cat " doing some scathe,"
ran it twice through with his sword. It escaped, but he
found it again and hit it over the head with a pikestaff,
still failing to kill it. Putting it, therefore, still living, into
a sack, he laid it under the stairs, intending to remove it
the next morning. But when he went to look the cat was
no longer there ; nor was it ever seen again.

The neighbours were probably convinced that the cat
was supernatural. It is, however, quite possible that the
ruffian had left enough life in it for it to escape away to die
unseen.

The cat and the dog are the usual forms of the animal
familiar ; but often it is a mouse or a toad, occasionally it is a rat, a mole, a ferret, a "coney," a bird,
or something so described that it is impossible
to identify. Whatever it was, its association with a
witch was ominous for both. The witches themselves,
by their reported confessions, encouraged the belief that
there was something uncanny in the relationship. In
some of the earlier English trials the accused admitted
to pricking herself, in the hand as a rule, to give drops of
blood to mix with her pet's food. Later, this developed
into allowing the animal to suck blood, and any abnormal
mark upon the witch's body was taken to be the place of
the suckling. Thus these marks were regarded as a twofold
proof of guilt. They were given to the witch by the
Devil ; and they were the "teats" for the animal
familiar.

The subject will often crop up again. The evidence
concerning it is grotesque and unpleasant. But its importance lies in what it *seems* to show about the witch's belief
in the more than natural character of her favourite animal,
quite other than some modern spinisters' all-but-idolatry
of a pet dog. The mingling of any real " religion " in the
relationship between man and animal may seem strangely
remote. Two stories, however, given in J. Ceredig Evans's

Welsh Folklore bring the idea down as far as the early Nineteenth Century.

Two old women of Llanddewi Brefi, states the first, went to Communion and kept the consecrated bread in their mouths until after the service. On leaving the church they walked round it nine times, whereon the Evil One came out of the church-wall in the shape of a frog, to which they gave the bread.

The other story was told by an old man in North Pembrokeshire, who said that at his first Communion he had put the bread in his pocket, giving it to a dog that met him after leaving church, and thus obtaining the power of a witch.

In both stories the act of bestowing the bread was interpreted as a symbol of the selling of the soul to the Devil. It may be compared with what the boy James Device was asked by his grandmother to do in Lancashire over two hundred years earlier.[1]

The familiars in these two Welsh instances were not " living in," any more than James Device's hare. Mostly the animal familiar was kept in the witch's home, sleeping in some household vessel and regularly fed. It is easily explained as a real animal if we leave the preternatural attributes out of account. But when we come to the other sort of familiar, in devil's or man's shape, the affair is different. This does not live in, but comes upon summons, by name or incantation. Though we have said in devil's or man's shape, it very often appears as an animal, mostly as a dog ; but it is of human speech and acts as a man, though called variously a devil, demon, spirit, fiend, and in one set of stories " puckrel."

As to how the familiar came to the witch originally, the witch's tale varies from its having been a gift from the Devil, obtained by magic, or, in the case of animals, given by another witch or left as a bequest.

The metamorphoses of the familiar are another complication. The Scottish witch Jonet Watson, for instance, at Dalkeith in 1661, confessed to having met the Devil first as a pretty boy, in green clothes. But he departed from her as a black dog ; and later, as she was changing her

[1] See p. 72.

" schirt," a great bee settled upon her naked shoulder and left there the mark that was found upon her. She became the Devil's servant, and afterwards was at a meeting at Newtowndene, where he had green clothes upon him and a black hat, and bestowed on her the name of " weill-dancing Jonet."

The witches were not reticent about their going to meetings, and some of them gave information as to the means of getting thither that is truly astonishing. One of the most talkative of Scottish witches was Isobel Gowdie, of Aldearne,[1] who in 1662 gave the following account, in which we change the spelling somewhat from the record :

" I had a little horse, and would say, ' Horse and hattock, in the Devil's name ! ' and then we would fly where we would, even as straws would fly upon a highway. We will fly like straws when we please. Wild-straws and corn-straws will be horses to us, and we put them betwixt our feet and say ' Horse and hattock, in the Devil's name ! ' When we would ride we take windle-straws or bean-stalks and put them betwixt our feet, and say thrice :

> ' Horse and hattock, horse and go
> Horse and pellatis,[2] ho ! ho ! '

and immediately we fly wherever we would."

The Council of Aquileia had denounced as heresy the opinion that witches were miraculously conveyed through the air as they claimed. But Boguet could not agree with the Council's ruling, being fully convinced to the contrary, " both because of the authority of those who have upheld this view, and by reason of the confession of nearly all

[1] Isobel Gowdie appears as a great romancer, whether by nature or distraught under the torture to which she was subjected. It was she who described the ploughing-ceremony near Kinloss, when " paddokis did draw the plewgh as oxen . . . and we all of the Coven went up and downe with the plewghe, prayeing to the Divell for the fruit of that land."

Still, she may have been describing an actual magic ceremony with toads yoked to a miniature plough. The " Divell" was present, and held the plough, while the officer of the coven of witches drew it.

[2] I can find no other explanation of " pellatis " than a sheep-skin without its wool. A Fifteenth Century Scottish poem speaks of " plucking the pellotis or even the scheip be slaine." Is the sheep-skin used as a saddle ? Commonly witches ride bareback.

witches that they have been conveyed to the Sabbat." He goes on to say that " there have even been cases of persons who were not witches, but who, following the example and at the instigation of witches, rubbed themselves with a certain ointment, and of farmers who were carried as much as a hundred or two hundred leagues from their homes, so that they had great difficulty in finding their way back again."

Boguet quotes from some of the witches' confessions received by himself, showing such varying means of transport as a white staff, a broomstick, a black horse, a black goat, a black man, or the Devil himself like a great wind.

A curious point has been raised lately by Mr. Arnold H. Kamiat, in an article in *The Psycho-analytic Review* (January, 1936). The article is entitled " Male Masochism and Culture," and, dealing with the "impulsion in the male toward the derivation of erotic pleasure from the domination, actual or fancied, of the feminine over the masculine," touches on the subject of riding-witches, though he does not use that term.₁ " The Icelandic female Maras, or nightmare-spirits," he says, " deserve mention here. The folk-tale of Vanland, who is done to death by one of them, carries an appeal to the masochist. Dreams with a similar content must have been common among Norse masochists, for Gray and MacCulloch's *Mythology of All Races* speaks of an ecclesiastical law prescribing a fine or outlawry for the woman proved guilty of being a Mara and riding a man or his servants. This law was in a class with the Norse statute imposing a fine of three marks on any troll-woman convicted of riding a man or his servants."

The Mara is clearly a sort of witch. But the charge seldom if ever comes up in British witchcraft of turning a man into a steed. Miss Murray does not quote any instance in her section on " Locomotion to the Sabbat " in *Witch-Cult in Western Europe*. There are cases of women being said to act as the steed, including the remarkable one of Ann Armstrong in Northumberland in 1673, who accused other women of having ridden her, putting upon her head an enchanted bridle, which changed her into the likeness of a horse until it was removed, when she stood up in her own

proper person. One of the women " rides her in the name
of the Devill." Isabell Shirie, of Forfar in 1661, on the
other hand, was alleged to have asserted that she was the
Devil's horse, that the Devil did always ride upon her, and
that she was shod like a mare or a horse.

Nevertheless, as Miss Murray remarks, " the method of
locomotion which has most impressed the popular imagination and has become proverbial was riding on a stick,
generally a broomstick." We shall see this in the Salem
chapter.

When we find witches claiming the power of preternatural locomotion, we very often too hear of a magic
ointment for anointing the body before the flight—
which may be made without any steed or such substitute
as a stick. Various formulas appear for the compounding
of the ointment, an ingredient in some being the fat of
infants, either slain for the purpose or resurrected from the
grave. Common ingredients are the deadly poisons
aconite and belladonna ; and Professor A. J. Clark, who
contributes an appendix on flying-ointments to *Witch-Cult
in Western Europe*, calls the employment of aconite interesting. He cannot say whether it might produce the impression of flying ; but " irregular action of the heart in
a person falling asleep produces the well-known sensation
of suddenly falling through space, and it seems quite
possible that the combination of a delirifacient like belladonna with a drug producing irregular action of the heart
might produce the sensation of flying."

This suggestion has some importance in instances of a
witch confessing to having made a journey to the Sabbat,
when it could be proved by trustworthy witnesses that she
was lying in her bed all the time.

Despite Boguet's dissent, it would seem that the Council
of Aquileia was wise as well as prudent in declaring it
heretical to hold that witches could fly through the air ;
since all that has remained for argument is how they
should have come to think they could.

One more question would be worth discussion, if there
were hope of getting a satisfactory answer to it, and that
is to what extent the witches considered themselves to be
connected with the fairies ; but the evidence is scanty,

and in England at least there seems to have been considerable reluctance in bringing the name of the fairies into court. The Yorkshire trial referred to above is exceptional. In Scotland there was not the same apparent shrinking from the subject. The Fairy Folk, the Court and Queen of Elfame (Elfin), the Good Neighbours, occur from time to time in the records of trials. It is the prisoner, not the prosecution that introduces the name, however. In a comparatively late case, at Inverary in 1677, the accusation against a man was " the horrid crime of corresponding with the Devil." The evidence, which only the accused was qualified to give, was to the effect that he had entered a fairy-hill, meeting with many men and women there, and playing on a " trump " (jews' harp) to them when they danced.

Where fairies are mentioned it is commonly in connection with a hill in which they dwell, and into which a visitor can be introduced. A person may be taken away by them and perhaps disappear for ever ; a woman may return with child by one of them. To witches they seem to be friendly people, with " piping and merriness and good cheer " ; but their gifts are vain, their money for instance turning into horse-muck within twenty-four hours, and those who disobey them will get little good of them. Those who listened to them, however, could gain from them, knowledge as to life and death.

The witch was not exempt from the dread of the folk who were called the Good Neighbours on the principle on which the Greeks spoke of the Erinnyes, the Furies, as the *Eumenides*, the Kindly Ones ; and how great this dread was can be gauged to some extent by the slowness with which it has died in the race-soul ; still surviving, indeed, low-down it may be, but there nevertheless.

Some two years ago the author (whose name can be guessed) of an article on " The Fair Folk " in *The Independent* recalled the excavation in Ireland of a fairy rath, known as such by perpetual tradition, when were found a deep place hollowed out in the earth, where the little dark people had lived, and a shaft, once communicating with the hilltop above, which confirmed the country people's story of those who imprudently ventured near

KNIGHT VISITING A FAIRY HOUSE

From illustration to a book by Olaus Magnus in 1558

THE POWERS OF EVIL

From an engraving by Coeck, after the painting by Brueghel

the place at night and saw flames leaping from the summit
of the fairy fort.

" Are we to conclude," asks this writer, " that the genuine
fairy tradition is a tradition of the dark, pre-Celtic people,
who lived under the hills ? Largely, perhaps ; but I
believe that there is something more. A party of tourists,
who climbed Mount Nephin in county Mayo, about
June 20th, 1929, were strangely misled and bewildered
by ' small persons ' who looked like children—but were
not children."

* * * * *

The cult of the Witches, as well as their " magic "
powers, has plausibly been explained as taught to them by
the race now only perpetuated under the name of the
Good and the Fair Folk—because they were reputed
bad and were certainly dark—or more shortly the Fairies.
Whether the witches, or some of them, had fairy blood in
them is arguable. The suggestion has seriously been
put forward in the case of Gilles de Rais, and there is
nothing inherently improbable about it, provided that we
grant that there was such a thing as fairy blood. The
witches commonly handed down their witchery from
parent, nearly always the mother, to offspring, and therefore, given the original start in a physical legacy, we have
a complete theory of the reason for the survival of witchcraft. The only thing missing is that we know nothing
about the Fairies.

CHAPTER II

THE SHORT WAY WITH WITCHES

THREE books mainly determined the course of procedure to be adopted when those accused of witchcraft were brought up for examination and trial; the *Malleus Maleficarum*, by Heinrich Krämer and Jacob Sprenger in 1489; *De la Démonomanie des Sorciers*, by Jean Bodin in 1580; and the *Discours des Sorciers*, by Henri Boguet in 1590.

To the *Malleus* reference has been made in the preceding chapter, where its tremendous influence on witch-prosecutions was noted.

Bodin was that dangerous combination, a lawyer-theologian. Studying law at Toulouse, he was an unknown man when at the age of forty he came to Paris in 1560; but he soon made a name as a writer on legal matters. It was the burning of a confessed witch at Ribemond eighteen years later that particularly drew his attention to the subject of sorcery and induced him to compile *De la Démonomanie*. The book was a success, ran through several editions, and was translated into a number of languages. The Church did not regard it as quite sound, in spite of its considerable debt to the *Malleus*; but it succeeded in establishing itself as an authority on the habits and the proper treatment of witches.

It is the third book, however, that we choose rather to take as the most suitable guide to the manner of dealing with the unfortunates who fell into the hands of the powers that were. Boguet had the advantage of coming later into the field than the authors of the *Malleus* and Bodin, and he was also a clearer and conciser writer. Born in Franche-Conté near the middle of the Sixteenth Century, after a good general education he devoted himself to the Law, and advanced rapidly till he became chief justice of the Bur-

44

gundian district of Saint-Claude, through the patronage
of the Archbishop of Besançon. He had an unquestionable
religious orthodoxy to recommend him, and, having in
the course of his duties to handle a very large number
of witch-trials, he gave full satisfaction by his procedure.
As he is said to have condemned six hundred people to be
burnt at the stake, it may be gathered that he was deemed
a strong judge. So that his experience should not be
wasted he compiled his book, of which the original
publication is supposed to have been made at Lyon in
1590.[1] This took its place very soon as the best textbook
on its subject, particularly as Boguet completed it with
a code of seventy articles, setting out the manner of a
judge's procedure in a case of witchcraft. It is true that
the *Discours* met with opposition. Copies of early editions
are rare. According to the Rev. Montague Summers, this
was due to the fact that wealthy members of Boguet's own
family bought them up and burnt them as they came out,
being suspected of being witches themselves. On the
other hand, the same accusation was brought against
Boguet himself, after his death in 1619, for the reason that
he knew so much about sorcery. The language of his
dedicatory epistle to the Archbishop of Besançon should
have preserved him from such a charge, for he fervently
expressed his wish that all witches might be " united in a
single body, so that they might all be burnt in a single
fire."

He viewed the state of Europe, and found all countries
" infested with this miserable vermin." Germany was
almost entirely busied in building fires for them ; Switzer-
land had wiped out whole villages because of them ; in
Lorraine they might be seen bound to thousands of stakes ;
Savoy had not escaped them. " We in Burgundy see that
the execution of witches is a common occurrence. . . .
And what shall we say of France ? " Britain, however, he
does not mention.

[1] The earliest edition of *Discours des Sorciers* in the British Museum
Library is the second, published at Lyon, 1608.

An English translation by E. Allen Ashwin was published in 1929,
under the title of *An Examen of Witchcraft*, edited with an introduction
by the Rev. Montague Summers. I have to some extent followed this
version.

In spite of great amount of material he was able to put into the earlier part of his book, drawn from the trials before him in the district of Saint-Claude, Boguet complains that witches never confess more than half of what they know ; though " we learn from one and the other," he admits. As to their evidence against one another, Satan makes them take a solemn oath not to give such information, a point to which judges should pay great attention. The only right course with them is the death-penalty on the slightest pretext, for they never change their manner of life. It is waste of time to show any mercy to witches.

We may now look at Boguet's code. It consists, as has been said, of seventy articles ; but not all of them call for notice.

" Witchcraft," he says, " is a crime apart, both on account of its enormity and because it was usually committed at night, and always secretly. Therefore the trial of this crime must be conducted in an extraordinary manner, and ordinary procedure cannot be strictly followed " (Article II).

A witch should always be imprisoned even on the accusation of but one accomplice ; and, as to accusation by common rumour, " this is almost infallible where witchcraft is concerned " (Article III).

At the witch's arrest search should be made for any ointment or powders, and particular notice should be taken of looks and words. When the witch is taken by surprise, much may escape that will serve as direct evidence (Article IV).

Examination should immediately follow arrest. Satan at that moment forsakes the witch, who is consequently confused, so that the truth may be more easily extracted. In prison Satan may visit and advise the witch. To the fact of this assistance all witches confess (Article VII).

The judge should ask the witch whether he [or she] has any children, and if they are dead of what they died ; for it is known that witches commonly dedicate their children to Satan, or kill them, even before or as soon as they are born (Article IX).

The witch being usually ashamed to confess his abominations in public, and being frightened by seeing his answers committed to writing, the judge should be alone with him, keeping his clerk and assessors in concealment (Article XI).

A witch should be confronted with an accusing accomplice, since nothing will so confound him as to see one who has been at the Sabbat with him (Article XII).

It is not improper to have the accused stripped and shaved, as some judges do. He may have concealed on him a charm for keeping silence (Article XIV).

The ordeals by ducking and by red-hot iron are both wrong, being condemned by the canons of the Church (Article XV).

It is lawful to search for witch-marks, since witches are usually marked ; but a very expert surgeon should be the searcher, since the marks are difficult to find (Article XVI).

Confinement in a dark and narrow cell is good in the case of an unconfessing prisoner. Hardship often compels, especially young persons, to confess (Article XVII).

As witches may corrupt their accusers, it is not advisable to lodge them near together (Article XIX).

Judges have often been known to promise impunity in return for the truth, and afterwards to condemn the accused to death. Though this seems to be approved commonly by doctors of civil law, Boguet gravely doubts its morality, and quotes the opinion of the theologians against it (Article XX).

The judge should as far as possible avoid the use of torture, for witches have charms about them that prevent them from feeling pain (Article XXII).

It is not, therefore, humanity that should limit the exploment of torture, as we may see by a number of the succeeding Articles, including XXV : " In this crime it is lawful to submit the accused to torture on a Holy Day, even if the day be sacred in honour of God." The better the day . . . !

A witch's confession is sufficient warrant for the use of torture on an accomplice if such confession is substantiated otherwise. But a voluntary confession is always of more weight than one extracted by torture (Article XXVIII).

The association of the accused with a witch is sufficient

to warrant torture, if it is substantiated by other evidence (Article XXIX).

If the accused is possessed of certain powders or oint-ments, this warrants torture (Article XXXI).

Lying and discrepancies during examination, when there is other evidence, are sufficient warrant for torture (Article XXXIII).

Torture is warranted when there is a mass of what the doctors term " light indications." These are : (1) If the accused turns his eyes to the ground, and some say if he has a frightened look ; (2) If the accused's parents were witches, considered by Bodin an infallible proof, but by Boguet only as " light " ; (3) If the accused has a mark ; (4) If the accused is prone to fall into madness and trembling rage, and to blaspheme ; (5) If, making as though to weep, the accused sheds no tears or only very few ; (6) If there is no cross on the accused's rosary, or it is otherwise defective[1] ; (7) If the accused had, when reproached in the past with being a witch, let it pass without seeking redress by law " or otherwise "—does Boguet mean violently ? ; (8) If the accused requests to be re-baptised (Articles XXXIV–XLII).

It is asked whether, when the accused has confessed under torture, he should be made to repeat his confession later, and in another place than that of the torture. Boguet thinks so, but adds that care must be taken that no accom-plice shall speak to him in the meanwhile, lest he should corrupt him, and also that he shall not be left alone, lest the Devil should come to advise him (Article XLIII).

If the confessed witch recants, torture should again be employed. The judge may order this three times, but no more. If denial is persisted in, the prisoner must be released. " But I shall always hold," says Boguet, " that one accused of witchcraft must never be unconditionally released, whatever torture he may have undergone, if there remains the slightest indication against him. For he who has once given himself to the Devil cannot easily escape from his clutches " (Articles XLIV–XLV).

[1] Boguet notes with regard to Françoise Secretain, who may be called his chief witch, that she could not shed tears though she tried, and that her rosary was defective though she was always busy with it.

If the accused cannot prove that his confession was false, the judge must proceed to pass sentence upon him, even if he afterwards commutes it (Article XLVIII).

Retractation of a confession is always suspicious, for it is known that the Devil instructs witches in prison and very often causes them to retract what they have confessed (Article LI).

Witchcraft is an exceptional crime, in which only equally guilty accomplices can furnish the proof of the accused's guilt. A man of good life never attends a Sabbat except by accident—and so cannot be admitted as a witness in the matter (Article LII).

A son may be admitted as witness against a father, a father against a son, and so on, though the Law does not otherwise allow this unless in cases of high treason (Article LIII).

Infamous and notorious characters are legal witnesses in witchcraft-cases (Article LIV).

The evidence even of children under the age of puberty must be allowed, since witches take their children to the Sabbat (Article LVI).

The usual penalty for witchcraft is burning, but there is doubt whether the condemned should be burned alive or strangled first. Boguet considers the second course the more reasonable, in order not to reduce the criminal to despair because of the harshness of his punishment. The practice, however, with regard to those who turn themselves into wolves[1] and in that shape kill people, is to burn them alive (Article LXII).

Children under the age of puberty, when they are witches, should only be punished with the lash, Bodin says ; and Binsfeld, suffragan Bishop of Treves, maintains that a child under sixteen should never have the death-penalty. But Boguet disagrees entirely, maintaining that not only a child-witch who has reached the age, but even one who has not, should be sentenced to death, if it can be proved that he has acted out of malice. He would not advocate the full penalty, but some gentler means, such as hanging.

---

[1] Boguet himself had many cases of lycanthropy to try, and condemned many to burning because of it. Lycanthropy does not come up in English witchcraft-trials, because of the absence of actual wolves.

" It is better to condemn child-witches to death than to
suffer them to live in contempt of God and to the public
danger " (Article LXIII).

If a father has compelled his young son to attend a
Sabbat and give himself to the Devil, Boguet would only
inflict the lash or banishment. But if the son continues to
go repeatedly, then he shows consent and evil intention and
should be punished with death (Articles LIV–LV).

Daughters and servants acting under their masters'
orders should be treated as sons (Article LVI).

The judge should attend the condemned witch's execution, so that he may know whether he takes back anything
he may have said concerning accomplices or accuses fresh
persons, and whether he dies penitent or not (Article
LXVIII).

A puisne judge may not grant to anyone at all a witch's
body for burial in consecrated soil. Nor does Boguet
think that the Supreme Court would ever permit this, in
view of the enormity of the crime (Article LXIX).

If a witch dies in prison before sentence, his body should
be buried in consecrated soil, even though he may have
confessed, provided that he has proved contrite and
penitent (Article LXX).

So here we have the picture of the complete judge of the
witches, the writer of what some admirer called " a book
precious as gold." Nothing is odder in Boguet's code than
the very few touches of humanity, as in Articles XV, XX,
XXII (very illusory), and, if it counts for anything,
LXX. These do little more than enhance the general
grimness of the picture.

It might be pleaded for Boguet that he had to deal with
many cases of lycanthropy—Lecky says that it was the
chief ground for his burnings—and that that crime, where
proved, deserved no more mercy than that of the *Anyoto*,
or " Leopard Men," of the Congo, with which in some few
instances there was a ghastly similarity. But Boguet did
not draw up his code solely for use in dealing with wer-
wolves. It was intended to be applied in witchcraft
trials generally, regardless of the sex or age of the accused.
Underlying all his rules is the assumption, which indeed he
makes repeatedly in the earlier part of his book, that

Satan is the worker of all sorcery. For instance, in the matter of waxen images (the "pictures" of so many English tales of sorcery) it is not the image, nor the witch who makes it, that inflicts the injury ; it is Satan himself. But this does not exonerate the witch, whom Boguet refuses to look upon as an ignorant, deluded creature. Deluded, indeed, he or she may be, but, as this is the result of a selling of the soul to Satan, "on the slightest pretext the witch should be put to death."

There is certainly unanimity between the Inquisitors of the *Malleus*, Bodin, and Boguet in this matter ; and De l'Ancre in his two books carries on the tradition. But it is Boguet who best represents the attitude of the sworn foe to all witchcraft, in deed and in word—though it was Bodin who demanded for all witches, harmful or harmless, "the most cruel death."

PART II
THE WITCH-HUNTERS

CHAPTER I

LANCASHIRE

IN the three chapters that follow, the main object will be to study the course of three great outbreaks of a campaign against witches, occurring in English territory in the Seventeenth Century : Lancashire, in 1612 ; Essex and adjoining counties, in 1645–6 ; and Massachusetts (which was then truly New England), in 1692–3. They were all celebrated manifestations of the persecuting spirit as directed against people believed or alleged to be practisers of the art of witchcraft in one form or another. We make the distinction between " believed " and " alleged," because, while the general popular belief of the period[1] was undoubtedly in the actuality of witchcraft, there were also two motives for the allegation of it, without necessarily any belief behind ; the malicious desire to do harm by accusations against disliked neighbours, and the still worse intention of making a profit out of accusations.

We will, however, proceed straight to the ascertainable facts of the three persecutions, without attempting to link them up in advance. It will be seen that there are features at once of great resemblance and of considerable difference in the three. The differences may be explained as largely due to the varying environments of Lancashire, the Eastern Counties, and Massachusetts ; Lancashire, with its painful memories of the struggle between Rome and Reform, and its wide support for the old Church, the Eastern Counties

---

[1] Indeed, as Frank Podmore says, in his chapter on Possessions and Witchcraft in *Modern Spiritualism*, belief in the continual intervention of spiritual beings (an essential part of witchcraft) underlay the whole of the popular thinking and much of the philosophy of the Middle Ages.

mainly Puritan, and Massachusetts almost entirely Calvinistic. As for the resemblances, this is a matter which pertains to the main question of what is witchcraft and what do its enemies represent it to be ; which it would be premature to discuss yet.

We take now, therefore, the " discovery " of witches in Lancashire, with special attention to a batch of trials which took place at Lancaster in August, 1612, in the tenth year of James I, royal author of the book *Dæmonologie*, wherein he so strongly exposed his view on the reality of witchcraft. The prisoners who were tried, and ten of them executed, at Lancaster were mostly drawn from the district known as the Forest of Pendle ; but there were a few others, some associated with them and some not. In spite of the remoteness of the place, in those days, the accused became famous, or infamous ; and as "the Lancashire witches," their name passed into a byword of the period and for some considerable time after. Thomas Heywood and Richard Browne produced a comedy in 1634, *The Later Lancashire Witches ;* and in 1681 Thomas Shadwell brought out his comedy *The Lancashire Witches and Tegue O Divelly the Irish Priest*. It was only the comic aspect of the affair that struck these playwrights ; the tragic side was ignored. It will be seen that there was indeed one.

The chief source of information concerning the happenings in the Forest of Pendle, then a desolate district, north of the river Calder and not far south of the Yorkshire boundary, is *The Wonderfull Discoverie of Witches in the Countie of Lancaster*, a pamphlet written by Thomas Potts and published in 1613, the year after the trials.[1]

Thomas Potts, whose origin and date of birth are unknown, was brought up under the charge of Sir Thomas Knyvet, of Escrick, and studied the Law in London, being described as of Chancery Lane. In 1612 he went as clerk on circuit with Sir Edward Bromley and Sir James

---

[1] A facsimile edition of this was published in 1926, under the title of *The Trial of the Lancaster Witches, A.D.* 1612, with a valuable introduction by G. B. Harrison.

The original dedication is to the Rt. Hon. Thomas Lord Knyvet, Baron of Escrick, " my very honourable good Lord and Master," and to his wife, Lady Elizabeth Knyvet.

Altham, Barons of the Exchequer, and was with them for
the assizes at Lancaster in August, when the chief business
was the trial of a number of persons accused of witchcraft.

After the assizes, at the request of the judges, he prepared
an account, which Bromley revised before its publication.
We have therefore the contemporary story, based on the
evidence at the trials. There is nothing to show that
Potts previously took an interest in witchcraft, and he did
not, apart from his duties as clerk, do anything to secure
the conviction of the prisoners. He was not himself a
finder or hunter of witches, but merely a recorder of the
prosecution. He is only heard of again in 1618, when he
was granted a small legal office. What claim he has to be
remembered is through his authorship of *The Wonderfull
Discoverie*. In it, despite some extraordinary spelling and
some looseness of grammar, he gives proof of good education. His religious views are decidedly Puritanical.

It is about twenty years before the trials, in 1591 or
1592, that the drama opens. A woman of sixty, by name
Elizabeth Southernes, but usually known as " Old Demdike," was then living at her home Malking[1] Tower, in
the Forest of Pendle, which Potts calls " a vaste place, fitte
for her profession." What she committed in her time, he
says, no man knows ; but she was " a generall agent for
the Devill in all these parts," and he speaks of her " barbarous and damnable practices, murders, &c." He makes
her out to have been, in 1612, a witch for fifty years. That,
of course, is merely hearsay.

By what was described as her " voluntarie confession,"
when she was arrested and examined in April, 1612, it was
about twenty years past that one day near to a stone-pit
at Gouldshey, in the Forest, she met " a Spirit or Devill in
the shape of a Boy, the one halfe of his coate black, and
the other broune," who bade her stay, and promised that
if she would give him her soul she should have anything
she might request. When she asked him his name, he said
it was Tibb. So she gave him her soul, the ceremony not
being described. Then for the space of five or six years
Tibb reappeared at sundry times, enquiring what she

---

[1] " Malking " is said to mean a hare ; and we shall meet with hare
" spirits " soon.

would have or do. Her answer was always " Nay, nothing "—for she wanted nothing yet.

After the five or six years, she continued, one Sabbath morn, as she was sitting in a slumber with a little child upon her knee, the spirit came in the shape of a brown dog and forced himself on to her knee, to get blood under her left arm. In this he succeeded, as she was only in her smock. She awoke, saying : " Jesus save my child ! " But she could not, she added, say Jesus save herself ! The brown dog vanished, after which she was almost stark mad for about the space of eight weeks.

Her daughter, it may be added, testified that Elizabeth Southernes had " a place on her left side by the space of fourty yeares."

The story is carried on by another of the accused, Anne Whittle, otherwise Chattox, who, in 1612, alleged that, about fourteen years ago (which gives us the date 1598, near that of Tibb's apparition as the brown dog), through the wicked persuasions of Elizabeth Southernes, *alias* Demdike, she agreed to " become subject unto that divelish abhominable profession of Witchcraft." Soon after the Devil appeared to her in the likeness of a man, about midnight at the said Demdike's. She was with difficulty, she asserted, persuaded to become the Devil's subject. He asked her for one part of her body to suck upon, choosing a place on her right side, near her ribs ; and to this she agreed.

Anne Whittle had more to tell. There was a thing like a spotted bitch that came with the spirit to Demdike, and told her she should have gold, silver, and worldly wealth at her will. What they had, however, by her story was flesh, butter, cheese, bread, and drink ; and they were bidden to eat enough. But, " although they did eate, they were never the fuller nor better for the same."

Two spirits were in attendance, who gave them light to see by (though they had neither fire nor candle), and cleared the remnants of the meal away. Anne Whittle is not at all clear about the sex of these. She speaks of " the Devill called Fancie and the other Spirit calling himself Tibbe," but also says that " they were both shee Spirites, and Divels."

Elizabeth Southernes and Anne Whittle, whom it may be more convenient in future to call by their soubriquets of Old Demdike and Old Chattox, were roughly the same age. Potts, in 1612, writes of the former as " a very old woman, about the age of foure score years," and of the latter as " a very old, withered, spent and decreped creature " of four score. Demdike had been blind for two years, and had to be led about by her granddaughter Alison ; Chattox was going blind.

It is obvious that the two women were at one time close friends with a bond of witchcraft between them, whatever importance we attach to the details of their " voluntarie confessions." No husbands are mentioned, and they always figure as widows ; but they had families, whoever the fathers. Old Demdike had a married daughter, Elizabeth Device, and a son, Christopher Howgate ; Old Chattox a daughter Anne, married to Thomas Redfearn. The two witches initiated their children into the secrets of their profession, Old Demdike extending her instruction to two grandchildren, James and Alison Device, while a third was too young to be initiated yet. Some neighbours of the witches were also drawn into their circle ; and we cannot get away from the conclusion that they succeeded in organising some sort of witch-society.

The friendship between the families continued until 1601, when it changed into a very different feeling, matters of witchcraft being only part-cause of the estrangement. In the neighbourhood there was a large family of the name of Nutter, of whom the principal man was Robert senior, owner of some property called Greenhead, in the Forest. The relationship of all the Nutters is impossible to trace ; but we know that old Robert had a son Christopher, and two grandsons, Robert junior and John. His wife Elizabeth bore no goodwill towards the younger Robert, and was very desirous that succession to the property should not go to him. She took the step of consulting Old Chattox as to how he might be removed. The witch was ready to do the job for her, but was dissuaded by her son-in-law, Thomas Redfearn, who was a tenant on the Nutters' land.

Young Robert, however, though a married man, made the mistake of trying to seduce Anne Redfearn in her own home, and, failing to persuade her, swore that if ever he came into the property she should never dwell upon his land. After this Thomas Redfearn no doubt withdrew his opposition to Old Chattox's intervention to help Elizabeth Nutter ; and soon after Old Demdike, passing the Redfearns' house, saw Anne and her mother making " pictures " of Christopher Nutter, Robert junior, and his wife Marie.

The description of the scene by Old Demdike of the making of the pictures (which are the same as the images, puppets or " poppets " in other witchcraft stories) is interesting. After she had passed the Redfearns' house, she said, there appeared to her the spirit Tibb, in the shape of a black cat, who bade her go back and do as the others were doing. She refused, whereon the spirit, seeming to be very angry, shoved or pushed her into a ditch, causing her to spill a kit or can, full of milk, which she was carrying. Tibb then vanished, only to reappear in the form of a hare, which accompanied her for about a quarter of a mile upon the road, without speech with her !

It is notable in these animal-metamorphosis stories the hare seldom seems to speak. Black dogs, brown dogs, speckled bitches, and here a black cat, talk ; but not usually the hares. An instance to the contrary, however, will be found on page 72.

The success of the piece of sorcery against Robert Nutter, junior, was apparently rapid, for he soon fell ill ; and he suspected the cause. His brother John, in testimony which he gave at the Lancaster trials, said that one day, as he was returning from Burnley to Pendle in the company of his father and brother, he heard Robert say : " Father, I am sure I am bewitched by Anne Chattox and her daughter Anne Redfearn. I pray you cause them to be laid in Lancaster Castle." Christopher Nutter called him a foolish lad, but Robert was not to be persuaded that his illness was not due to witchcraft. He went away from Lancashire into Wales, intending to return shortly, but died in Cheshire on his way home, about half a year, or even less, after the making of his picture. This was about eighteen or nineteen years before the trials, and the quarrel between the witches had not broken out yet. Probably

young Nutter's death caused some ill talk at the time
against Old Chattox and her daughter, but as long as the
witches held together, evidence against them was hard
to procure. Unfortunately for them, about 1601, an
affair occurred that caused a split in the society, with very
serious results for them all. Some goods of the Devices
were stolen, including a band and coif belonging to Alison,
who when she saw Anne Redfearn next Sunday wearing
them, claimed them back insistently. John Device, who
had a dread of witchcraft, in spite of his family's connection with it, not only restrained his daughter, but actually
agreed to pay blackmail to Old Chattox, in the form of
a quantity of meal each year, so long as she hurt neither
him nor his daughter. Ultimately he failed in his payments
—and then he died.

Though Potts says of Old Chattox that she was " in her
witchcraft always more ready to do mischief to men's
goods than themselves," the two cases of Robert Nutter,
junior, and John Device do not bear him out. She did
not herself claim to be a " good " witch.[1]

There was open enmity now between the Demdike and
Chattox factions, and as for the heads of them " whom
the one favoured," Potts says, " the other hated deadly."
This state of dissension led to a fatal readiness of the
witches to accuse one another when the growing talk
against them began to suggest action to stop their activities. Only the evidence, to which we are coming, can show
to what extent the hostility had developed.

The blow descended on the witches at the beginning of
April 1612, when the local justice of the peace had the blind
Elizabeth Southernes, the nearly blind Anne Whittle,
with the former's granddaughter Alison and the latter's
daughter Anne, arrested and brought before him on
charges of witchcraft, some including murder by the same.
The first of whom Roger Nowell, J.P., got hold was the
girl Alison Device, whom he examined at his house at
Read (or Reade) in the Forest of Pendle, on March 13th.
She was induced to make statements against both her
grandmother and the other old woman.

[1] See her remark about Margaret Pearson, p. 78. But there is the
story on p. 65, where she starts to do good, though she finishes with evil.

Her grandmother, she thought, had bewitched a child, which afterwards died, because the father, Richard Baldwin, would not let her come upon his land in the Forest. She had heard her curse Baldwin sundry times. With regard to Old Chattox, her story was stranger still. About six years ago, she said, Anne Redfearn had been to the house of John Nutter, of the Bull-hole, to beg a dishful of milk, which she took to her mother, who was about a field's breadth from Nutter's house. Old Chattox took the milk, put it in a can, and " did charne [*sic*] the same with two sticks across in the same field." Thereupon Nutter's son came to Chattox and, misliking her doings, put the can of milk over with his foot. The next morning a cow of the said John Nutter fell sick—and then died.

Demdike, Chattox, and Anne Redfearn were seized and examined " at the Fence in the Forrest of Pendle " at the beginning of April. Nowell had *reos confitentes et accusantes invicem*. They all made confessions, stated to be voluntary, of witchcraft, and with regard to murder freely accused each other.[1] After their examination " at the Fence in the Forrest of Pendle," they were committed to Lancaster Castle, to await the assizes in August.

The arrest of these prominent witches is alleged to have caused consternation in the witch community of Pendle Forest ; and it seems beyond a doubt that there was a meeting within a week (in fact, on Good Friday) at Malking Tower, where those interested in the practice of witchcraft took counsel how to rescue the prisoners at Lancaster. We may leave this, however, until we come to the assizes, except to mention that Elizabeth Device, daughter of one and mother of another, is said by Potts to have used her liberty to procure this " solemn meeting of the Grand Witches of the Counties of Lancaster and Yorke."

[1] Old Demdike did not deny murder herself. In her statement she said that the speediest way to take a man's life by witchcraft was to make " a picture of clay like unto the shape of the person," and to prick with thorn or pin in that part where the illness was desired, or to burn the picture when it was desired that the whole body should consume away.

Old Chattox, not accusing herself in this respect, stated that Demdike had shown her how she bewitched to death one Richard Ashton. But Demdike accused Chattox of young Nutter's murder.

Elizabeth Device was not long at liberty, for her arrest, and that of her son James, came before the end of April, Elizabeth being charged with several murders. As the result of the usual voluntary confessions, largely about others' misdeeds, and of accusations made by persons claiming to have been bewitched, the net was widened until the number caught in it rose to eighteen, who were all lodged in Lancaster Castle. This included some from outlying places who had only visited Pendle Forest, and were not residents.

Potts being the official recorder of the case against the witches, we do not hear anything about their treatment at the Castle. All we know before the trials is that Old Demdike died there, and so escaped the death by hanging that would undoubtedly have been hers. She could not even be tried ; but there was no name more prominent in the trials than hers.

Sir Edward Bromley and Sir James Altham, with Potts as their clerk, opened the Lancaster Assizes on August 17th. They had just come from the York Assizes, where they had had a witchcraft case before them, that of Jennet Preston, of Gisborne-in-Craven, who was accused of bewitching to death Thomas Lister, of Westby. As her name comes into the Pendle story we may stop to consider her case, wherein there are points of considerable interest.

Jennet Preston, it was stated, had been for many years well thought of by Master Lister, and had free access to his house, " nothing denied her she stood in need of." It would seem that she visited Lister's house, the Sowgill, in quest of charity ; for there is no suggestion of the relationship having been other than that of patron and client. Though she had a husband living, " old Preston," she was perhaps one of those wandering witches of whom Reginald Scot writes :

" These miserable wretches . . . go from house to house and from doore to doore for a pot of milke, ye[a]st, drinke, pottage, or some such releefe ; without which they could hardlie live : neither obtaining for their service and paines, nor by their art, nor yet at the divel's hands (with whome they are said to make a perfect and visible bargaine) either beautie, monie, promotion, welth, worship, pleasure, honor, knowledge, learning, or anie other benefit whatsoever."[1]

That Jennet Preston had the established reputation of a witch is shown by the fact that only so recently as the Lent Assizes at York she had been brought up on a charge of causing the death of a child of one Dodg-sonnes (as Potts writes the name) by nefarious arts. The prosecutor in that case had been Leonard Lister, son of Thomas ; though it might appear from some of the evidence at the Lancaster trials that it was Thomas himself. Anyhow, she considered that the prosecutor had borne malice unto her and had thought to have her put away. But she was acquitted.

Between the Lent and the next assizes at York old Lister died. How soon a new charge was brought against Jennet Preston is not clear. Potts writes that, " having cut off Thomas Lister Esquire, . . . she revenged herself upon his son, who in short time received great loss in his goods and cattell by her meanes." But he also records evidence at her trial which suggests that she was quickly arrested after Thomas Lister's death. Witnesses testified that on his deathbed old Lister had cried out to them that Jennet Preston was in the house. " Look where she is, take hold of her ! " he had cried ; and also " Jennet Preston lies heavy upon me, Preston's wife lies heavy upon me, help me, help me ! " With singular lack of grammar for a man of his education, Potts adds that " when brought to him laid out, to touch him, they [what ?—for we hear of no wounds] bled fresh blood presently, which has ever been held a great argument to convince a jury to hold the accused guilty."

It looks as if Jennet Preston was required to come to touch the corpse. Her trial was at York Castle on July 27th, when she was condemned to be hanged. Her execution followed speedily. She died impenitent, confessing nothing, says Potts, whence her friends and relatives claimed she died an innocent woman. But " old Preston, her husband, was fully satisfied his wife had justice and was worthy of death."

Fresh from this case at York, the worthy Barons of the

---

[1] R. Scott, *The Discoverie of Witchcraft* (1584), from which a further quotation following close upon this, occurs on p. 67.

Exchequer arrived at Lancaster Castle for a whole batch of witchcraft trials, beginning with that of Anne Whittle, *alias* Chattox, on Monday, August 17th, against whom the chief accusation was the murder of Robert Nutter, of Greenhead, in the Forest of Pendle. Of this " very old withered spent and decreped creature, her sight almost gone," Potts also says " her lips ever chattering and walking [? talking], but no man knew what." Her voluntary confession, made in gaol in May, was put in, of which we have already heard, and also some further admissions. She now stated that about fourteen or fifteen years ago " a thing like a Christian man " came to her at sundry times for four years together, and asked her to give him her soul, which in the end she did. He then said, " Thou shalt want nothing, and be revenged of whom thou list." She was told to call him Fancie, and when she summoned him he would be ready.

After young Robert Nutter's attempt on her daughter, she said, she called Fancie unto her and bade him revenge her on Nutter, with the result that in about a quarter of a year he was dead.

The deceased Demdike's story of the making of the " pictures of clay or marl " having been put in, one James Robinson testified that young Nutter, before he went to Wales, several times complained that he " had harm by them," whom he explained as being Anne Whittle and Redfearn's wife. Robinson was at the time at old Robert Nutter's house, where young Robert dwelt in the summer.

Yet another voluntary confession by Old Chattox was produced next, which had nothing to do with Nutter's death. It related, however, to her character as a witch. She was sent for, she said, by John Moore's wife to " help drink that was forspoken or bewitched." (The witch, therefore, in a benevolent aspect, undoing the harm done by another witch.) She made use of " a charme," giving the words as follows :

Three biters hast thou bitten,
  The Hart, ill Eye, ill Tonge,
Three bitter shall be thy Boote,
  Father, Sonne, and Holy Ghost
    a God's name.

Five Pater-nosters, five Avies,
  and a Creede,
In worship of five wounds of
  of our Lord.

This is obviously a distorted version of something older than the " old decreped creature " herself. But it is to be noted that it is a distinctively Christian charm, of a pre-Reformation Christianity, and therefore likely to linger in Lancashire ; though its use by a witch was not altogether to be expected.

John Moore's wife was not pleased with the charm, but " did chide her and was grieved at her," we are not told why. The witch thereupon abandoned her benevolent intention, and " called her Devill Fancie and bade her[1] go bite a brown cow of Moore's by the head." Fancie, in the likeness of a brown dog, bit the cow, which went mad and died in about six weeks.

Two witnesses called against the prisoner were her former friend's grandchildren, James and Alison Device, who on their arrests had already incriminated her. James's story was to the effect that, at a burial at the new church in Pendle twelve years ago, Chattox took three " scalpes " (i.e. skulls) of people who had been buried and then cast out of a grave. She had taken eight teeth out of the said " scalpes," whereof she kept four herself and gave four to his grandmother. On being shown four teeth found in Old Demdike's house, he identified them as the same that were given to her. We might suggest that " James Device, labourer," as he was described, was hardly an expert witness on teeth.

Alison Device, an alleged young witch herself, testified to the guilt of Old Chattox in four instances, whereby the death by witchcraft was caused of a girl, a " child," a man, and a cow respectively. The case of the girl was the most full. She was one day at Anthony Nutter's house, she said, in the company of his daughter Anne, when Old Chattox came to the house. The girls, were laughing, and Old Chattox insisted that it was at her. " Well," she remarked, " I will be meet with the one of you ! " On the next day Anne Nutter fell ill, and in three weeks she died. James Device's evidence was brought that a picture found " about a yard over in the earth," and " almost withered away," was Anne Nutter's.

[1] Note again Old Chattox's inconsistency as to the sex of the " Devill."

There is no record of any cross-examination of Old Chattox, her evidence being all in the form of confessions alleged to have been obtained from her without the use of constraint. They give the impression of coming from a rambling creature, who really believes that she has extraordinary powers. She answers well to Reginald Scot's description in his *Discoverie of Witchcraft*, published twenty-eight years before the Lancaster trials :

" The witch . . . expecting hir neighbour's mischances, and seeing things sometimes come to passe according to hir wishes, curses, and incantations, being called before a Justice, by due examination of the circumstances is driven to see hir imprecations and desires and hir neighbour's harmes and losses too concurre, and as it were to take effect : and so confesseth that she (as a goddess) hath brought such things to passe. Wherein not only she, but the accuser and also the Justice are fowlie deceived and abused ; as being through hir confessions and other circumstances persuaded (to the injurie of God's glorie) that she hath doone or can doo that which is proper onelie to God himself."

The bewitching to death of John Moore's cow also reminds us of Reginald Scot, when he tells how witches, not getting what they ask for, " wax odious " and curse " from the maister of the house, his wife, children, cattell, &c. to the little pig that lieth in the stie "—so that if some ill actually befalls it is attributed to the witch's curses.

Old Chattox's trial lasted for part of a day, and was immediately followed by that of Elizabeth Device, of whom Potts draws a most unprepossessing picture. She had from birth a left eye standing lower than the other, the one looking down, the other looking up ; which Potts calls " a preposterous marke in nature." Apart from this, she was " a barbarous and inhumane monster beyond example, so far from sensible understanding of thy own misery "— he is apostrophizing her—" as to bring thy own natural children into mischief and bondage." At the bar she was not able to contain herself within the limits of any order or government ; exclaiming in very outrageous manner against her children, the prosecutors, and the witnesses, " sparing no man with fearefull execrable curses and banning." In fact, " there was not a more dangerous and

devillish Witch to execute mischiefe." Among the charges
against her were three of murder by witchcraft.

Elizabeth Device would confess nothing[1] "untill it
pleased God to raise up a yong maid, Jennet Device, her
owne daughter, about the age of nine yeares (a witness
unexpected) to discover all their practises, meetings, con-
sultations, murthers, charmes, and villanies."

It is strange to think that one day this child was to know,
as a mature woman, the bitterness of the accusation of
being a witch.[2]

When little Jennett was put forward by the prosecution,
"her mother, according to her accustomed manner,
outragiously cursing, cryed out against the child in such
fearefull manner as all the Court did not a little wonder at
her, and so amazed the child as with weeping eyes shee
cryed out unto my Lord the Judge and told him shee was
not able to speake in the presence of her mother." The
judge therefore ordered Elizabeth Device to be taken away,
and the child to be set on a table to give evidence.

Before we come to this evidence we may look at two
documents which were put in, each purporting to be a
"voluntarie confession" made by Elizabeth Device on
April 27th, when she was arrested in Pendle Forest.

In the first confession the woman told of her spirit, Ball,
in the shape of a brown dog, appearing to her about four
years ago at her mother's house and bidding her make a
picture of John Robinson. She made the picture, dried it
by the fire, and crumbled it all away within a week; and
in about another week Robinson died. He had, she said,
"chidden and becalled" her for having a bastard child
by one Sellar. She also confessed to the murder of James
Robinson, John's brother, and (aided by her mother, now
dead, and by Alice, wife of Richard Nutter) of Henry
Mytton; but she gave no details of these bewitchments.

The second confession was chiefly about the Good Friday
meeting at Malking Tower, shortly before her arrest. We
may leave it until we have heard what her children said
of this famous meeting.

[1] But she *had* confessed earlier, as we shall hear; and Potts writes
about her confessions.

[2] See p. 89.

Jennet Device, on her table, gave evidence that her mother was a witch, as she knew, for she had seen her spirit come unto her sundry times in the likeness of a brown dog, which she called Ball. Once Ball had asked what her mother would have him do, and she said " to help kill John Robinson." About a year ago her mother had summoned Ball and said she would have him kill James Robinson ; and about three weeks later James died. Similarly Henry Mytton died the same period after an appeal to Ball.

With regard to the Malking Tower meeting—the first details of which were originally extracted from her by the Pendle justice of the peace—she said that it was about noon on Good Friday that the people came. Her grandmother (Old Demdike) told her that they were all witches, and that they came to give a name to the " spirit " of her sister Alison. They had for dinner beef, bacon, and roast mutton; the last being from a wether belonging to Christopher Swyer,[1] which her brother James had " brought in " the night before. She knew the names of six of the witches : the wife of Hugh Hargroves, Christopher and Elizabeth Howgate, Dick Miles's wife, and Christopher Jackes and his wife. There was also a woman from Craven, whose name she did not know, and whom she could not recognise among the prisoners in the dock at Lancaster.

Of the witches named, Christopher Howgate was Old Demdike's son. (It is hardly necessary to call him a natural son ; the Pendle witches were decidedly promiscuous.) He, and presumably his wife with him, had fled to escape arrest with their associates. The woman from Craven was Jennet Preston, whose trial has been reported on pp. 63–4. She could not of course be seen in the dock at Lancaster, as she had been hanged at York.

James Device had already, on his arrest in April, incriminated his grandmother and his sister Alison. At Lancaster he had helped to convict Old Chattox. Now his evidence was to be used against his mother.

In the matter of Henry Mytton's death, he told that he

---

[1] As John Robinson is described as " *alias* Swyer," it would seem that there was a feud between the witches and this family.

had heard his grandmother say his mother had killed Mytton by witchcraft because he would not give her (Old Demdike) one penny. He testified also to the death of John Robinson after the summoning of Ball. But his most interesting information was about the witch-gathering on Good Friday. This, he said, was at 12 o'clock in the day-time, and was made up of three men, including himself, and the rest women. He gave the names as Hugh Hargrieves's wife; Christopher Bulcock's wife and her son John; Myles Nutter's mother; Elizabeth, wife of Christopher Hargrieves; Christopher and Elizabeth Howgate; Alice Gray; "one Mouldheele's wife (actually Katherine Hewit); his mother and himself. He does not mention the woman from Craven. If those named, Jane and John Bulcock and Katharine Hewit were among the prisoners in the dock.

His mother told him that the witches met for three causes. The first was the naming of his sister Alison's spirit; but they "did not name him because she was not there." The second was the delivery from gaol of his grandmother and sister, and of Anne Chattox and her daughter, by killing the gaoler, Master Cowell, and blowing up Lancaster Castle before the assizes. The third was the killing of Master Lister, of Westby, for assistance in which Jennet Preston, of Gisborne, had come to the meeting to ask. Her power, she explained, was not strong enough to do the business herself, "being now less than it was before."

All present, averred James Device, gave their consent to put Master Thomas Lister to death, and "to joyne together to hancke Master Leonard Lister when he should come to dwell at the Sowgill and so put him to death."

Jennet Preston, he said, had a spirit with her like unto a white foal with a black spot on the forehead. He speaks also of all the witches going out of the house in their own shapes and likenesses, and riding away on mounts like unto foals, some of one colour, some of another. They all presently vanished out of his sight; but before parting they arranged to meet at Jennet Preston's house that day twelve months, when she promised them a great feast. If they were to meet in the meanwhile, it would be by notice, "upon Romleyes Moor."

Elizabeth Device in her second " voluntarie confession "
in April had agreed to what her son said of the gathering at
Malking Tower, adding to the list of those present two
women from Burnley parish and one Anne Croucksey, of
Marsden.[1] She had also confessed " all touching the
christening of the spirit and the killing of Master Lister,"
but denied any talk, to her remembrance, of killing the
gaoler or blowing up Lancaster Castle.

On her son's evidence now being read out in court, she
cried out for mercy, and was removed.

James Device's own trial followed on August 18th.
When it was necessary for him to come to the bar, Potts
says that he was " so insensible, weake, and unable in all
thinges as he could neither speake, heare, or stand, but
was holden up when he was brought to the place of
arraignment "—which hardly suggests to us that he had
been mildly treated as a prisoner. The principal charges
against him were the killing by witchcraft of Anne, wife
of Henry Townely, of the Carre, gentleman ; of John
Duckworth ; and of two people named John and Blaze
Hargraves. He pleaded not guilty.

His statement made on April 27th, after his arrest, was
put in as first evidence against him. In this he confessed
to the making of a clay picture of Mistress Townely, at
the bidding of his spirit Dandy, which was like unto a black
dog. The picture was dried by the fire, and crumbled or
" mulled " away. Two days later Mistress Townely was
dead. She had offended him one day, when he called at
the Carre, by accusing him and his mother of having
stolen some turves of hers. She had also bidden him " packe

[1] The three accounts given by Elizabeth Device and her children
of the attendance at this meeting may be compared with the prosecution's list on p. 92. I must say that I can see no reason for calling this
gathering, as Mr. Harrison and some others do, an example of a
" Witches' Sabbat." A dinner of beef, bacon, and stolen mutton,
such as Jennet Device testified to, does not constitute a diabolical orgy.
If there were " spirits " present, there was no Black Man mentioned.
It appears to have been a business-meeting (of the coven or several
covens, if you like) to decide what to do about the prisoners at Lancaster
Castle and in Jennet Preston's case against Master Thomas Lister.
Nothing orgiastic was stated to have occurred. But clerical interference
was lacking in the Pendle cases !

the doores," giving him a knock between the shoulders as he went out.

In the matter of Duckworth he said that he had willed Dandy to kill him, because Duckworth had promised him an old shirt and then denied him. There is no mention of a clay picture being made.

In James Device's confession, as read out now, there is a curious passage, which indicates that he was not always a willing sorcerer. He related how his grandmother, Old Demdike, " on Sheare Thursday two years ago," told him to go to church, and at the Communion not to eat the bread, but to bring it away and deliver it to such thing as he should meet on his way home. He disobeyed, and ate the bread. On the way home he met a thing in the shape of a hare, which asked him had he brought the bread. When he said no, the thing threatened to pull him to pieces. But " he marked himself to God, and so the said thing vanished."

Here we have the rare phenomenon of the talking hare-spirit.[1]

Jennet Device was called as a witness against her brother, giving her evidence with " modestie, governement, and understanding, wonderful to the Court," Potts says. She stated that James had been a witch for three years. She told of his black dog Dandy, which he called to him and asked to help kill old Mistress Townely of the Carre ; as also happened in respect of the deaths of John and Blaze Hargraves.

James Device did not deny the truth of his young sister's evidence. He was, it is true, hardly in a condition to do so ; and moreover he had already accused himself of sorcery against Mistress Townely.

A minor piece of evidence given by the child related to less harmful witchcraft. Her mother, she said, had taught her a " prayer " by which to get drink ; and her brother had told her he had so gotten drink. " Within an hour after saying it drink hath come into the house after a very

[1] James Device had another unpleasant experience with a hare. He told how once, after seeing some pictures being " crumbled " at the Redfearns' house, he had an apparition of " a thing like a hare, which spit fire at him."

strange manner." This prayer or charm, for the benefit
of any thirsty modern sorcerer, is simply : " *Crucifixus hoc
signum vitam Eternam. Amen !* "

Yet another, much more elaborate charm was repeated
by little Jennet as being said by her brother to be a cure for
one bewitched. We give it in the form in which it was
taken down from her recitation, with no alterations except
in the matter of stops :

> Upon Good Friday I will fast while I may
> Untill I heare them knell
> Our Lord's owne bell.
> Lord in his messe
> With his twelve Apostles good,
> What hath he in his hand ?
> Ligh in leath wand.
> What hath he in his other hand ?
> Heaven's doore key.
> Open, open Heaven doore kcyes.
> Steck, steck hell doore.
> Let Crizum child
> Goe to its Mother mild.
> What is yonder that cast a light so farrandly ?
> Mine own deare Sonne that's nail'd to the Tree.
> He is nail'd sore by the heart and hand,
> And holy barne Panne.
> Well is that man
> That Fryday spell can,
> His Childe to learne ;
> A Crosse of Blew, and another of Red,
> As good Lord was to the Roode.
> Gabriel laid him downe to sleep
> Upon the ground of holy weepe :
> God Lord came walking by.
> " Sleep'st thou, wak'st thou, Gabriel ? "
> " No, Lord, I am sted with sticke and stake
> That I can neither sleepe nor wake."
> " Rise up, Gabriel, and goe with me,
> The stick nor the stake shall never deere thee."
> Sweete Jesus our Lord, Amen.

As in Old Chattox's charm on p. 65, we have here
preserved something from more ancient days ; not so much

distorted in this instance, though in places marked by unfamiliar dialect.[1]

The case against James Device being brought to an end, the jury were called upon to give their verdicts in respect of the three prisoners whom they had seen before them. They brought them all in guilty of the several murders by witchcraft.

At this point the prosecution of the Pendle prisoners was interrupted to allow that of a distinct set of witches—or alleged witches, we should say ; for the accused were acquitted. The Salmesbury case may be left until we have finished with Pendle. It only took part of a day, allowing the trial of Anne Redfearn to be concluded on August 19th.

One charge against Anne Redfearn, as a matter of fact, was dealt with on the night of the 18th, immediately after James Device's case. This was the accusation that she had by witchcraft caused the death of young Robert Nutter. Of this she was acquitted, Potts admitting that the evidence against her was "not very pregnant." Now she was charged with the death of his father, Christopher Nutter, of which we have not previously heard. The Nutter family were certainly unfortunate in their contact with witches.

Anne Redfearn seems to have been at one time a more prepossessing witch than Old Demdike, Old Chattox, or Elizabeth Device, if we may judge by young Robert Nutter's attraction to her—though even the hideous Elizabeth Device had had a lover, as we know, and Old Demdike in her younger days had " affairs " resulting in children of different surnames. Anne was found guilty on the new charge, to the satisfaction of Potts, who remarks : " All men that knew her affirmed she was more dangerous than her mother, for she made all or most of the pictures of clay that were made or found at any time."

The next case was that of Alice Nutter, described as the

[1] I submitted the charm to Mr. Arthur Machen, who wrote back : " It no doubt preserves, as you wrote, the better religious atmosphere of a former age. But this is not at all remarkable ; it would be remarkable rather if age-old feeling and observance and tradition had been annihilated in seventy years. But, on the other hand, the old formulas —especially in the case of a charm—may well be used mechanically, without any specific assent to the dogmas implied."

wife of Richard Nutter, of the Rough-Lee. She was one of those at Malking Tower on Good Friday ; but the principal charge against her was that she was concerned in the death of Henry Mytton (also of the Rough-Lee), for which Elizabeth Device had already been condemned. As the last-named had confessed to association with Alice Nutter in the bewitchment of Mytton, the result of the trial was practically a foregone conclusion. It was a verdict of guilty.

Potts finds it difficult to explain her connection with the other witches, who were nearly all of the labouring class. " It is certain," he says, " she was a rich woman ; had a great estate and children of good hope ; in the common opinion of the world, of good temper, free from any envy or malice ; yet whether by the means of the rest of the witches, or some other unfortunate occasion, she was drawn to fall to this wicked course of life, I know not."

He records that when, according to her sentence, she was hanged she died very impenitent, " insomuch as her own children were never able to move her to confess any particular offence or declare anything, even *in articulo mortis.*" It looks at least possible that Alice Nutter was merely a well-to-do amateur interested in the mystery of witchcraft. If so, she paid a terrible penalty for her curiosity. Nowadays she might have gone in for Spiritualism, which would not have got her hanged ![1]

Three short trials followed also on August 19th. The first was that of Katherine, wife of John Hewit, *alias* Mouldheele, or Mould-heeles—was he a cobbler ?—for the murder of a child by witchcraft ; according to Elizabeth Device, she had an associate, one Alice Gray, of Colne, where the child lived. The other two were of Jane and John Bulcock, mother and son, for the similar murder of a woman. All three were found guilty. There were no special features of interest in their trials.

For one reason or another, to the present writer, the

---

[1] Frank Podmore compares the witchcraft epidemic with modern Spiritualism in its effects on popular belief. He adds that " it is not clear that the bulk of witchcraft manifestations had much bearing upon the *evidential* aspects of spiritualism—the evidence being so untrustworthy." (*Modern Spiritualism*, p. 16.)

case of Alison Device has more pathos in it, though Potts does not feel it, than the cases of the other witches with whom she was associated. For one thing she was much younger than most of them. Her age is not stated ; but her little sister was only nine. Even Potts, who calls her " this odious witch," admits that she was but a young witch, of but a year's standing, who was "induced" by her grandmother Demdike.

Then there is the charge on which she was tried and condemned to death ; the laming by witchcraft of a petti-chapman, or poor pedlar, John Law, so that his body wasted and consumed. Though Potts make capital, in his denunciation of the accused, of the "poore Pedler, not well able to go or stand," and led into court by his " poore sonne," we cannot give such sympathy as Potts does to his tale of suffering at the hands of the accused.

It is true that Alison "confessed," at the time of her arrest in Pendle Forest. We must look at what she said.

According to her account, her grandmother had about two years ago advised her to have " a Divell or Familiar " appear unto her, which she did. Accordingly there came a thing like a black dog, to which she gave her soul, and a place to suck at below her breast. (It was this devil, familiar, or spirit which was to have been christened at Malking Tower on Good Friday, had Alison been able to be present.) Then on March 18th, 1612, she met the pedlar, of whom she wanted to buy some pins ; but he would not unloose his pack. Her black dog appearing and asking what she would have him do, " What canst thou do at him ? " she enquired. " Lame him," replied the black dog, and went after the pedlar, who had departed on his way.

John Law confirmed this tale, except that he said Alison was very earnest with him for pins, but that he would *give* her none ; while his son Abraham said that the girl wanted to *buy*, but had no money, and that his father told him he did give her some pins.

When he had passed Alison Device, the pedlar's story went on, he fell down lame. He went into an ale-house at Colne, and lay in great pain. He then saw a great black dog, very fierce, with fiery eyes, looking him in the face ;

and immediately after Alison Device came in, looked on him, and went away. Since that time he had continued lame and unable to travel.

Turning to the prisoner, Law said, " This thou knowest to be too true ! " She humbly acknowledged that this was so, and on her knees, weeping,[1] she begged him to forgive her wicked offence.

Witnesses came forward to say that John Law had been " a goodly man of stature." Now Potts describes him as having his head drawn awry, his eyes and face deformed, his legs lame as well as his left arm, and his hands turned out of their course, while his speech could not well be understood.

When asked if she could help him, the unfortunate young witch answered no ; but that had her grandmother lived she could have helped.

Alison Device was " convicted upon her own confession," and made no protest. Was this the vanity of a witch, thinking—to quote Reginald Scot's words again—that " she (as a goddess) hath brought such things to passe " ?

She had also been accused, in her brother's confession in April, of the bewitching of a child ; but apparently this charge was not pressed.

Still on August 19th, for Altham and Bromley were certainly expeditious judges, two more prisoners were tried, Margaret Pearson and Isabel Robey. Margaret Pearson, of Padiham, is called by Potts " a wicked and ungodly witch," whose third trial for the offence it was ; once for murder by witchcraft (she must obviously have been acquitted), once for bewitching a neighbour, and now for goods. The goods in question were a horse, or mare, belonging to a man named Dodgeson, that she was said to have killed by her art. Old Chattox's evidence was produced against her, that Pearson's wife had a spirit, which came to her first in the likeness of a man, and cloven-footed. She and her spirit had gone in at a loophole to Dodgeson's stable, and together sat upon his horse or mare, which died.

Old Chattox had also testified that Margaret Pearson had

[1] Yet common experience, according to Henri Boguet (*Discours des Sorciers*), shows that witches are unable to shed a tear !

confessed to bewitching the wife of one Childers. She claimed that Margaret was as bad as herself. The judges, however, did not agree with her. When Margaret was found guilty they only sentenced her to the pillory on market-day at four places, a year's imprisonment, and then to be bound over with substantial sureties to be of good behaviour. The death of a horse was not murder.

Isabel Robey was less fortunate. She was charged with several bewitchments, the principal one being that of Peter Chadwick, who married her god-daughter when she wished him to marry her instead. He had told her he did not care for her, whereupon he became sore in all his bones, and suffered other ills. She threatened that he should never mend until he begged her forgiveness. He would not do this ; and he said he was fearful to meet her. Though none of her bewitchments seemed to have a fatal end she was condemned to death.

Five (as we shall see) of the accused in the Pendle affair were acquitted. Ten were sentenced to be hanged, and one to the pillory. In his judgment Sir Edward Bromley, addressing the condemned, said :

" As you stand simply (your offences and bloudie practices not considered) your fall would rather move compassion than exasperate any man. For whome would not the ruine of so many poore creatures at one time touch, as in appearance simple and of little understanding ? But the bloud of these innocent children and others His Majestie's subjects, whom cruelly and barbarously you have murdered and cut off, with all the rest of your offences, hath cried out unto the Lord against you, and solicited for satisfaction and revenge, and that hath brought this heavie judgement upon you at this time."

To his clerk this address of Bromley's seemed admirable.

Having dealt with the guilty, Bromley proceeded to address those who had been found not guilty. And here, it must be pointed out, that there is a mistake of very long standing with regard to the number of these latter. It has been thought best to relegate the proof of this mistake to a note at the end of this chapter. Here it may suffice to say that there were three women (Elizabeth Astley, Alice Gray, and Isabel Sidegraves) and two men (Lawrence

Hay and John Ramsden) to whom the judge directed
words that are very much in the spirit of the traditional
Irish verdict, " Not guilty, but we hope they won't do
it again." Though they were by the Law to be acquitted,
they must not presume further of their innocence than they
had just cause to do. Without question, he continued,
they were as deep in the matter as any of the condemned,
and it was time now for them to forsake the Devil and pray
to God they might not fall again. He ordered them to
find sureties to appear at the next Lancaster Assizes,
and in the meantime to be of good behaviour.

Potts states that the condemned witches were executed
at " the common place of execution near unto Lancaster "
on the day after the judgment.

Before looking at a few aspects of the witchcraft epidemic
(as it is sometimes called) that was dealt with at Lancaster
in August 1612, we may complete the story by including
the remaining trials on the like charge at the same assizes.

The case of " the Salmesbury witches " that made a
brief interruption in the Pendle case was a much simpler
matter. There were three accused persons, an old woman
named Jennet Bierley, her unmarried daughter Ellen, and
a widow named Jane Southworth ; and only one accuser
of importance, Grace Sowerbuts, a girl of about fourteen,
granddaughter of Jennet Bierley. The girl did indeed
include in one statement a fourth woman, " Old Doewife,"
like the others of Salmesbury, but the name was not again
mentioned.[1]

The charge against the accused was that they had practised divers devilish and wicked arts called witchcrafts,
etc., upon Grace Sowerbuts, whereby her body wasted
and consumed. What made it particularly atrocious was
the relationship between some of the parties ; and there
was also a religious question involved, as soon appeared.

Grace said that for the space of some years she had been
haunted and vexed by these women, who used to come to
her, carrying her off—once by the hair of her head—and
laying her on the top of a hay-mow, on a barn floor, or

[1] With reference to the statement so often made, that there were
six women and two men involved in the Salmesbury case, see the note
at the end of this chapter.

elsewhere. Once the three of them took her to Red Bank,
north of the river Ribble, where they met " foure black
things, going upright, and yet not like men in the face,"
who first danced with them and then used their bodies,
including hers. She further accused her grandmother of
the murder of a little child and, with her aunt, of first
partaking of its flesh and then making an ointment from
its bones, " that thereby they might sometimes change
themselves into other shapes." This, of course, is a common
charge against witches ; but it seldom comes from the lips
of a young girl.

Potts in this case does not come out against the alleged
witches. When he wrote his account not only had the
accused been acquitted, on the judge's direction, but it
had been revealed that behind Grace Sowerbuts was " a
Seminarie Priest, or, as the best in this Honorable Assembly
[at the Lancaster Assizes] thinke, a Jesuite." So he de-
nounces Grace as " this impudent wench," and goes on :
" The Jesuite forgot to instruct his scholler how long it is
since she was tormented. It seems it is long since he read
the old badge of a lyer, *Oportet mendacem esse memorem.* He
knows not how long it is since they came to Church, after
which time they began to practise Witchcraft. . . . How well
this project to take away the lives of three innocent poor
creatures, to induce a young scholler to commit perjury, to
accuse her own grandmother, aunt, etc., agrees either with
the title of a Jesuite or the dutie of a religious priest, who
should rather profess sinceritie, and innocencie than practise trecherie. But this was lawful ; for they are heretikes
accursed, to leave the companie of priests, to frequent
Churches, hear the word of God preached, and profess
Religion sincerely."

In very different language from what he had used about
Old Demdike, Old Chattox, and Elizabeth Device, Potts
speaks for Jennet Bierley. " The wrinkles of an old wive's
face is good evidence to the jurie against a witch. And how
often will the common people say, ' Her eyes are sunk in
her head, God bless us from her ! ' "

The way in which the religious background to the trial
had been shown up was this. Sir Edward Bromley, the
judge presiding, after hearing the evidence, asked the

accused what answer they could make ; whereon, kneeling
and weeping, they begged him to examine Grace Sowerbuts as to who had set her on to make her charges against
them. Immediately, says Potts, her countenance changed,
while the witnesses behind began to quarrel and accuse
one another. Bromley questioned the girl, " who could
not for her life make any direct answer, but, strangely
amazed, told him she was put to a master to learn, but he
told her nothing of this."

Bromley turned to the Court, and remarked that " if a
priest or a Jesuit had a hand in one end of it, there would
appear to be knavery and practice in the other end of it."
He then called on Thomas Sowerbuts, Grace's father, to
say who was the girl's master. The father " in general
terms denied all " ; but the accused at once asserted that
Grace " went to learn with one Thompson, a Seminarie
priest, who had instructed and taught her in this accusation
against them because they were once obstinate Papists and
now came to Church."

Grace was at this point committed to Mr. William Leigh,
" a very religious preacher," and another justice of the
peace, to be questioned privately. To them she denied her
story about the killing of a child by her grandmother and
aunt, as well as all the rest of her testimony. She also said
that she took Master Thompson to be really Master Christopher Southworth ; and that he had advised her to give
what evidence she gave.

It seems that the priest Christopher Southworth was a
kinsman of Jane Southworth's late husband. There had
been a quarrel in the Southworth family, presumably over
religion, and old Sir John Southworth, now dead, was
alleged always to have shunned Jane's house, saying that
he doubted not she would bewitch him. She was perhaps
his daughter-in-law, as her husband's name was also John.

Bromley directed the jury to acquit the prisoners, which
they did. And so was laid open, writes Potts, " this bloudie
practice of the priest." He records with satisfaction that
Grace Sowerbuts, in her examination by the two justices
of the peace, confessed that she had never been at the
church, but promised to go hereafter, " and that very
willingly."

Therefore " the Witches of Salmesbury," as Potts states that the county called them, were admitted not to have employed witchcraft at all. The whole trouble arose through the bitterness of religious feeling in Lancashire, where the Pilgrimage of Grace and its sequel were still deeply remembered ; especially the hanging of John Paslew, last abbot of Whalley Abbey, in March 1537. The efforts of the Reformers to suppress Roman Catholicism in the county had met with little success below the surface of things.

The Salmesbury case came to a very different ending from that of the Pendle cases. It was a much simpler affair altogether, arising out of family and religious feuds. With regard to the child whose evidence was relied upon by the prosecution, though she may have had a dislike for her grandmother and her aunt, she was clearly the carrier of others' malice besides her own. Sir Edward Bromley and Thomas Potts eagerly seized on the direction of the priest Southworth ; and it really does not seem as if he can be acquitted. The charges against the accused women smack too strongly of the *Malleus Maleficarum* and like works, which can hardly have come within the reading of Grace Sowerbuts herself. In particular there is the tale of " the foure black things, going upright, and yet not like men in the face," with the carnal orgy at its end.[1] Then there is the cannibalism and anointing of the witches. Doubtless we should have heard more, had not the judge quickly made up his mind as to the falsity of the charges.

We get nothing about witch-marks in the Salmesbury case ; nor about familiars, unless we class the four black things as such.

In the Pendle cases, on the other hand, there is a little about one and much about the other of these attributes of witches. Old Demdike had the place on her left side ; Old Chattox one on her right side ; Alison Device one below her breast ; Elizabeth Device, from birth, a " preposterous marke in nature." We are not told of any searching for marks, as is so regular in the later Essex cases.

[1] Friedrich von Spee's *concubitus contra naturam cum creatura spirituali*, the unnatural intercourse with a spiritual being, which he allows to be an occasional part of the " most enormous, most heavy, most atrocious " crime of the witch (*Cautio Criminalis*, 1631).

Spirits, devils, or familiars were positively rife in the Forest of Pendle, one to each witch being the regular allowance, their shapes and sex varying. Old Demdike had Tibb, on first appearance a boy, in a coat half black, half brown ; later a brown dog, once a black cat. Old Chattox had Fancie, at first " a thing like a Christian man," later a brown dog, male or female. (It has been remarked how uncertain Old Chattox was about the sex of her own and Demdike's familiars.) Elizabeth Device had Ball, a brown dog, and her son James Dandy, a black dog ; both of which little Jennet Device claimed to have seen as well as they. Alison Device had her black dog, which failed to receive its name at Malking Tower. Jennet Preston, from Yorkshire, had a white foal with a black spot on the forehead.

The witches are not accused, either by themselves or by others, of going about in a preternatural manner, the nearest approach being the appearance of Alison Device, after her black dog, to John Law in the ale-house, which he does not assert to be strange. When they meet at Malking Tower the witches " go out of the house in their own shapes and likenesses," and mount foals to depart. James Device, the witness, does not say that they came in any other shape than their own, and there is no suggestion of pole- or broomstick-riding at Pendle.

Clay pictures or images are much in evidence in the trials, and are indeed the instruments for compassing the murders charged against the witches. The confessed ones had no doubt of the pictures' efficacy. A few other " charms " have been noted.

There is a child witness, as in the Salmesbury case ; but Jennet Device, who so favourably impressed the Court and Thomas Potts, does not seem to have been actuated by malice. She had certainly been brought up in a strange atmosphere in the forest. She gave her evidence straightforwardly, though we cannot tell to what extent she had been coached by the prosecution. It is easy to believe that she saw something of the Good Friday meeting, for it actually took place in the house where she lived. She saw, too, dogs called Ball and Dandy, there is no reason to doubt. What nature she attributed to them is a matter of what she was told by their owners, her mother and brother. They believed in witchcraft, their neighbours believed in witchcraft, most people of the day believed in it, and the legal gentlemen with whom the trials brought Jennet in contact urged her to testify to things which must have seemed to her to be based on it. Therefore she is not to be dismissed as a lying child like Grace Sowerbuts.

Have we seen enough of the business of the Lancashire witches to come to any conclusion about it? Were they " witches," as most of them were induced to confess, and as so many, if not all, of those who knew them charged them with being? We cannot resist taking refuge again in a quotation from Reginald Scot, where he says : " My question is not (as manie fondly suppose) whether there be witches or naie ; but whether they can doo such miraculous works as are imputed unto them."[1] On the latter point he has no hesitation in rejecting the evidence as " frivolous," and the alleged proofs against the witches as " incredible, consisting of ghesses, presumptions, and impossibilities contrarie to reason, Scripture, and nature."

Scot might well have been writing of some at least of the Lancashire witches, twenty-eight years after the appearance of his book, when he says :[2]

" One sort of such as are said to bee witches are women which be commonly old, lame, bleare-eied, pale, fowle, and full of wrinkles ; poore, sullen, superstitious, and papists ; or such as knowe no religion : in whose drowsie minds the divell hath gotten a fine seat ; so as, what mischief, mischance, calamitie, or slaughter is brought to pass, they are easilie persuaded the same is doone by themselves ; imprinting in their minds an earnest and constant imagination thereof. They are leane and deformed, shewing melancholie in their faces, to the horror of all that see them. They are doting, scolds, mad, divellish ; and not much differing from them that are thought to be possessed with spirits ; so firme and stedfast in their opinions as whosoever shall onelie have respect to the constancie of their words uttered would easilie beleeve they were true indeed."

Is not this description readily applicable to Old Demdike

[1] *The Discoverie of Witchcraft*, 2nd prefatory epistle.
[2] *Ib.*, Bk I, Chap. 3.

and Old Chattox? The "sort" of whom Scot writes is none other than theirs.

Scot's rationalising, sceptical attitude did not please his contemporaries at all. King James I denounced in *Dæmonologie* these "damnable opinions," and accused Scot of being a follower of the Saducees. He further ordered all copies of *The Discoverie* to be burnt. James and hosts of others who agreed with him in condemning Scot's view of witchcraft were especially vexed at the inadequate position assigned to the Devil. They would have in the words of George Gifford, a Malden minister, writing a few years before James, that a witch is " one that worketh by the Devill, or by some develish or curious art, either hurting or healing, revealing thinges secrete or foretelling thinges to come, which the Devill hath devised to entangle and snare men's soules withal to damnation."[1]

Though they could not agree as to the spelling of the Devil's name, the writers about witchcraft practically all insisted on retaining him as the chief actor and inspirer among the witches. This tenet has died hard, if it can be said to have died at all. In the very instance before us, of the happenings in Lancashire, G. B. Harrison, the learned editor of, and writer of the introduction to, Thomas Pott's book, refuses to abandon the diabolical explanation, differing as he no doubt does from King James, etc., on the question of the personality of the Devil.

Mr. Harrison has no doubt as to the complete guilt of the Pendle witches. To him their trials reveal the witch-cult " in its full horror." Anne Chattox, he points out, collects "scalps" and teeth of the dead from the churchyard ; James Device is told by his grandmother to steal consecrated bread at Communion ; enemies of the coven are cursed by means of clay images ; and there is at least a suspicion that poison is used. (This last supposition, it is true, would help to explain the numerous exceedingly rapid deaths mentioned in the trials.) At any rate, the Pendle witches had such a hold over their neighbours that they could kill or paralyse by suggestion ! He instances the paralysis of the poor pedlar by the shock

[1] *A Discourse of the subtile Practises of Devilles by Witches and Sorcerers* (1587).

of seeing Alison Device's " spirit." But here we may note
that John Law's story was not to the effect that he saw the
great black dog before he fell down lame. His lameness
came on previous to his visit to the ale-house at Colne,
where he was lying in pain before he saw the dog. If it were
not for Alison's confession we should be inclined to scout
Law's account entirely.

And, with regard to confessions, we cannot share Mr.
Harrison's opinion that there is no sign of force in the
depositions produced at Lancaster. The use of the word
" voluntary " conveys little. It is a conventional term,
which perhaps means that actual torture, the omnipotent,[1]
was not applied. But there are other means of extracting
from prisoners the kind of statement desired, as we shall
hear fully in the Essex and Salem cases. The official
Thomas Potts would not think it necessary to record such
matters. We may be wrong in inferring anything from Old
Demdike's death in gaol, or from James Device at the bar
being " so insensible, weake, and unable in all things as
he could neither speake, heare, or stand, but was holden
up." There may have been no ill-treatment, short of
positive torture, applied to the prisoners from the moment
of their arrest. But is that probable in the year 1612, in a
neighbourhood seething with hatred and fear of "witches"?

Like Mr. Harrison, the Rev. Montague Summers has
no hesitation in condemning the Pendle witches as diabolical ; but we may leave his attitude towards witches
until later.[2]

The notoriety of the Lancashire witches did not result
in a spread of their practices throughout the county.
The executions at Lancaster had shown how dangerous it
was to be suspected of even dabbling in witchcraft. It is
rather curious that witch-hunting ceased when the tempta-
tion was so great to destroy or at any rate seriously injure

---

[1] " *Quid possint torturae et denunciationes?* " asks von Spee in the
appendix to his *Cautio Criminalis* ; and he answers : " *Possunt paene
omnia. Unde quidam nuper non illepide torturam appellabat Omnipotentem.*"

[2] See, with regard to the Salem cases, pp. 168–9, 173–4 ; and, on the
witch in general, p. 169, footnote.

I leave Miss Margaret Murray's attitude also to the Salem chapter.
She accepts the Pendle witch-cult as real, but does not call it diabolical.
To her it is Dianic.

detested neighbours in this way. The one particular covert
of the Forest of Pendle had no doubt been successfully
drawn ; but there must have been others where the sport
could have been carried on. There was certainly no
outcry against the sentences in 1612. Yet in Lancashire,
at any rate, alleged witches were left in comparative peace
for twenty-one years, when there came another crop of
accusations. It looked at first as if the tragedy of the gallows
at Lancaster in 1612 were to be repeated. But the good
sense of Charles I (during whose reign, up to the Rebellion,
only five persons are definitely known to have been executed
for witchcraft) prevailed over the malice of the persecutors.

In May 1634 Sir William Pelham wrote to Viscount
Conway that the greatest news from the country was of a
huge pack of witches lately discovered in Lancashire,
whereof it is said nineteen are already condemned and at
least sixty more discovered. Divers of them are of great
ability, and they have done much harm. It is suspected
they had a hand in raising the storm in which His Majesty
was in great danger at sea in Scotland.[1]

Then on June 15th there is a letter from the Bishop of
Chester to the two Secretaries of State. He had been
ordered, he says, to examine seven of the condemned
witches at Lancaster. Three of them, John Spencer, Alice
Higgins, and Jennet Loynd had lately died in gaol, and a
fourth, Jennet Hargraves, was sick past recovery. He had
examined the other three. One was an old woman,
Margaret Johnson, *alias* the penitent witch, who, with tears
in her eyes after his exhortation, said : " I will not add sin
to sin. I have done enough already, and will not increase
it. I pray God I may repent."

Her confession, somewhat abbreviated, is as follows :

" Margaret Johnson, widow, aged sixty, says she had
been a witch about six years ; was brought thereto upon
some vexations of her bad neighbours. About that time,
walking in the highway in Marsden in Whalley, there
appeared to her a man in black attire, with black points,
who said to her, if she would give him her soul, she should

---

[1] *Calendar of State Papers (Domestic)*, 1634–5. This volume contains
all the information we have concerning the second witchcraft business
in the Forest of Pendle.

want nothing, but should have power to hurt whom she would. She refused, and he vanished. In this manner he oft-times resorted to her till at last she yielded, and he gave into her hand gold and silver ; but it vanished soon again, and she was ever bare or poor though oft he gave her the like. He called himself Mamilion, and most commonly at his coming had the use of her body. After this he appeared in the shape of a brown-coloured dog, a white cat, and a hare, and in those shapes sucked her blood. . . . There were seven or eight of her neighbours who were witches, but most of them are dead. . . . Since her imprisonment her familiar never came near her. . . . She frequented the church till her compact with the Devil, but seldom since."

The others he examined, says the Bishop, will soon discover their guilt or innocence. But he expresses the opinion that " conceit and malice are so powerful with many in these parts that they will easily afford an oath to work revenge upon their neighbour." He clearly did not think much of the evidence against the accused.

The second survivor of the condemned at Lancaster was Mary Spencer, of Buckley, aged only twenty, who protested her innocence. Both her parents had been condemned at the last assizes and were since dead. (We have heard of John Spencer as having lately died in gaol ; his wife may have predeceased him there.) She complained of the malice of Nicholas Cunliffe against her and her parents for the past five or six years, and of his recent wrathful abuse of them. Apparently his accusation against her was that she could make a " collock," or pail, come running to her of its own accord, which she utterly denied. She was not afraid of death, she declared, for she hoped it would make an entrance for her into Heaven.

The last of the seven was a married woman, Frances Dicconson, who protested of the wrong done to her by a boy, son of Edmund Rough, *alias* Robinson. The father, she said, had bought a cow of her husband, and because Dicconson would not let it go without surety had " maliced " her and her husband. He had offered to have her freed if her husband would give him forty shillings. A second witness against her had " maliced her upon a bargain of butter."

It was decided to have the accused examined for witch-marks in London. On June 20th the Privy Council ordered the two surgeons to His Majesty to choose midwives to search the bodies of the three women, after instructions from Dr. Harvey, the Royal physician, and themselves.

An endorsement on this order shows that the prisoners were already at the Ship Tavern, Greenwich. On July 2nd a certificate was issued from Surgeon's Hall, Mugwell Street, attested by the two Royal and five other surgeons and by ten certificated midwives. They had inspected the women from Lancaster, and found on Jennet Hargraves, Frances Dicconson, and Mary Spencer nothing unnatural. On Margaret Johnson were " two things which may be called teats " ; but they were evidently unconvinced that these might not be explained naturally.

Another proof of the care taken in the case was the examination of the boy accuser before George Long, Justice of the Peace for Middlesex, on July 10th. Edmund Robinson junior, *aged ten*, of Newchurch, Lancashire, con-fessed that all his story had been false ; " but only he had heard tales and reports made by women, so he framed his tale out of his own invention, which once told he persisted in till he came to the King's coachman, to whom he confessed the truth."

The principal tale was a preposterous rigmarole about two greyhounds that refused to chase a hare. He was beating them, when one turned into one of the accused women, another into a boy. The woman offered him twelvepence to say nothing about the matter. Then she put a bridle into the boy's mouth, and he became a white horse, on which the woman took the examinate with her to a place called Horestones, in Pendle Forest. Here young Robinson saw a number of persons gathered together, who gave him meat, etc.

This childish description of a witches' Sabbat was brought up again at young Robinson's second examina-tion six days later, when he confessed that his accusations against the prisoners Dicconson and Hargraves, Jennet Devys (note the name, evidently Device), her half-brother William, and another as having been at the witch-feast at Horestones were inventions. He had heard neighbours talk of a witch-feast at " Mocking Tower " in Pendle Forest about twenty years since, to which many came who were apprehended and executed at Lancaster. " Thereupon he framed those tales concerning the persons aforesaid, because he had heard neighbours repute them as witches. . . . Nobody was acquainted with any part of his fiction . . . but it merely proceeded out of his own brain." He denied that he said to the King's majesty or to any other person that he had been set on to make his original statements.

It seems as if Charles I, like his son Charles II so often in later days, took a personal share in the examination of the case.

The upshot of it all was that the King decided to grant a pardon to all the condemned. And so—except for those who had died in gaol—the new crop of " Pendle witches " escaped the doom that was intended for them by their ill-wishers.

NOTE.—It is to Thomas Potts's *Discoverie of Witches* itself that is due an error in respect of the persons acquitted on the charge of witchcraft at the Lancaster Assizes in August 1612 ; an error that has been perpetuated ever since, without (as far as I know) anyone drawing attention to it. Yet a careful study of Potts's book reveals it clearly.

It is true that on a page in the original edition of 1613[1] there are two lists in which are given the names of those purported to have been involved in the two sets of trials, and among " the Witches of Salmesbury " are included, with the names of Jennet Bierley, Ellen Bierley, and Jane Southworth, five other names—Elizabeth Astley, John Ramsden, Alice Gray, Isabel Sidegraves, and Lawrence Haye [*sic*]. So we get the six women and two men who are commonly alleged to have been charged with, and acquitted of, witchcraft at Salmesbury.

An examination of the actual trials, however, shows

[1] There are no page-numbers in this, which may be seen in the North Gallery of the British Museum Library (reference no. C. 27 b. 37), but in G. B. Harrison's facsimile edition of 1929 it is p. 29.

that the five other names are wrongly included in the
Salmesbury list ; and the concluding part of Sir Edward
Bromley's "judgement"[1] makes this plain beyond all
doubt. I cannot do better than reproduce the judge's
words to "the prisoners found not guilty by the juries,"
as set out by Potts and passed by Bromley himself as being
a correct report of what he said.

These are Bromley's words, taken from the actual edition
of 1613 :

> " ELIZABETH ASTLEY.
> JOHN RAMSDEN.
> ALICE GRAY.
> ISABEL SIDEGRAVES.
> LAWRENCE HAY.

" To you that are found not guiltie, and are by the Law
to be acquitted, presume no further of your Innocencie then
you have just cause : for although it pleased God out of his
Mercie to spare you at this time, yet without question there
are amongst you that are as deepe in this Action as any of
them that are condemned to die for their offences. The
time is now for you to forsake the Devill. Remember how
and in what sort hee hath dealt with all of you : make good
use of this great mercie and favour : and pray unto God you
fall not againe. For great is your happinesse to have time
in this world to prepare your selves against the day when
you shall appear before the Great Judge of all.

" Notwithstanding, the judgement of the Court is,
You shall all enter recognizances with good sufficient
sureties, to appeare at the next Assizes at Lancaster, and
in the meane time to be of the good behaviour. All I can
say to you :

> JENNET BIERLEY,
> ELLEN BIERLEY,
> JANE SOUTHWORTH,

is, that God hath delivered you beyond expectation, I
pray God you may use his mercie and favour well, and
take care you fall not hereafter : and so the Court doth
order you shall be delivered."

[1] Pp. 167–8 in the facsimile edition.

Is it not now obvious that Bromley first addressed himself to those found not guilty in what we may call the Pendle cases, and then to those in the Salmesbury case, which had been taken in the middle of the others?

Additional proof, if any is required, is furnished in the list that Potts gives elsewhere of the witches who were at the Good Friday meeting at Malking Tower. This is as follows:

Elizabeth Device, Alice Nutter, Katherine Hewit *alias* Mould-heeles, John and Jane Bulcock, Alice Graie, Jennet Hargraves, Elizabeth Hargraves, Christopher Howgate, Grace Hay, Anne Crunckshay, Elizabeth Howgate, Jennet Preston, " with many more, which being bound over to appear at the last Assizes are since that time fled to save themselves."

Here we have the name of Alice Gray at least of those so grudgingly acquitted by Bromley; and we have heard the name before, in connection with Katherine Hewit's trial. Perhaps the identity of surname in Grace Hay and Lawrence Hay is not of any significance.

Presence at the Malking Tower meeting, of course, was only a part of the charges against the witches, so that it need not be a matter for surprise that the names Astley, Ramsden, and Sidegraves are not in the above list.

I think that it is correct to assume that in the *Discoverie of Witches* the inclusion of five names among " the Witches of Salmesbury " is a mere error, whether due to Potts's own carelessness in reading his proofs or to a blunder by his printer which did not come under his eyes.

CHAPTER II

ESSEX

ALTHOUGH only thirty-two years elapsed between the Lancashire witch persecution and those that may roughly be classed under the head of the Essex persecutions (though extending to several neighbouring counties), we shall find some striking differences in the campaigns. The first is that we see, as the originator of the trouble in Essex, a man who made a profession of the seeking out of witches ; " a trade," says his contemporary, the Rev John Gaule, vicar of Great Staughton, " never taken up in England till this." Matthew Hopkins was to have numerous imitators, both in England and in Scotland. But the infamy of being the pioneer, at least in England, was his. That he was proud of his distinction is shown on the very title-page of his pamphlet *The Discovery of Witches*, where he describes himself as " Witch-finder."[1] He found a colleague worthy of himself ; but it was his name that was always recalled in connection with his trade. In his play, *The Lancashire Witches*, Shadwell makes Sir Jeffery Shacklehead (" a simple justice, pretending to great skill in witches, and a great persecutor of them ") say : " You shall turn me loose against any witch-finder in Europe ; I'd make an ass of Hopkins if he were alive."

Matthew Hopkins was the son of James, Puritan minister of Wenham, about eight miles from Ipswich, the year of his birth being unknown. He studied the Law, and practised

---

[1] *The Discovery of Witches : in answer to severall queries lately delivered to the Judges of Assize for the County of Norfolk, and now published by Matthew Hopkins, Witch-finder, for the benefit of the whole Kingdome* (London, 1647). A frontispiece shows a picture of " Matthew Hopkins, Witch Finder Generall." It is reproduced in the present work.

This pamphlet was reprinted in 1928, with a valuable introduction by the Rev. Montague Summers.

at Ipswich, apparently with no marked success. He then moved to Manningtree, in Essex, where he was in 1645, the year of his rise to notoriety.[1] According to his own account his first acquaintance with " that horrible sect of witches " was at Manningtree, where seven or eight lived near him, with divers other adjacent witches of other towns. He discovered their existence in the month of March. He asserts that on Friday every six weeks they met close by his house, and " had their severall solemne sacrifices there offered to the Devill." One night he heard one of them speaking to her imps and bidding them go to another witch, who was thereupon apprehended and searched.

Now we know that the first charge in the Essex prosecutions concerned an old one-legged woman, Elizabeth Clarke *alias* Bedinfield, who lived in great poverty at Manningtree. It was said that her mother and others of her family in the past had been executed for murder by witchcraft. A neighbour of hers, John Rivet, tailor, laid an information against her in March, 1645, that, his wife having fallen sick and lame, he went to " a cunning woman " at Hadleigh, Suffolk, who told him his wife had been cursed by two women, near neighbours ; whereupon he believed that Elizabeth Clarke had bewitched her.

What was the connection between Rivet and Hopkins does not appear. Perhaps Rivet made clothes for Hopkins ; but that does not explain why the lawyer put the tailor up to bringing a charge of bewitchment against an old beggar-woman. Hopkins may have had his interest in witchcraft aroused by the past records of the county where he had come to live. In 1566 two women had been hanged as witches at Chelmsford ; in 1579 three more ; in 1582 there had been the St. Osyth case ; and in 1589 three witches were hanged at Chelmsford.

Elizabeth Clarke was arrested and charged before two justices of the peace, Sir Harbottle Grimston and Sir Thomas Bowes. When she was searched—we are not told whether this was done by Goody Phillips, who was after-

---

[1] Hopkins gives the date of his discovery of the witches as March 1644 ; but this must be Old Style, unless we are to suppose that he waited a whole year before revealing what he had found out.

MATTHEW HOPKINS, WITCH-FINDER

From an engraving by R. Cooper

HOPKINS, WITH WITCHES AND IMPS

From illustration to "The Discovery of Witches," 1647

wards Hopkins's regular female "searcher"—she was
"found to have three teats about her, which honest
women have not," says Hopkins. The witnesses who
followed Rivet against her were "Matthew Hopkins,
of Manningtree, Gent.," and John Stearne, also living at
Manningtree, who joined Hopkins in the profession of
witch-finder.

The evidence, which was read afterwards at Elizabeth
Clarke's trial at the Chelmsford Assizes,[1] shows that she
was subjected to the ordeal of being "watched." Hopkins,
in his information, stated that, by the justices' direction,
he and Master Stearne went to the woman's room on
March 24th, when she offered to call one of her white
imps and play with it in her lap ; but they would not
allow it. According to what he admits in his *Discovery*,
she had been kept from sleep two or three nights before
this, and it was on the fourth night that this offer was
made, there being then "ten of us" in the room. This
he does not mention in his evidence, which goes on to say
that she then confessed to having had carnal connection
with the Devil for six or seven years. He appeared to her
three or four times a week, in the shape of a proper gentleman, with a laced band, and would say : "Besse, I must
lie with you," which he did for half a night together.

Within a quarter of an hour after she told them this,
continued Hopkins, there appeared an imp like a white
dog with sandy spots, very fat and plump, with very short
legs, which forthwith vanished away. This was Jarmara,
the old woman said. Then came another imp Vinegar
Tom, like a greyhound with long legs, and a black imp
like a polecat. She told them she had five imps of her
own, and two of the old beldam Weste's. She also said
that the Devil would not let her rest till she killed the hogs
of one man and the horse of another at Manningtree.

In his *Discovery* Hopkins amplified his description of the
imps, who were Holt, like a white kitling ; Jarmara, like a
fat spaniel ; Vinegar Tom, a long-legged greyhound with
a head like an ox, who, when Hopkins bade him go to the

---

[1] The record is in Cobbett's *State Trials*, IV, pp. 817 ff., and is
supplemented by Hopkins's pamphlet and by Stearne's *Confirmation
and Discovery of Witch-Craft* (London, 1648).

place provided for him and his angels, "immediately
transformed himself in the shape of a child of four years
old, without a head, and gave half a dozen turns about the
house, and vanished at the door "; Sack-and-Sugar, like
a black rabbit; and Newes, like a polecat. All these
vanished in a little time. Then the prisoner " confessed
several other witches, from whom she had her imps, and
named to divers women where their marks were, the
number of their marks, and imps, and imps' names, as
Elemanzer, Pyewacket, Peckin the Crown, Grizzel Greedi-
gut, &c., which no mortal could invent."

Stearne's information against Elizabeth Clarke roughly
agreed with Hopkins's. He gives her imps' names as
Hoult, Jarmara, Vinegar Tom (in the likeness of a dumb
dog !), and Sack-and-Sugar. She further confessed that
" she had one imp for which she would fight up to the
knees in blood before she would lose it ; and that her imps
did commonly suck on the old beldam Weste, and that
the said old beldam's imps did suck on her likewise."

In his *Confirmation and Discovery*, Stearne adds that when
Hopkins asked Elizabeth Clarke, " Besse, will they do us
no harm ? " she replied, " What, did you think I am
afraid of my own children ? " With regard to her intercourse with the Devil, when she was asked by Hopkins in
what manner or likeness he came, she said : " Like a tall,
proper, black-haired gentleman, a properer man than
yourself." And asked which she had rather lie withal, she
answered, " The Devil ! " Hopkins did not record this
himself, it may be noted. In the circumstances, it was
perhaps difficult to know how to take such remarks.

From the testimony of the " watchers " it would appear
as if they saw some of the imps themselves. Mr. Montague
Summers maintains that " they must have seen something
to account for these phenomena." But is it really a case
of " must " ? *Credo quia. . . .*

Other witnesses before the justices testified to what the
accused had told them of successful bewitchments, some to
death, by old beldam Weste. Then she herself in examination told how about six months previously she had met
Anne Weste, widow, in a field where she was picking up a
few sticks. Weste had pitied her for her lameness and her

poverty, and said there were ways and means for her to live much better. She would send her a thing like "a little kitlyn," which would fetch some victuals for her. Within two or three nights there came a white thing to her one night, and a grey thing the next, which told her they would do her no hurt, but would help her to a husband, who should maintain her ever after. These things would then come into her bed by nights and suck upon her.

It is not quite clear at what point we leave the proceedings before the justices of the peace, Grimston and Bowes, in March to May, 1645, and change to the Chelmsford Assizes in August, under the presidency of the Earl of Warwick. Elizabeth Clarke and some of her alleged fellow-witches were sent to the assizes, and the previous testimonies and confessions were produced there. It would be tedious to examine all that came up at Chelmsford in detail ; but some items merit attention.

Anne Weste "hath been suspected for a witch many years since, and suffered imprisonment for the same." She is accused of several murders. Elizabeth Gooding is " a lewd woman," who has kept company with Clarke, Weste, and Anne Leech. The last-named herself confesses to having joined with Clarke and Gooding to send imps to kill a cow, and with Gooding to kill a child, both belonging to the same man ; and also to sending her imp alone to kill a woman who had refused her a coif.

Another woman named Clarke, Helen, a married daughter of Anne Leech, was charged with bewitching a neighbour to death, after having been heard to say that she " should rue for all "—the victim's death occurring within six weeks. She had been arrested at once, when she confessed that the Devil had appeared to her about six weeks ago, in the shape of a white dog, which became her familiar Elimanzar, and was fed by her on milk-pottage. The imp spoke to her audibly and bade her deny Christ, and she should never want. She assented to this, but maintained that she had never bewitched a woman to death.

Rebecca, daughter to Anne Weste, confessed to having been at a meeting in Elizabeth Clarke's house with several of the other accused women, six in all. " They together spent some time in praying unto their familiars, and everyone in order went to prayers. Afterwards some of them read in a book, the book being Elizabeth Clarke's. Then the familiars appeared, and the women told them what they desired to effect.

Hopkins gave evidence against Rebecca Weste, that she had told him at Colchester, not only how she had been initiated into witchcraft at Elizabeth Clarke's, but also how she had sent the Devil to kill a man, who died within a fortnight—after which " she took him for her god, and thought he could do as God."

Women searchers came forward to give evidence as to finding " bigges " or " teates " (*alias* witch-marks) on various parts of the prisoners' bodies. One of the accused, according to her own sister, had cut her " bigges " off and laid plasters to the places.

The imps in the cases were almost legion.[1] In addition to the names we have already had, we hear of Wynowe, Panu, Jesus, Jockey, Sandy, Mrit, Elizabeth, Collyn, etc. One woman, Margaret Moone, admitted that she had twelve of them. She was charged with the deaths of both human beings and animals, and also with spoiling a brewing of beer and a batch of bread. From her confession she would appear to have been half-witted ; but she did not admit anything worse than a " sending " of lice to a very cleanly woman !

Some of the accused were from the St. Osyth neighbourhood, where there had been a famous witchcraft-trial as long ago as 1582, the twenty-fourth year of Queen Elizabeth. The strangest of the tales from St. Osyth now was told by one Joyce Boanes, who said she had been to Rose Hallybread's house, and met Susan Cook and

[1] Miss Margaret Murray, in *The God of the Witches*, seems rather pained by all these imps. " The Domestic Familiar," she says, " came into such prominence during the trials of the Essex witches, owing to the sensational records of the two witch-finders, that it has ever since been regarded, though erroneously, as an essential part of the outfit of a witch."

It may not be essential. But when Miss Murray states that the Domestic Familiar is found almost entirely in the eastern counties of England, we are entitled to ask whether she is not going too far. Have we not seen the D. F. much in evidence in Lancashire ?

Margaret Lindish.[1] Each of them took an imp of hers to a carpenter's house, in order to kill his man-servant, who had refused Cook a sack of chips. The victim did not die, however, but " hath oftentimes crowed like a cock, barked like a dog, sung tunes, and groaned "—which must have been annoying to his master.

Joyce Boanes's imps were " in the likeness of mouses," and she used to give them suck.

Another St. Osyth woman, Rebecca Jones, had as imps three black things like moles, with four feet but no tails. She was accused of killing by their means a man and his wife. The man had beaten her son for eating some honey he had found in his house.

Much more evidence was given at the Chelmsford Assizes as to the possession by the accused of imps or familiars, always in animal shape ; and it is to be noted that this had been a constant feature in Essex witchcraft-cases from a long time back. There were the Chelmsford witches of 1579, whose story was set out in a pamphlet picturesquely entitled *A Detection of Damnable Driftes*. Of these one, Elizabeth Fraunces, late of Hatfield, admitted having cursed Poole's wife for having refused her yeast ; where-upon suddenly she heard a great noise, and there appeared to her a spirit of a white colour, " in seemying like to a little rugged dogge," who asked her whither she was going. For such things as she wanted, she replied, and then told about the refusal of the yeast. She willed the spirit to go to Poole's wife and plague her. The spirit bade her first give him something. She had a crust of white bread in her hand, which she bit, throwing a piece on the ground. The spirit took this and went on his way, after having been willed to plague Poole's wife in the head.

Since that day, Elizabeth Fraunces said, she had never seen the spirit. But she heard from neighbours that not long after Poole's wife was grievously pained in the head, and remained so still.

---

[1] There is recorded in *State Trials* (IV, 828 *n.*) the trial for witchcraft at Worcester in 1649 of Margaret Landis, Susan Cook, Rebecca West, and Rose Holybread, all four being condemned and executed. These women are obviously, by their names, of those who were lucky enough to escape death at the Chelmsford Assizes.

Another of those charged at Chelmsford in 1579, Ellen Smith, was accused by a man of having caused a very great pain in his body, because he had driven her young son from his door. The same night, as he sat by the fire with a neighbour, they saw a rat run up the chimney and presently fall down again in the likeness of a toad. This they took up with the tongs and thrust into the fire, which burned " as blewe as azure," and was almost out. The result of this was great pain to the witch herself.

Here we have not Ellen Smith's alleged confession, but an accusation made against her ; but the rat-toad is clearly her familiar.

The St. Oses (St. Osyth) case in 1582[1] involved no fewer than thirteen women, who were charged with causing the deaths of two dozen people and a number of cattle and swine, besides other wicked acts. Against one of the witches, Ursley Kempe, *alias* Grey, her eight-year-old base son bore witness that she had four spirits ; and she confessed that it was true. The four were Tyffin, like a white lamb ; Tyttey, like a little grey cat ; Pygine, like a black toad ; and Jacke, like a black cat. The son said that he had seen his mother give them beer to drink, and of a white loaf or cake to eat, and that in the night the spirits would come and " sucke blood of her upon her armes and other places of her body."

The woman herself confessed to having been the death of her brother's wife for calling her " whore and witche." This death was accomplished by the agency of Jacke ; while Tyffin had been sent to take revenge on another woman by rocking her child's cradle over, " so as the child might fall out and break the neck of it." She explained as the origin of her evil career as witch that about ten or eleven years ago, being troubled with a lameness of the bones, she went to one Cocke's wife, of Weley, now deceased, who told her she was bewitched and, at her entreaty taught her how herself to become a witch—no pleasant process.

[1] The contemporary pamphlet on this case is entitled *A true and just Recorde of the Information, Examination, and Confessions of all the Witches taken at St. Oses*, the author's name being given as W. W. He deals only with the preliminary investigation of the case before the Justice of the Peace at St. Osyth.

Ursley Kempe in her confession involved several other women, who in their turn made confessions implicating others till the number of thirteen was reached. The details, which were given to Bryan Darcy, Esq., J.P., in February, preparatory to trial at the assizes, are much the same as in most cases of the kind, and need not detain us. Three items only seem worth mention.

One woman, Elizabeth Bennet, had a spirit called Lyard or Lyerd, "like a lyon or a hare." (Truly these familiars were Protean in shape!) Another, Annis Hird, had twelve imps or spirits, of which six were like kine, of the bigness of rats, which she fed on straw or hay. Usually the term "spirit" is employed, more rarely "imp."

The third item, from the confession of Ales Manfield, of Thorpe, is indeed curious. She had four imps, Robin, Jack, William, and Puppet *alias* Mamet. A little before Michael-mas they had said to her : "I pray you, Dame, give us leave to go unto Little Clapton, to Celles [another witch]. We would burn barns, and also kill cattle." After their return they told her they had burnt Rosse's barn, with corn. "Celles his wife knewe of it, and they all foure were fedde by her at the time they were away, was about a sevennight." This is a defence that modern barn-burners do not make.

It is not clear what exactly happened to these St. Osyth witches. Francis Hutchinson, who in *An Historical Essay concerning Witchcraft* gives a long list of all the cases of which he could obtain information, merely says (under the wrong date, 1576) : "About this time seventeen or eighteen were condemned at St. Osith in Essex," giving no clue as to whether they were hanged, either at Chelmsford or in their own neighbourhood.

We may now return to 1645, where the facts are better substantiated.

As a result of the witchcraft trials at Chelmsford, Hopkins records with pride that "in our Hundred in Essex 29 were condemned at once, 4 brought 25 miles to be hanged"; and Stearne says that "those which were condemned, there being about 28, at Chelmsford, in the summer 1645, were (as I remember) all women." It would appear that Elizabeth Clarke and Anne Leech were two of the four executed at Manningtree, as Stearne specifically mentions their names ; Anne Weste is sure to have been another, seeing how she was implicated by the rest of the accused.

Hutchinson states that one of the condemned died in gaol, another on going to execution.

Having purged Essex, the witch-finders transferred their activities to the adjacent county of Suffolk, guided by what had been elicited from the confessions produced at Chelmsford. In Suffolk they seemed likely to obtain a still larger number of victims. The gaol at Bury St Edmunds, where the assizes were to be held at the end of August, was soon full, the prisoners on charges of witchcraft being possibly as many as two hundred.

When the assizes began, the Court had the assistance of two leading Puritan ministers in Suffolk, one being Edmund Calamy, who, according to Richard Baxter, listened to the confessions of the accused in order to see that there were no fraud or wrong done them ! As Calamy was almost as credulous as Baxter on the subject of witchcraft, his presence was of little promise to the accused.

It would be well if we could think that the ministers' influence was used in the removal of one gross torture inflicted upon some of the accused, that of " swimming," or the ordeal by water, when the victim, after having thumbs and big toes tied together, was lowered into a pond by a rope round the waist. The theory was that a witch would swim, an innocent person sink. Among those charged at Bury St. Edmunds who were submitted to this ordeal was the Rev. John Lowes, eighty years old, whose case we refer to in detail on pp. 104-5 ; while Hopkins's defence of " swimming " will be found on p. 109. Perhaps in consequence of the Lowes scandal, the Court at Bury-St. Edmunds condemned the employment of the ordeal by water. But we do not hear that the ministers assisting were responsible for that condemnation.

What we do hear is Baxter's calm comment in *The Certainty of the World of Spirits*—long after the witch-trials in Suffolk, it may be admitted—that " an old reading parson named Lowis was one that was hanged ; who confessed," etc. No word of reprobation for his torturers. But then

Lowes was "an old reading parson," that is to say one who daily read mattins and evensong in his church, which did not commend him to Baxter. Hopkins the Puritan, on the other hand, the upholder of the ordeal by water, is by him described as "famously known for his work in Essex and Suffolk." Such was the effect of religious bias upon a man commonly held up for admiration.

More hopeful to the prisoners at Bury than the presence of ministers in Court was a turn in the fortunes of the Civil War. The Assizes were actually interrupted when, as Stearne writes, "an Allarum at Cambridge" caused adjournment of the gaol-delivery at Bury. But after a few weeks it was seen that the forces of the more enlightened Royalists would not be able to come, and the Puritans resumed their grim work. Altogether Stearne puts the number of those condemned, "most women, all at one goale [sic] delivery" at sixty-eight. Owing to there being no precise record of the second session at Bury, the total number of those condemned and executed is uncertain. Francis Hutchinson was told "near forty at the several times of execution, and as many more in the county as made up threescore," but says others made it more.

The persecution spread. Norfolk was affected not long after Suffolk, and about twenty alleged witches had been hanged before the Yarmouth corporation in August invited Hopkins to visit the town, offering him such a fee as he thought fit.[1] He paid two visits before the end of 1695, and secured the condemnation of six women, one of whom was reprieved. Cambridgeshire and Huntingdonshire were next visited, but with less success. In the latter county John Gaule, vicar of Great Staughton, made a determined stand, both in the pulpit and out of it, with the consequence that Hopkins left Great Staughton alone.

Gaule was himself a Puritan, who called himself "Preacher of the Word," and believed in the evil reality of witchcraft. But he strongly condemned the professional witch-finder. Before the end of 1646 he published in

[1] Concerning his fees, see his own account on p. 110. That his work in Norfolk and before, however, was called in question may be inferred from the title of his book, with its reference to " queries lately delivered to the Judges of Assize for the County of Norfolk."

London his *Select Cases of Conscience touching Witches and Witchcraft.* On p. 88 of this he states his sixth case : "Whether witch-seeking or witch-finding is an Art, Vocation, Profession, Occupation, Office, or Trade of Life, allowable by a Christian Church or State ?" On p. 108 he gives as his conclusion : "Though the Authority be commendable, yet the case is doubtfull, the undertaking difficult, the. profession dangerous, but the usurpation damnable."

Hopkins and Stearne, not finding Huntingdonshire profitable, went on to Bedfordshire, but there too met with considerable hostility, which decided Hopkins at least to give up his work about May, 1646. He was perhaps already feeling the symptoms of the illness that was to carry him off next year. He was certainly influenced by objections made against his methods of "discovering" witches, and determined to publish a defence.

Stearne continued his work a little longer, and was able, when he came to sum up the whole results of the campaign, to boast of "about 200 executed since May, 1645," in the various counties visited, whereof "the women farre exceeded the men in number."

Before coming to an examination of the defences put up by Hopkins and Stearne of their activities, we may look at a few of the cases ; two of which made a considerable stir at the time.

The first is the case of the Rev. John Lowes, a man of eighty, who had been vicar (and "a reading parson," as we have heard) at Brandeston, Suffolk, over forty years before he was brought up at the Bury St. Edmunds Assizes on the charge of witchcraft. According to Stearne, more than thirty years before "Parson Lowis" had been "indited for a common imbarriter,[1] and for witchcraft, and the grand jury found the bill for a common imbarriter." He plainly had enemies in his parish, and the accusation of witchcraft was now renewed.

The old man was submitted to the ignominy of being

[1] This word I have been unable to find anywhere ; but it appears to have the same meaning as barrator (or -er), in its secondary sense of "a person who buys or sells ecclesiastical preferment, a simoniac or simonist." See Murray's *Dictionary*.

searched for witch-marks. These were duly found. Then a confession was extracted from him. Stearne says he confessed that, " in pride of heart to be equal, or rather above God, the Devill took advantage of him, and he covenanted with the Devill, and sealed it with his blood." He admitted, too, that he had three familiars, which " sucked on his marks," and did much harm, as when they once sank a ship with all hands. He was joyful, he said, to see what his imps could do. He also asserted that he had a charm to keep him out of gaol and hanging.

As to how the confession was obtained from the wretched man, there is the evidence of a letter written by a Mr. Rivett, of Brandeston, to Dr. Hutchinson. Rivett's father had been acquainted with Lowes, so that the evidence may be regarded as contemporary.

The " watching " of the accused (which was probably under the direction of Hopkins) was particularly cruel in this case, in view of his age. He was kept awake several nights together, and run backwards and forwards about the room until he was out of breath. After a rest he was run again. This went on for several days and nights, " till he was weary of his life, and scarcely sensible of what he said or did." He was also swum, at Framlingham, which Rivett says was " no true rule to try him by, for they put in honest people at the same time, and they swam as well as he."

We should rather wonder that the old man swam! But he was evidently of strong physique. He was condemned, as a matter of course—having the marks, having confessed, and having swum—and was hanged. It is recorded that he " dyed very desperately " ; though this may mean no more than that on the point of death he protested his innocence.

As a result of a visit by Hopkins to Ipswich in 1653, a woman named Jane Lakeland was executed there on September 9th. There is some doubt as to the manner of her death. It is commonly said that she was burnt at the stake, not hanged ; which is possible, since there was a charge against her of murder of her own husband by witchcraft, and this was " petty treason," punishable by burning at the stake until the penalty was changed in 1790.

Dr. Francis Hutchinson, who had been perpetual curate of St. James', Bury St. Edmunds, in 1692, merely says (in the second edition of his *Historical Essay*, 1720), "About this time Jane Lakeland was either hanged or burnt at Ipswich."

Hopkins mentions the case of one Meggs, baker, living seven miles from Norwich, who was hanged for witch-craft at the assizes there. At the time of the scare in Norfolk, it appears, he came voluntarily to Norwich to be searched for witch-marks. Unfortunately he had some kind of marks, and so was tried, condemned, and executed. His fate is regarded by Hopkins as an instance of persuasion by the Devil, misleading his followers.

Stearne gives the fourth story. There was a young man, Henry Carre, of Rattlesden in Suffolk, "a scholler fit for Cambridge (if not a Cambridge scholler) and well educated." He fell into "the grievous sin"; and, what was worse, into Stearne's hands. He was searched, and marks were found on him. He then confessed to having two imps that for two years had sucked on those marks, coming in the likeness of mice, "which he felt oft, and said they were hairy and heavy."

Carre said that he had forsaken God, and God him. But he would confess no more until he came to the gallows, and then he would confess all. He resisted all importunity to change his attitude ; and, his trial being delayed " by reason of an Allarum at Cambridge," he died in gaol at Bury St. Edmunds.

It was conceived to be pride of heart, says Stearne, which was the original cause of his sin. "Yet I confess that he fell into poverty before his death, but, as for that, I think it is seldom or never that any get estates or thrive that thus give themselves over to Satan, but rather consume their estates, if they have any."

Another remarkable tlae of Stearne's is about one Clarke's wife, at Keyston, Huntingdonshire. The ending is somewhat enigmatic. Clarke's wife, it appears, "skipped out at a hole in a stone wall, about half a foot thick, which was some nine inches long, and some foure and a halfe broad, all the one side head and all, and but little to be seen of her but one leg ; and the hole was near a yard and halfe from the ground, and yet one pulled her back againe, and afterward went away, nobody knew how." Does Stearne mean it to be understood that Clarke's wife was one of the vanishing witches, of whom we shall hear more in the next chapter ? There is, at any rate, no mention of her having been hanged.

We now turn to Hopkins's apologia. His *Discovery of Witches* is defined by himself as " Certaine queries answered, which have been and are likely to be objected against Matthew Hopkins, in his way of finding out Witches." It provides us with information which otherwise we should have been without, or should have been far less assured about. His answer to the queries are frank, for a man of his character, and show no sense of shame for what he had done. The text on the title-page is " Thou shalt not suffer a witch to live."

To Query I, that he must be " the greatest witch, sorcerer, and wizzard himself, else he could not doe it," his answer is, " If Satan's kingdome be divided against itselfe, how shall it stand ? "

Query II is that he certainly must have met the Devil and cheated him of his Book, in which were written the names of all the witches' names in England ; and also that if he looked on a witch he could tell by her countenance, so that his help was from the Devil. If he had been too hard for the Devil, he replied, and got his book, " it had been to his great commendation, and no disgrace at all." He disclaimed any more judgement of physiognomy than other men had.

The next two queries were as to how he gained his skill ; if by experience, how was that gained. His answer was mainly a relation of his discovery of the Manningtree witches in 1644 and of what he found out from Elizabeth Clarke. This we have already heard.

Query V is concerned with " papps or teats," the supposed marks of a witch. " Whereas many people (especially antient people) are troubled with naturall wretts on severall parts of their bodies, and other naturall excrescences," it is asked whether these people are to be judged by the searcher alone, and so accused or acquitted. There seems perhaps an allusion to the case of old John Lowes here.

The parties so judging, answers Hopkins, can justify their skill, and show good reasons why the marks are not merely natural. One of the proofs is that they are " most commonly insensible, and feel neither pin, needle, aule, etc., thrust through them." He speaks, of course, as an actual searcher ; for he and Stearne did this work themselves where men-prisoners were concerned.

Query VIII is the next of importance ; and with the answer, it is indeed of importance, in view of the weight that some modern writers attach to the " confessions " of the witches. When the marks have been discovered on the accused, it is queried, " yet that will not serve sufficiently to convict them, but they must be tortured and kept from sleep two or three nights, to distract them, and make them say anything ; which is a way to tame a wilde colt, or hawke, &c."

" In the infancy of this discovery," runs the answer, " it was not only thought fitting, but enjoined in Essex and Suffolk by the magistrates, with this intention only, because they being kept awake would be more the active to call their Imps in open view the sooner to their view, which oftentimes happened ; and never or seldom did any Witch complain in the time of their keeping for want of rest, but after they had beat their heads together in the Goale [sic] ; and after this use was not allowed by the judges and other magistrates it was never since used, which is a year and a half since, neither were any kept from sleep by any order or direction since ; but peradventure their own stubborn wills did not let them sleep, though tendered and offered to them."

Query IX continues on the subject of torture, asking about the accused being " extraordinarily walked till their feet were blistered," to force confessions from them. The gist of Hopkins's answer is that the accused were " walked " only to keep them awake. He admits that " diverse have been by rusticall people (they hearing them confess to be witches) misused and abused, diverse whereof have suffered for the same, but could never be proved against this Discoverer to have a hand in it or consent to it." Who, we may wonder, was responsible for the " running " of John Lowes ?

Query X referred to the ordeal by water—" a tryall not allowed by Law or conscience." " It is not denied," Hopkins answers, " but many were so served as had papps, and floated, others that had none were tried with them and sunk, but mark the reasons," which he gives as follows :

(1) The Devil persuaded many to come of their own accord to be tested, their witch-marks being " so close they shall not be found out." Some came ten or twelve miles to be searched, and were hanged for their labour. (He gave the instance of one Meggs, baker, hanged at Norwich, which we have heard.) The Devil, he goes on, advises them to be " swome " and tells them they shall sink ; when they are tried that way and float, they see the Devil has deceived them again.

(2) The question of their floating or sinking was never brought in as evidence against any of the accused at their trials.

(3) King James I in his *Dæmonologie* approved of the test, since God had appointed that " the water shall refuse to receive them in her bosom that have shaken off them the sacred Water of Baptisme, and wilfullie refused the benefite thereof."

As for the matter of confessions wrung by torture from " stupified, ignorant, unintelligible, poore silly creatures," which is posed in Query XI, Hopkins utterly denied that a witch's confession was of any validity when elicited by torture or violence. Though some *had* suffered after being watched, walked, swum, " yet peradventure magistrates with much care and diligence did solely and fully examine them after sleepe and consideration sufficient." He also denied the validity of confessions drawn from a witch by flattery (" you shall not go to the gaol, nor be hanged, &c.") ; of those involving improbabilities or impossibilities, such as flying through the air, riding on sticks ; and of those where the words are in the interrogation put in the mouth of " a silly (yet witch wicked enough) " and agreed to by her.

It is indeed strange to see Hopkins assuming this humane and reasonable attitude ! And in his next answer he actually says : " I would that the magistrates and jurats

would a little examine witnesses when they hear witches
confess such and such a murder, whether the party had
not long time before, or at the time when the witch grew
suspected, some disease or other predominant which might
cause that issue or effect of death." Could more plausible
words come from the mouth of a Hopkins?

What perhaps he considered the strongest part of his
defence of himself as witch-finder, Hopkins reserved to
the end of his book. The fourteenth and last Query
suggests that all the witch-finder does is to " fleece the
country " ; to go to towns and make fair promises, and
maybe to do nothing for it. You do him a great wrong,
he answers. In the first place, he never went to a town
except on invitation. He never " detected " a witch, nor
said to one, " Thou art a witch ! " except after a test by
search and confession. As to the accusation of fleecing,
we may give his closing passage verbatim :

" He demands but 20s. a town and doth sometimes ride
20 miles for that, and hath no more for all his charges
thither and back again (and it may be stayes a weeke
there) and findes there 3 or 4 witches, or if it be but one,
cheap enough, and this is the great summe he takes to
maintaine his Companie with 3 horses."

Judicet ullus, he writes in conclusion, as though sure of
the verdict.

What happened to him actually between his retirement
from witch-finding in the first half of 1646 and his death
in August, 1647, has not been established. The story that
he, in consequence of the accusations against him of being
a witch himself, suffered the same fate that he had brought
upon so many others, and was hanged, is an example
of the idea of " poetic justice " influencing legend.
What Hutchinson says in his *Historical Essay on Witchcraft* is
that Hopkins " went on searching and swimming the poor
creatures until some gentleman, out of indignation at the
barbarity, took him and tied his own thumbs and toes,
as he used to tye others, and when he was put in the water
he himself swam as well as they did. This cleared the
country of him ; and it was a great deal of pity that they
did not think of the experiment before." Apart from there
being no confirmation of this, the statement certainly does

not make out that Hopkins was hanged.[1] There are two
pieces of evidence to the contrary.   One is what is said
by his ally Stearne one year after his death : " Concerning
him who is dead, who likewise was an agent in the business,
for my part I never knew that he either unjustly favoured
any, or received bribes, or used such extremity as was
reported of him.   Only at first, before he or I ever went,
many towns used extremity of themselves, which after
was laid on us.   And I do not deny but at first he might
watch some ; but, to my knowledge, he soon left it, or at
least in such a way as not to make them uncapable ; but
if he ever did at first, evidence was not taken till after
they rested. . . . To my knowledge, we have been both
much injured in words, and he since his death ; but I am
certain (notwithstanding whatsoever hath been said of him)
he died peaceably at Manningtree after a long sickness
of a consumption, as many of his generation had done
before him, without any trouble of conscience for what he
had done, as was falsely reported of him.   And, though
many of these things may seem very strange and hardly
to be believed, yet this is the very truth ; and that he was
the son of a godly minister, and therefore without doubt
within the Covenant.   Therefore let no man take upon
him either to speak or write more than he knoweth to be
truth ;   for this I am able to manifest and prove to
be truth."

The other piece of evidence is the entry in the parish-
register of Mistley-cum-Manningtree of his burial at
Mistley on August 12th, 1647.   So it may be taken that
Matthew Hopkins was not hanged, but died in his bed.

In 1648 John Stearne, " now of Lawshall neere Burie
Saint Edmunds in Suffolke, sometime of Manningtree in
Essex," published in London his *Confirmation and Discovery
of Witch-Craft*.   This is described on the title-page as

---

[1] The Rev. Montague Summers dismisses even the story of the
swimming as a mere figment. As to Samuel Butler's lines (*Hudibras* II,
canto 3),

> Who after prov'd himself a witch
> And made a rod for his own breech,

he very reasonably maintains that they imply Hopkins's fall from
success, not his death as a witch.

" Containing there several particulars ; that there are
Witches called bad Witches, and Witches untruely called
good or white Witches, and what manner of people they
be, and how they may bee knowne, with many particulars
there unto tending. Together with the Confessions of
many of those executed since May 1645 in the severall
Counties hereafter mentioned. As also some objections
answered."

Stearne is more uncompromising than was Hopkins in
part at least of his " queries answered." For him there
is only one treatment for any witch. In his address to
Courteous Reader he states that " the sinne of Witchcraft, and the diabolical practise thereof, is *omnium scelerum
atrocissimum*,[1] and a few pages later he guards against any
idea that he may wish to treat good or white witches more
leniently than those called bad. " I say all Witches to be
bad, and ought to suffer alike, being both in league with
the Devill : for so is the good, so untruly called, as well
as the other, either open or implicit. And therefore I
conclude, all that be in open league with the Devill ought
to die."

Stearne insists much on the predominant number of
women among the witches. In the just quoted address he
remarks : " Of Witches in generall there be commonly
more women than men. This is evident. First from God's
Law against Witches, *Exod.* 22. In the feminine gender,
præstigiatricem ne sinito vivere. . . ."

He repeatedly returns to the point ; and it is of course a
fact that in witchcraft, as in Spiritualism and most modern
" freak " religions, the majority of the adherents are
women. In the evidence set out by him the women's
names far outnumber the men's.

That Stearne, like Hopkins, believed in the reality of his
evidence we need not doubt. Nor need we wonder. What
may cause wonder is that so many writers to the present
day do not hesitate to accept what Stearne, Hopkins,
etc., thought evidence as valid. Podmore observes,
somewhat guardedly, in *Modern Spiritualism* that the

---

[1] Compare F. von Spee's *enormissimum, gravissimum, atrocissimum*.
But this does not prove that Stearne had read the *Cautio Criminalis*.
The epithet was constant.

evidence of the professional witch-finder is perhaps no more worthy of credence than that of the professional " medium " of to-day.

Why perhaps ? Surely Gurney is justified when—criticising Glanvil's maintenance in *Sadducismus Triumphatus* of the " overwhelming evidence " and the " attestation of thousands of eye and ear witnesses, and these not of the easily deceivable vulgar only, but of wise and grave discerners "[1]—he asks : " If thousands of wise and grave discerners *saw* the incredible marvels with their own eyes, how is it that in not a single case has the record been preserved ? If on the other hand they *saw* only the credible marvels—fits and the like—and *believed* the incredible ones, on extraordinarily feeble testimony but under an extraordinarily strong prepossession, in what sense can it be asserted that there was then ' overwhelming evidence ' for what would now be denied ? "

Stearne, with the mediæval mind, which persists so pathetically to-day, believed in the reality of the incredible things that he related. That was not his enormity. What was enormous was the fact that he made money out of witch-finding. He was well aware of the suspicion that this aroused ; and near the end of his sixty-page pamphlet he defends himself. He denies that he ever made gain, or favoured any and persecuted others, or took bribes. Never, one time with another, he asserts, did he make as much (by witch-finding) as by his calling and practice towards the maintenance of his family ; nor had any money save what he openly took in sight of the townsmen where he came.

In short, he did not make gain ; he took money legitimately for his good work. And, as for ever accusing anyone wrongfully, he concludes, his conscience was clear before God !

This unctuous rascal, as the Rev. Montague Summers

[1] As an example of what the Rev. Joseph Glanvil, a little after the time of the Essex witches, regarded as valid evidence, we may take his story of the panting old woman who was suddenly seen in the place of a hunted hare. A huntsman vouched for the fact. Glanvil accepts it, and explains that the hare was a demon, the old woman a witch, who was invisibly hurried along with the hare, so as to put her out of breath.

well calls him, is not honoured by a place in *The Dictionary of National Biography*, though two eminently respectable namesakes are.   James Crossley, who edited Potts's *Discovery* for the Chetham Society of Manchester in 1845, speaks of him, in a communication to *Notes and Queries* (June, 1852), as " the reverend author " of his book, and says that he was " no theorist, but a thoroughly practical man," who " has the subject at his fingers' ends and discusses it so scientifically that Hopkins sinks into insignificance by the side of him."   When he adds : " Pity is it that such a philanthropic individual should have had occasion to complain :   ' In many places I never received a penny as yet, nor am like, except that I should sue,' " we cannot help but wonder if this is sarcasm too thickly veiled ! But Mr. Crossley seems to have been serious.

If he is right in talking of the reverend author, then Stearne's crime is all the greater, whatever his scientific learning, so-called.

CHAPTER III

SALEM

NO apology will be made for the length of the chapter which is to follow; because the events which centred at Salem Village, Essex County, in the province of the Massachusetts Bay, New England, in the year 1692, were of notable importance and painful interest in the history of witch-persecution. Nowhere is there more strikingly illustrated the outbreak of the mania with which this part of our study deals, in a community of inferior intellectual development, isolated to a large extent from the outside world, and brought up in exceedingly narrow views of the religion which it professed.

It may be objected that Salem had the advantages of the neighbourhood of Boston and of Harvard College, whose tercentenary is being celebrated this autumn. The answer is to refer to the representatives of Boston and of Harvard with whom we shall meet in the course of the story. It may be stated in advance that, for the most part, they do not impress anyone who wishes to be impartial as an influence that can be described as humanising or conducive to that charity without which no religion can claim respect. In whatever other ways they strove for good, their conduct in the matter of the " witches " was a horrible blot upon the chronicles of New England, and on the annals of mankind at this period. The tale, however, may be left to tell itself, without any further introduction.

* * * * *

Stories of witchcraft were not unknown before in New England. In the section of his *Wonders of the Invisible World*, entitled " Wonders Encountered," the Boston minister, Cotton Mather, wrote in 1692 or 1693 : " We have been advised by some Credible Christians yet alive that a Malefactor, accused of Witchcraft as well as Murder, and Executed in this place more than Forty Years ago, did then give notice of an Horrible Plot against this Country by Witchcraft, and a foundation of Witchcraft then laid, which if it were not seasonably discovered, would probably Blow up, and pull down all the Churches in this Country. And," he continues, " we have now with Horror seen the Discovery of such a Witchcraft ! An Army of Devils is openly broken in upon the place which is the Center, and after a sort the first-born of our English Settlements : and the houses of the Good People are fill'd with the doleful Shrieks of their Children and Servants, Tormented by Invisible Hands, with Tortures preternatural."

Cotton Mather therefore had no doubt that the Salem phenomenon was no new thing.

Now in *Records of Salem Witchcraft, 1691–2*,[1] there is mention of a charge made against one John Bradstreet— this name we shall hear again later—who was brought before magistrates at Ipswich, near Salem, in 1652, " for suspition and having familiarity with the devill." Upon examination of the case it was found that Bradstreet " had tould a lye, which was a seconde, being convicted once before " ; and the sentence was " a fine of 20s. or else to be whipt." This is obviously not Cotton Mather's Horrible Plot.

In 1662 there was a witch named Greensmith executed at Hartford, as is barely recorded in Increase Mather's *Remarkable Providences*.[2]

There are more details, in *Records of Salem Witchcraft*, of a case in 1669, when a widow named Burt was accused

---

[1] Published in 1864 by W. (*sc.* W. Elliot Woodward), of Roxbury, Mass., from the original documents in the archives of Essex County, Mass. This work contains all the examinations, confessions, etc., of the accused persons at Salem, as well as some other valuable information connected with the affair and with some antecedent cases.

[2] This work shows its author to have been a remarkably credulous and bigoted man. In his sixth chapter, headed " That there are Dæmons and Possessed Persons," he writes : " It must sadly be confessed that many innocent persons have been put to death under the notion of witchcraft, whereby much innocent blood hath been shed ; especially it hath been so in Popish times and places."

by various people of evil practices. A girl Bethiah Carter, aged 23, testified that she had heard Sara " townsan "— her married sister, it appears—say that when she was a maid and lived with Goodwife Burt the latter told her if she could believe in her god she would cure her body and soul. The said goodwife added that she had not been able to cure her husband because he would not believe in her god.

Sara had also informed Bethiah and others that she had often seen Goodwife Burt appear at her bed's foot and at divers other places, by day and by night.

A physician testified that he had attended Sara when she was ill with " noe naturall fitts," and that she had informed him that " Burt " had afflicted her, and had told her that if she ever related it to anyone she would afflict her worse.

The two girls' father's evidence was that both his daughters were at one time sorely afflicted, " and in their greatest extremity would cry out and roar and say that they did see Goody Burt, and say ' There she is, do you not see her? Kill her, there she is ! ' and that they said several times."

Other witnesses were two brothers named Knight, of whom the elder had nothing of more importance to reveal than that he had seen old Goody Burt come out of a swamp once, and suddenly she was gone out of sight. When he met her indoors afterwards he asked her if he had seen her in the swamp just now. " No, I was in the house," she replied, whereon he called her a light-headed woman !

The younger Knight had formerly lodged at the same house as the widow Burt in Salem and met with several unexpected appearances of her. On his way to Salem once he momentarily saw first a cat, then a dog, and then widow Burt, of whom he also lost sight. The same night, looking out of his window in clear moonlight, he saw the widow, " or one in her shape," upon a grey horse. This vision disappeared, but she was next in the room with him. " Then I took up a piece of a barrel-head and threw it at her, and as I think hit her on the breast ; and then could see her no more that time."

The outcome of the case against Goody Burt is not stated. It is unlikely that the Knights' evidence counted for much. In view of later happenings, we cannot feel sure that the " afflicted " sisters' charges were disregarded.

Small cases came into court in 1674 and 1680, two Salem men being respectively dismissed with a caution and ordered to find security for 20s. An alleged witch-woman in 1680 failed to appear, having managed somehow to make herself invisible ; but that was a faculty of witches.

Still more details than with regard to Goody Burt are given of a case at Boston in 1688, which is notable as apparently first causing Cotton Mather to take an active interest in the investigation of witchcraft. It forms the chief part of his book, *Late Memorable Providences relating to Witchcrafts and Possessions*, published by him at Boston in 1689 and re-issued in London two years later. The first edition was " recommended by the Ministers of Boston and Charleston," and evidently reflected the predominant local religious opinion of the day.

The particular providence illustrated concerned the family of John Goodwin, a mason, who lived in Boston with his wife and four children. Mather emphasises the family's piety. In the summer of 1688 the eldest child, a girl of thirteen, saw cause to examine the washerwoman about some missing linen, which it was feared had been stolen. This washerwoman was the daughter of " an ignorant and scandalous old woman in the neighbourhood, whose miserable husband before he died had sometimes com-plained of her that she undoubtedly was a witch." The old woman, by name Glover, who was Irish, took up her daughter's defence, and bestowed very bad language upon the Goodwin girl when she questioned her about the linen, whereupon the child became indisposed in her health and soon was visited with " strange fits." Before long her sister and two brothers were similarly seized, and within a few weeks all four were grievously tormented.

John Goodwin laid a complaint against the old woman Glover, and she was brought to trial ; " at which," writes Mather, " thro' the efficacy of a charm, I suppose, used upon her by one or some of her Crue,[1] the court could receive answers from her in none but the Irish, which

---

[1] I retain Mather's spelling, but not his capital letters hereafter.

was her native language, although she understood the English very well." The services of two interpreters were therefore called upon.

A search of Glover's home revealed "several small images, or puppets, made of raggs, and stufft with goat's hair and other such ingredients." When these were produced in court she acknowledged that her way to torment the objects of her malice was by wetting her finger with her spittle and stroking one of these images. Moreover, when she took one in her hand in court, one of the children fell into "sad fits" before the whole assembly, the experiment being repeated with the same result. The conduct of the accused, however, was such that the magistrates appointed five or six physicians to examine her very strictly "whether she were not craz'd in her intellectuals, and had not procured to herself by folly and madness the reputation of a witch." Surprisingly, the physicians found no discourse come from her but what was "pertinent and agreeable." She owned herself a Roman Catholic, and could repeat the *Paternoster*, though imperfectly. In the upshot they found her *compos mentis*, and sentence of death was passed upon her.

There were other charges of witchcraft against her, including the causing of the death of a woman who had declared she saw Glover sometimes come down her chimney.

In his capacity of minister at the Second Church, Boston, Cotton Mather visited the old woman after her condemnation. He says that she never denied the guilt of witchcraft, but "confessed very little about the circumstances of her confederacies with the Devils ; only she said that she us'd to be at meetings which her *Prince* and four more were present at." She told who the four were, and, "for her *Prince*, her account plainly was that he was the *Devil*."

Before she went to execution Glover predicted that the Goodwin children would not be relieved by her death. And so it was, declares Mather, who gives fantastic details of their afflictions. He took the eldest to his house to cure her, which in some considerable time he did, after a last violent fit, when she appeared nearly to die.

Such was the story which Mather had to tell of the particular providence which resulted in the hanging of the old woman Glover ; and he was well assured of the good which the publication of his narrative would do. "Go then, my little book," he exclaims in his introduction to it, " as a lackey to the more elaborate essays of those learned men [Baxter, Glanvil, More, etc.]. Go tell mankind that there are devils and witches." Four Bostonians, who signed a commendation to the book as " eye and ear-witnesses of many of the most considerable things related " in it, also stated that it would afford clear confirmation that " there is a God, and a Devil, and Witchcraft." Truly these pious gentlemen got great comfort out of the Devil !

We now come to the history of the Salem witch-persecution proper ; a sufficiently ghastly tale, though lacking the atrocious presence of a professional witch-finder like Hopkins. In his place we have the intervention of various congregationalist ministers, and in particular of the two Mathers, father and son, who have left their ample records of the whole affair, without the slightest indication of remorse for the part which they played in it.

In view of the Mathers' importance in the story of the Massachusetts Bay colony, it was not to be expected that they should be treated otherwise than tenderly in *The Dictionary of American Biography*. But it might seem to the impartial reader that their biographer—in both cases Mr. Kenneth B. Murdoch—has allowed his admiration for their championship of the rights of Massachusetts and of their religious faith to blind him to the evil which they helped in doing. We will try to set out the facts dispassionately, beginning with those concerning the origin of the Mather family in America, which help to explain to some extent their fierce sectarianism.

The founder of the family in the New World was Richard Mather, born at Lowton, Lancashire, in 1596, who after a brief residence at Brasenose College, Oxford, returned to his native county to become a preacher at Toxteth Park Chapel. He later received ordination from the Bishop of Chester ; but, having been first suspended and finally forbidden to preach, on account of his Puritan doctrines, he decided to leave England for America, and in May, 1635, sailed from Bristol for Boston in " the province of the Massachusetts Bay." By George Offor, editor in 1856 of his son Increase's *Remarkable Providences*, he is called one of those seventy-seven pious clergymen who, with four thousand followers, took refuge in the wilds of America from "the ferocious tyranny of Archbishop Laud." How liberty was used by these pious refugees, or their immediate descendants, remains to be seen.[1]

Richard Mather, soon after his arrival in New England, was invited to become Congregationalist minister at Dorchester, Massachusetts, and here he remained until his death. Here too was born, in 1639, Increase, the youngest of his surviving five sons by the widow of the Rev. John Cotton, all but one Congregationalist ministers. Increase was brought up at Dorchester in severely Calvinistic principles before going to the recently founded Harvard College. He took his degree at Harvard at the age of seventeen, and was made a Fellow. To complete his training he was sent to the Old World. When only nineteen he became M.A. of Trinity College, Dublin, and proceeded to England. In 1659, while the Commonwealth still ruled, he accepted the invitation of the Governor of Guernsey to become preacher to the garrison in the island. But with the Restoration came the Act of Uniformity, with which he refused to comply, accordingly losing the chance of what is described as a valuable living in England.

In 1661 Increase Mather was back in Boston, where he received a call to be minister of the Second, or New North, Church. His academic distinctions, coupled with his success as a preacher and a name which he had begun to make for himself as a writer, gained him the offer of the presidency of Harvard in 1681. He declined it, but four years later agreed to be acting-president ; and in 1685 he took the substantive post, with the title of Rector.

Before this happened he had been drawn into the political life of his native Massachusetts, which had been greatly agitated by action from England. Up to 1684 the province had been under charter-government ; but that year Charles II, in pursuance of a plan to weld the separate

---

[1] Offor writes of Increase Mather having, during his long ministry at Boston, "sowed the seeds of religious and political liberty." This statement might have been more ready accepted if Mather had not left so very many works behind to perpetuate his opinions.

American colonies into one dominion, largely for the sake
of military unity against France in the New World, withdrew the charter. In Boston there was indignant opposition to the scheme, and Increase Mather was foremost in
giving expression to the protests. A temporary governor,
Joseph Dudley, with a council nominated by the King
from the various colonies, could do little to pacify the
independent people of Massachusetts ; and the arrival,
at the end of 1686, of Sir Edmund Andros, chosen as
Governor by James II, made matters worse ; for he
insisted on his right to levy taxes on a community which
had no direct representation. Andros succeeded in
suppressing an outbreak in Essex County, but feelings
were the more embittered thereby. Early in 1688 it was
decided by the Congregational churches of the province to
send Increase Mather to make a personal appeal to the
King for the restoration of individual charter-government
for Massachusetts. He sailed for England in April, getting
away secretly, despite the efforts of Andros and the other
officials to prevent his departure.

There was not wanting another Mather to lead the
opposition at Boston. Increase had married Maria,
daughter of John Cotton, who was his father's step-daughter
by his second marriage ; and by her he had a large
family, of whom the eldest son, named Cotton after his
mother, was born at Dorchester in 1663. Cotton had
entered Harvard at the age of twelve, being the youngest
student ever admitted there, and obtained his M.A. degree
in 1681. Being ordained at the Second Church of Boston,
he remained a minister there for the rest of his life. With
his father's departure for England he took on a leading
role in the resistance to dominion-government. Andros
played into his hands by antagonising both the merchant
and the landowning classes of the colony through his
administration. The Revolution in England completed
the work. Cotton Mather wrote *The Declaration of the
Gentlemen, Merchants, and Inhabitants of Boston*, which was
published and was followed by open insurrection. Andros
and all dominion officers who could be found were made
prisoners, and, as the Bostonian Robert Calef says, within
seven weeks of the Revolution at home " there was not

such as the face of any government " in Massachusetts, many being against even the resumption of charter-government. For the time William Stoughton was chosen as deputy-governor.

However, in England Increase Mather had been working by more peaceful means. He had secured the support of the leading nonconformists in London, and had five interviews with James II. When William of Orange came into power, he obtained his ear also. In 1690, by which time Massachusetts had appointed him one of their temporary official agents in England, Increase succeeded in persuading William that the revolt in Boston was not against the royal authority, but merely against the tyranny of James. With some difficulty he carried the day also with his fellow-representatives from Massachusetts, that William's offer of a new charter, in place of a restoration of the old, should be accepted. In return William agreed to Increase Mather's choice of the next governor of Massachusetts.

The man chosen was Sir William Phipps, who had had a curious career. Born in 1651 of humble parents living on the border of Maine, he had started work as a ship's carpenter, married a widow with some money, and became a ship-building contractor in Boston and the master of a sailing vessel. Inspired by nautical friends with the idea of finding sunken treasure, he was ultimately successful in raising a ship off the coast of Hispaniola. In this venture he had as his patron the Duke of Albemarle, and with his share of the treasure in hand he obtained a knighthood in England and a post in Boston under Sir Edmund Andros. But he was soon uncomfortable in his new position, and returned to England to complain. Meeting with Increase Mather, he became a friend and ally, which led to his choice as Governor of Massachusetts. He had already in 1690 joined the Second Church of Boston, and thus was Mather's parishioner.

The two sailed back to America together to institute the new regime. They found an unexpected turmoil awaiting them in Massachusetts. The madness about witchcraft had broken out ; and Increase's eldest son was much involved in it. There was trouble also in the discontent of those who had demanded the colony's old charter. But

we may leave politics aside now and turn to our proper
subject of the campaign against the alleged witches, for
which we must go to Salem Village in the month of
February, 1692.

At this time the minister at Salem Village was Samuel
Parris, a Londoner by birth, who as a child had been
brought by his father to New England, and went to
Harvard, but left without taking a degree. Calef allows
him to have been a man of liberal education, but says that
" not meeting with any great encouragement or advantage
in merchandising "—both in the colony and in the West
Indies, it would appear—he " betook himself to the
ministry, Salem being then vacant, and met with so much
encouragement that he settled as minister among them."
He accepted the call to Salem Village in 1689, being then
thirty-six years of age. Though his narrow religious views
commended him to his parishioners, he soon had some
dispute over his stipend ; which, as we shall see, was not
an unprecedented occurrence at Salem. Calef says that
after about two years he obtained a grant from part of the
town that the house and the land he occupied should remain
to him as his own estate in fee simple, which was a cause of
dissensions among the inhabitants, and between a considerable part of them and the minister ; " which were a
prelude to what followed."

Parris was, however, living comparatively peacefully
in the minister's house at the beginning of 1692, with his
wife, their nine-year-old daughter, and a niece Abigail
Williams, aged eleven, as well two " Indian " (really
negro) servants, or slaves, one male and one female.

About the end of February the young persons of Parris's
family and one or more of the neighbourhood began to
act strangely ; according to Calef's account, getting into
holes and creeping under chairs and stools, using sundry
odd postures and antics, and uttering foolish and ridiculous
speeches, of which neither they nor anyone else could make
sense. Parris's remedy was fasting and praying, and he
invited several neighbouring ministers to his house for a
solemn day of prayer. At this the " sufferers " were mostly
silent, but as soon as a prayer was ended they would act
strangely and ridiculously, and a girl of eleven or twelve

(probably Abigail Williams) would sometimes seem to be in convulsive fits, with her limbs twisted several ways.

The next stage was the naming by the afflicted children of several people whom they said that they saw, when in their fits, afflicting them. The first named by them was Tituba, Parris's " Indian " woman. She did not deny the accusation at first, but owned—almost certainly in words given to her in which to make her confession—that the Devil had urged her to sign a book and to work mischief against the children. Later her account was that her master had beaten her and otherwise abused her, and that he made her give the names of what he called her sister-witches. Anyhow, she seems to have mentioned one Sarah Good, wife of a labourer in Salem Village.

The children also accused Sarah Good, long counted " a melancholy or distracted woman," says Calef, and also a bed-ridden old woman named Osborne, as afflicting them. Both these unfortunates were already so ill thought of in the village that the accusation was readily believed ; and they, with Tituba, were committed for trial.

In the *Records of Salem Witchcraft* the first document is a warrant against Sarah Good, dated February 29th, issued on the complaint of four yeomen of Salem Village " for suspition of witchcraft by her committed and thereby much injury done " to four women. An arrest followed on March 1st, and then a speedy trial. Three indictments show that Sarah Good was charged with that on divers days she had used " certaine detestable arts called witchcraft and sorceries upon and against Sarah, wife of John Vibber ; against Elizabeth Hubbard ; and against Ann Putman—each of the two last being described as " singlewoman." There is no fourth name mentioned.

Sarah Vibber, wife of a husbandman in the village, was thirty-six years old. Elizabeth Hubbard was seventeen. There were two Ann Putmans, the wife and the daughter of Thomas Putman—the name appears very frequently as Putnam—parish clerk, and constable, who is sometimes styled sergeant and occasionally captain. Both mother and daughter were regular witnesses in the Salem trials, but more especially the daughter. Ann Putman junior, in fact, was one of the main instruments of the prosecution ; and it will be seen that she ultimately repented of her evil work. She was in 1692 barely twelve years old. The question of ages is of more importance than might be suspected at present.

It is clear from the charges against Sarah Good that the campaign was assuming a more serious aspect than it had when Parris's daughter and niece, and some of their young friends, complained against the negress Tituba. The last was arrested about the same time as Sarah Good, and her " confession " is the first of these documents in *Records of Salem Witchcraft*. It is taken from the note made by Ezekiel Chevers, whose spelling we retain.

Tituba charged Sarah Good with intent to hurt the children—Elizabeth Parris, Elizabeth Hubbard, Abigail Williams, and Ann Putman—" and would have her do it." She continues :

" Five were with her last night, and would have her hurt the children, which she refused, and Good was one of them. Good with others are very strong and pull her with them to Mr. Putnam's and made her hurt the child. Good. Cr.[1] rode with her upon a poole behind her, takeing hold of one another. Doth not know how they goe, for she never sees trees nor path, but are presently . . . [Here there is a hiatus in the record] Good came to her last night when her M[aster] was at prayer, and would not let her hear. Hath one yellow bird, and stopped her eares at prayer-time. The yellow bird hath been seen by the children, and Titabee saw it suck Good between the forefinger and long finger on the right hand. . . . Same Good have a catt besides the bird, and a thing all over hairy Cr. [*sic*] Sarah Good appeared like a wolfe to Hubbard going to Proctors', and saw it sent by Good to Hubbard. . . . Saw Good's name in the booke, and the devell told her they made the marks. C. said to her she made this marke C. It was the same day she went to prison. Good[wife] Cr. came to ride abroad with her. C. the man

---

[1] This appears to be Goodwife Martha Carrier, afterwards hanged as a witch. The simple " C " later in the record perhaps merely indicates a paragraph ; in which case " the man " who showed Good's name in the book is " the divell."

showed Good['s] name in the book. Good[wife] Cr. pinched her on the leggs. C. being searched found it so after confession."

Somewhat unintelligible in parts, this confession (which undoubtedly saved her life in the end) seems to have been made by Tituba in prison, and shows her admitting to have been at a Sabbat the previous night, not in the body, but as a disembodied witch. We can but suspect that the terrified negress was willing to confess anything that was put to her, after having been " beaten and otherwise abused " by her master. The introduction of a new name, Goodwife Carrier, shows the campaign spreading.

Sarah Good is now credited with familiars, the yellow bird which sucks between her fingers, and a cat. Her daughter Dorothy, only four or five years old, was brought into court to say that her mother " had three birds, one black, one yellow, and these birds hurt the children and afflicted persons."

This little child herself became suspect, as the " afflicted " stated that she bit them (without bodily contact) and showed marks as of small teeth on their arms, while when she looked on them they complained that they were in torment ! The farce of committing Dorothy for trial was carried through ; but there is no more heard about the matter. She was one of the nine children of tender age accused during the persecution.

The accused herself, in her examination in court at the village meeting-house on March 1st, was steadfast in her denial of familiarity with any evil spirit or of a contract with the Devil. When asked why she hurt the children, she replied : " I do not hurt them, I scorn it." John Hathorne, who with Jonathan Corwin was on the bench, now desired the children to look upon her and see if she were one of the persons that tormented them. " Presently," records Ezekiel Chevers, " they were all tormented." Thereupon the following passage ensued :

Hathorne. " Sarah Good, do you not see now what you have done ? Why do you not tell us the truth, why do you thus torment these poor children ? "

S. G. " I do not torment them. *H.* " Who do you employ then ? " *S. G.* " I employ nobody, I scorn it."

H. " How came they thus tormented ? " *S. G.* " What do I know ? You bring others here, and now you charge me with it. *H.* " Why, who was it ? " *S. G.* " I do not know, but it was some you brought into the meeting-house with you." . . . *H.* " Who was it then that tormented the children ? " *S. G.* " It was Osborne."

This is the usual feature. The accused, badgered by cross-examination, accuses someone else ; in this instance the old bedridden Sarah Osborne, who was already, however, charged by the children.

" Who do you serve ? " enquired Hathorne a little later. " I serve God." " What God do you serve ? " " The God that made heaven and earth."

" She was not willing to mention the word God," notes Chevers in his report. " Her answers were in a very wicked, spiteful manner, reflecting and retorting against the authority with base and abusive words, and many lies she was taken in."

At this point, as it had been stated that William Good had said he was afraid that his wife was either a witch or would be one very quickly, Hathorne asked him his reason for speaking so of her. Had he ever seen " anything by her ? " No, not in this nature, replied the husband ; but it was her bad carriage to him—" and indeed," said he, " I may say with tears that she is an enemy to all good." Whether this was a dreary jest on his part does not appear.

Numerous charges were brought against Sarah Good, striving to prove that she belonged to a " company " which mustered to observe unholy days of fast and thanksgiving and blasphemous sacraments. This story of a Witches' Sabbat was now taking full shape ; and on March 31st, a day set apart for solemn humiliation at Salem, Abigail Williams declared that she *saw* a great number of persons in the village at the administration of a mock sacrament, where they had bread as red as raw flesh, and red wine. Who was it that inspired this girl of eleven, the minister's niece ? There was evidently not to be a mere affair of accusations against a labourer's wife, a helpless old woman, and a negress slave. Religious fanaticism was aroused.

Deodat Lawson, Parris's predecessor at Salem Village,

had already arrived on the scene in March—though it is
not implied that he had come to foment the trouble.
Ministers generally were taking interest in the matter,
and quickly had new cases to claim their attention. Two
more women were accused of witchcraft, Goodwives Cory
and Nurse, members of churches at the village and at
Salem itself, and other names were added to the list.
At the examination of Martha Cory on March 21st she
had found ten " afflicted " ready to testify against her,
including Elizabeth Parris, Abigail Williams, and Ann
Putman junior ; " these three being not only the beginners
but also the chief in these accusations," says Calef. They
accused her of biting, pinching, and almost strangling
them, and said that in their fits of torment they saw her
likeness come to them with a book to sign.

Hathorne again took the lead in examination. Why, he
asked, did she afflict the children. She denied it. " Who
did then ? " " I do not know, how should I ? " The children were distracted creatures, she added, and no heed
should be given to what they said. Thereupon Hathorne
and Mr. Noyes, a minister assisting the magistrates,
declared that it was the judgement of all present that the
children were bewitched, and only she said that they were
distracted.

The afflicted now broke in to say that the Black Man
was at the moment whispering in the accused woman's
ear, and also that the yellow bird[1] which used to suck
between her fingers was present in the assembly. (The
bench saw neither Black Man nor yellow bird, but did not
rebuke the witnesses.) They also cried out whenever the
accused made any movement with her body, hands, or
mouth. If she bit her lip, they complained of being bitten.
If she grasped one hand with the other, they declared she
was pinching them, and produced the marks.

This feature recurs at the Salem trials, notably in that of
Bridget Bishop (see p. 161), and Edmund Gurney in his
Phantasms of the Living, compares it to the phenomenon of
hypnotic control, when the " subject " imitates postures
and gestures of the controller ; from which it appears

[1] It has been suggested that Sarah Good's and Martha Cory's
yellow birds were pet canaries !

that he accepts it as not mere pretence on the part of the alleged victims of the alleged witch. It becomes us not to question the theory of so great an authority ;[1] but the Salem " children " are really so unworthy of credence, and no one testifies to the marks now any more than in those of little Dorothy Good's teeth.

On Martha Cory being committed to prison, the crying out of the afflicted ceased.

At the examination of Rebecca Nurse, which followed, there was still more of a scene. Parris took the note of the trial, and writes that the noise of the accusing girls and speakers was so great that he could not proceed with his minutes. He was able to record, however, that when the accused looked round the meeting-house, and saw no sympathising countenance, she exclaimed : " O Lord, help me ! " Hathorne thereupon remarked : " It is very awful to see these agonies in all old professors, charged with contracting with the Devil ! " O upright judge !

Rebecca Nurse, according to Calef, was a most estimable and intelligent woman, to whose Christian life and care in bringing up her children many testified—after her execution, for no one came forward in court. She was one of three sisters, the other being Mary Easty (who likewise suffered death for witchcraft) and Sarah Cloyce. After Goodwife Nurse's committal to gaol the excellent Mr. Parris, on April 3rd, took as the text for his sermon : " Have I not chosen you twelve, and one of you is a devil." Sarah Cloyce, who was in the congregation, rose up and walked out, the wind shutting the door behind her forcibly, which made some suppose she went in anger ! Soon after she was complained of and committed, but she was more fortunate than her sisters, for she merely suffered imprisonment.

By April 11th, says Calef, the number of the accused and accusers was much increased, and there was a public

---

[1] Gurney says (*Phantasms*, I, 117) that there is " no feature in the evidence for witchcraft that more constantly recurs than the *touching* of the victim by the witch," and quotes De l'Ancre in 1612, who tells a story of some French children, believing themselves to have been taken to a Sabbat, and saying that the witch had passed her hand over their faces or put it on their heads.

examination at Salem, at which six magistrates and several
ministers were present. There were " hideous clamours
and screechings " in court from those who accused others.

The greatest sensation was now to come, by the implication of a congregationalist minister, directly named, in the
charge of witchcraft in its most heinous forms as then
considered. It is not certain when the name of George
Burroughs first came to be mentioned ; but a warrant for
his, arrest was procured from Boston on April 30th, and
was promptly served on him as he sat with his family at a
meal in the ministerial house at Wells, Maine. Before we
proceed to this most remarkable of all the Salem trials we
may give the principal facts known about the accused man
apart from the evidence offered against him and the record
of his fate.

The name Georgius Burroughs appears in the Harvard
graduates' list of 1670, so that he came between the
Mathers, father and son. He is described in a note in
Calef's book as a small black-haired man, of quick passions,
and possessed of great muscular strength, which was well
known while he was at Harvard. The date of his entering
the Congregationalist ministry is not certain, but he was a
preacher in Maine for some years before he received a call
to Salem Village in 1680. He stayed there only three years,
having financial and other troubles which made the post
uncomfortable. His stipend was not properly paid, his
wife died, and he had not enough money to discharge his
debt for her funeral. In 1683 he left and went to live at
Casco Bay, where he continued his religious work for a
number of years. He had recently become minister at Wells
when he was arrested. In the indictment against him he
appears as " late of Falmouth, in the province of the
Massachusetts Bay, in New England, clerk."

He was thrice married, and was a double widower with
seven children, the eldest fifteen at the time of his trial,
when he wedded his last wife, by whom he had a daughter.

He was taken to Salem on May 4th, and five days later
was brought up for examination at the usual meeting-
house, the local justices of the peace, Hathorne and Corwin,
being reinforced for the occasion by William Stoughton,
acting governor of Massachusetts, and Captain Samuel

Sewall from Boston. The evidence against him is contained in *Records of Salem Witchcraft* and in the section entitled " The tryal of G. B." in Cotton Mather's *Wonders of the Invisible World*, which are supplemented by what Calef has to say upon the subject. The accounts in the Essex County archives (reproduced in the *Records*) and in Mather's *Wonders* by no means tally exactly. Mather, by his own testimony, was not present at any of the witchcraft trials, and with regard to Burroughs he writes : " Glad should I have been if I had never known the name of this man, or never had this occasion to mention so much as the first letters of his name ; but, the Government requiring some account of his trial to be inserted in this book, it becomes me with all obedience to submit unto the order."

Unfortunately Cotton Mather did not refrain from comments on the trial which showed no reluctance to accept every charge that was made against the accused.

In the actual records from the archives it appears that Burroughs, in his first examination, was asked a number of questions, the substance of which, with the answers, was as follows. Called on to say when he (presumably last) partook of the Lord's Supper, he replied that it was so long since that he could not tell. " Yet he owned he was at meeting one Sabbath at Boston part of the day, and at Charlestown part of a Sabbath, when that sacrament happened to be at both, yet did not partake of either." Asked whether his house at Casco were haunted, he denied it, " yet he owned there were toads " ! He admitted that none of his children except the eldest was baptised.

The witnesses against him now came forward ; and the official note states that on his entry into the room many, if not all, of the bewitched were " grievously tortured." The witnesses were, in addition to Ann Putman junior, Elizabeth Hubbard, and Sarah Vibber, of whom we have already heard, Susan Sheldon, aged eighteen, Mercy Lewis, nineteen, Mary Walcott, seventeen, and Abigail Hobbs, age not stated ; and some men, of whom Thomas Putman alone was important.

Susan Sheldon came first, to testify that the ghosts of the accused's two former wives had appeared to her in their winding-sheets, saying " that man " had killed them.

Burroughs was told to look at the witness, whereupon " he looked back and knockt down all (or most) of the afflicted who stood behind him." This is a court record, it must be remembered !

When Mercy Lewis's deposition was about to be read, Burroughs looked at her, and she fell into " a dreadful and tedious fit." The same happened to Mary Walcott, Elizabeth Hubbard, and a second time to Susan Sheldon. The last, however, succeeded in joining in a statement with Ann Putman that Burroughs had brought them " the Book," and would have them write in it.

Being asked what he thought of these things, the accused answered that it was an amazing and humbling providence, but he understood nothing of it. " When they begin to name my name," he added, " they cannot name it." Was this an instance of hypnotic control, we may wonder? Ann and Susan now testified that the accused's first two wives and two of his children were destroyed by him. At this point some of the bewitched were " so tortured " that the magistrates ordered them to be taken out of court. It should have been the tortures of conscience that they suffered.

Some men next gave evidence as to the great strength of Burroughs, as shown by his holding out a heavy gun with one hand and lifting a barrel of " mallassoes " ; while Thomas Putman stated that Burroughs had made his wife enter into a covenant with the Devil.

Finally, Abigail Hobbs affirmed that Burroughs " in his shape appeared to her and urged her to set her hand to the Book, which she did ; and afterwards in his own person he acknowledged to her that he had made her set her hand to the Book."

This witness was brought from gaol, where she lay under a charge of being a witch herself. Her confession at her examination on April 20th is interesting as introducing the Witches' Sabbat. The note taken in court says :

" She confesseth further that the Devil in the shape of a man came to her, and would have her to afflict Ann Putnam, Mercy Lewis, and Abigail Williams, and brought their images with him in wood like them, and gave her thorns and bid her prick them into these images, which she did accordingly into each of them one ; and then the Devil told her they were afflicted, which accordingly they were, and cried out they were hurt by Abigail Hobbs. She confesseth she was at the great meeting at Mr. Parris's pasture, when they administered the Sacrament, and did eat of the Red Bread and drink of the Red Wine at the same time."

There is no mention of Burroughs by name here ; but it seems likely that Abigail Hobbs was induced to identify " the Devil in the shape of a man " with him before his arrest. The matter of the reality or otherwise of the meeting at Mr. Parris's pasture may be left for the present.

Burroughs was committed to gaol to await his trial at the beginning of August. He, with Tituba and some others were sent to Boston, where there was more room for prisoners. In the meanwhile, on May 14th, Sir William Phipps arrived in Boston with Increase Mather, to find the colony in an uproar. No arrests had been made outside the Salem neighbourhood, except that of Burroughs in Maine, but the scandal of the affair was widespread, and the ministers, including those of Boston, were all keenly interested. Cotton Mather in particular was engaged in investigation of the subject of witchcraft, as might have been expected of the author of *Late Memorable Providences*, now in its second edition, with a preface by his father's English friend, Richard Baxter—a man most credulous in the matter of witchcraft.

The Mather party were at this time the leaders of Boston opinion, and their enemies were mostly outside Massachusetts.[1] Phipps found in them his chief support, and he in

---

[1] The most determined opposition came from the Quakers of Pennsylvania, who had no sympathy with Calvinistic doctrines. One of them, George Keith, had published in *The Churches of New-England brought to the Test*—" an answer to the gross abuses, lies and slanders of Increase Mather." As Increase had written of " the blasting rebukes of Heaven upon the late singing and dancing Quakers " and declared that " the Quakers are some of them undoubtedly possessed by evil spirits," Keith's anger is intelligible. But Cotton Mather, in the appendix to his *Late Memorable Provinces* spoke of " those no less absurd than angry people, the Quakers," and complained of " the incivilities lately shown to my father by one Keith in a sort of a thing lately published at Pennsylvania." Keith, he says, had visited New England, where he fell foul of all the ministers of Boston.

turn listened to their advice. His first act as governor is
said to have been to order those in Salem gaol and at
Boston under the charge of witchcraft to be put in irons.
This was followed by the appointment of a special commission of oyer and terminer to try the cases ; and on June 2nd
the commission began its sessions at Salem with a quorum
from William Stoughton, lieutenant-governor, and six
others.

The first case was that of Bridget Bishop, *alias* Oliver,
of Salem. She kept a small beer-shop on the old Ipswich
Road, and the Rev. John Hale, of Beverly, in his deposition
stated that he was informed that she entertained people in
her house at night, drinking and playing shovel-board.
This does not savour much of witchcraft ; but it was
recalled that about twenty years ago a man had accused
her of it (though he had later, on his deathbed, repented
of the charge), and numerous living witnesses came
forward with fresh accusations. It is clear that considerable importance was attached to securing a conviction.

Search was made for a witch-mark on the wretched
woman ; and a " teat " was duly discovered. The trial
was short. She was pronounced guilty, condemned to
death, and hanged on June 10th, the first victim of the
witch-hunters at Salem. She refused to the end to make any
confession of her guilt. What some modern writers have
made of her will appear later.

Phipps seems to have been anxious to be assured of
religious approval of what was going on, for we read that
on June 15th several ministers in and near Boston, having
been consulted by His Excellency, declared that they were
affected by the deplorable state of the afflicted, but advised
a cautious proceeding, lest many evils ensue, and advised
that tenderness be used towards those accused. Nevertheless they " humbly recommended to the government
the speedy and vigorous prosecution of such as have
rendered themselves obnoxious, according to the directions
given in the laws of God, and the wholesome statutes of
the English nation for the detection of witchcraft."

So encouraged, the commission continued its sittings on
June 30th, when five women came up for trial, including
Sarah Good and Rebecca Nurse. The usual evidence was

forthcoming, all five were condemned, and on July 19th they were hanged.

There was great irregularity (to use no stronger word) with regard to Rebecca Nurse's condemnation. Two of the witnesses against her were Deliverance Hobbs and her daughter Abigail, confessed witches. When they appeared the accused remarked "What, do you bring her? She is one of us" or "What, do these persons give evidence against me now? They used to come among us"—for there are two versions of her words. She clearly meant that the Hobbses had been in gaol with her, as they had, and it was not until after the grand jury's verdict had been given in her favour that another interpretation was substituted. When she had been found not guilty, all the accusers in court, says Calef, and soon all the afflicted out of court, made "a hideous outcry," which influenced the judges. The president said that he would not impose upon the jury by a retrial of the case, but intimated that they had not well considered one of the prisoner's expressions, drawing attention to the words in question. The jury accordingly went out again, but could not agree. On their return Rebecca Nurse was asked to explain her words, which were repeated to her. She made no reply or explanation, and the jury, going out for the third time, brought her in guilty.

This example of judicial conduct is apparently to be imputed to William Stoughton.

One of the jurymen, challenged a few days later, by relatives of the condemned woman, as to the reason for the change of verdict, said that as she had not replied he took her previous words as principal evidence against her. When she was told, she put a declaration into court : " I intended no otherways than as they were prisoners among us, and therefore did then, and do now, judge them not legal evidence against their fellow-prisoners. And I, being something hard of hearing, and full of grief, none informing me how the court took up my words, therefore had no opportunity to declare what I intended when I said they were of our company."

Even now Phipps granted a reprieve ; but her accusers renewed their "dismal outcry," says Calef, and the governor was induced by some gentlemen's representations to withdraw it, thus completing the irregularity of the proceeding against her. She is reported to have died with Christian behaviour.

Not so Sarah Good, who was defiant to the end. On the execution-ground at Gallows Hill she was urged by the Rev. Mr. Noyes to confess, as " she knew that she was a witch." " You are a liar ! " she retorted. " I am no more a witch than you are a wizard, and if you take away my life God will give you blood to drink ! "

On August 5th six more of the accused came up for trial : George Burroughs ; John and Elizabeth Proctor, and John Willard, of Salem Village ; George Jacobs senior, of Salem ; and Martha Carrier, of Andover.

Burroughs and Jacobs had been searched for witch-marks, with no result in the first case ; but on Jacobs were found three " tetts," through two of which a pin was run without his being sensible of it. But there was no intention of letting the minister escape, in spite of the absence of incriminatory marks.

The first evidence now produced against him was that of a man who had lived at Casco Bay when Burroughs was minister there. He had heard much of his great strength, he says, and there was talk of it one day when Burroughs called on him. Burroughs told him that " he had put his fingers into the bung of a barrell of malases, and lifted it upon and carried it round him and set it down again." The minister was obviously proud of his muscular development.

Another man testified that at Casco Bay three years ago Burroughs gave an exhibition of his strength by holding out with one hand a heavy gun with a seven-foot barrel, which he himself could hardly do with two hands.

It was not considered possible that such feats could be performed without the Devil's aid !

More serious, however, than these charges of super-natural strength were those made of leadership of the witches at Salem, and of murder by witchcraft, the accusers here being female. Ann Putman, junior, was the most important, and her statements are worth quotation at some length, as showing the full virulence of the Salem madness. Attention must again be called to the fact that

this girl was twelve years of age when she made her astonishing statements. It must also be remembered that she was
the daughter of parents who took their share in the persecution, Thomas Putman being prominent in the Village
as parish clerk and constable.

Ann Putman's first deposition was made on August 3rd,
and was read in court two days later. It appears in the
records of the trial as follows, the spelling and punctuation
being somewhat altered :

" On 20th of April, 1692, at evening, she saw apparition
of a minister, at which she was grievously affrighted and
cried out, ' O dreadful, dreadful, here is a minister come.
What, are ministers witches too ? Whence come you, and
what is your name, for I will complain of you, though you
are a minister, if you be a wizard ? ' And immediately I
was tortured by him, being racked and almost choked by
him. And he tempted me to write in his book, which I
refused with loud outcries, and said I would not write in
his book, though he tore me all to pieces, but told him it
was a dreadful thing that he, which was a minister that
should teach children to fear God, should come to persuade
poor creatures to give their souls to the Devill. ' Oh
dreadful, dreadful, tell me your name that I may know
who you are.' Then again he tortured me, and urged me
to write in his book, which I refused ; and presently he
told me that his name was George Burroughs, and that
he had had three wives, and that he had bewitched the
two first of them to death . . . and that he had made
Abigail Hobbs a witch and several witches more ; and he
has continued ever since, by times tempting me to write in
his book, and grievously torturing me by beating, pinching,
and almost choking me several times a day. And he also
told me that he was above a witch, he was a conjurer."

On the same day Ann followed this with a second deposition. On May 3rd, 1692, at evening, she said the apparition
came to her again, grievously tortured her, and urged her to
write in the book, which she again refused.

" Then he told me that his first two wives would appear
to me presently and tell me a great many lies, but I should
not believe them. Then immediately appeared to me the
form of two women in winding-sheets and napkins about

their heads, and they turned their faces towards Mr.
Burroughs and looked very red and angry, and told him
that he had been a cruel man to them, and that their blood
did cry for vengeance against him ; and also told him
that they should be clothed with white robes in heaven
when he should be cast into hell. And immediately he
vanished away, and as soon as he was gone the two women
turned their faces towards me and looked as pale as a white
wall, and told me that they were Mr. Burroughs' two first
wives, and that he had murdered them : and one told me
that she was his first wife, and he stabbed her under the
left arm and put a piece of sealing-wax on the wound, and
she pulled aside the winding-sheet and showed me the
place. . . . And they both charged me that I should tell
these things to the magistrates before Mr. Burroughs'
face, and if he did not own them they did not know but
they should appear there."

Ann Putman's evidence was succeeded by that of Mercy
Lewis, aged nineteen, who had apparently been maid
with the Burroughs family. She, too, told of an apparition
of the minister to her, urging her to write in his book.
" And then he brought to me a new fashion book which
he did not use to bring, and told me I might write in that
book." Though she had known his study she had never
seen this book before ; but he said he had several books
in his study she had never seen.

She further deposed that on May 9th (which was five
days after he was brought in custody to Salem) Burroughs
had carried her to an exceeding high mountain and showed
her all the kingdoms of the earth, and told her he would
give them all to her if she would write in his book ; but
if she did not he would throw her down and break her
neck ! " But I told him they were none of his, and I
would not write if he throde me on a hundred pitch-
forks."

The seventeen-year-old Elizabeth Hubbard told of an
apparition of " a little black-haired man in blackish
apparel," who wanted her to sign the book, and tortured
her by biting, pinching, squeezing her body, and running
pins into her.

There was more testimony to the same effect, concerning

apparitions of Burroughs, demands for signature, and torturing. When older witnesses were produced the evidence grew more menacing to the accused. In particular there was Deliverance Hobbs, apparently an elderly woman. We have heard how at Rebecca Nurse's trial she and her daughter Abigail appeared as confessed witches to bear witness for the prosecution.

Deliverance Hobbs's story now was that she was—in April, it seems—at a general meeting of witches in the pasture near Mr. Parris's house, and that Mr. Burroughs preached and administered to them. When she had herself been charged with witchcraft on April 22nd she had made a confession, which was produced. In this she acknowledged herself to be a " Covenant Witch," and said that on the previous day she, having been warned to attend a meeting, was there with John Proctor and his wife, Goody Nurse, Giles Cory and his wife, Goody Bishop, and Mr. Burroughs, who was the preacher and " pressed them to bewitch all in the village, telling them they should do it gradually, and not all at once, assuring them that they should prevail." He administered the sacrament to them with " red bread and red wine like blood." Next the minister sat " a man in a long-crowned white hat," and they " sat seemingly at a table, and filled out the wine in tankards."

Two women named Lacy, mother and daughter, attested to having been with Martha Carrier at a diabolical sacrament where Burroughs administered to them. The mother told of a baptism, where " he dipped their heads in the water, saying they were his."

Abigail Hobbs was not quite so sensational as her mother, but she owned that she had made two covenants with the Devil and had been a witch for six years, and had killed children by witchcraft. Burroughs, she said, had brought poppets for her to stick pins into, but she could not remember that he had brought poppets of his wives. He was in his bodily person when he came to her, as he also was when he tempted her to set her hand to the book. There was no mere apparition, as with Ann Putman, Elizabeth Hubbard, and others.

Abigail Hobbs was one of those who was at once an

afflicter and an afflicted person, a self-accused witch[1] and
a witch-denouncer. When she appeared in court in
April she was immediately taken with " a dreadful fit " ;
and her mother affirmed that it was Goodman Cory who
hurt her, and that she saw him and a " gentlewoman from
Boston " striving to break her neck. In spite of her thus
being among the alleged sufferers, the daughter was
sentenced to imprisonment later (though nine years
afterwards she received £10 damages for this), while the
mother was let off, being a valuable weapon in the hands of
the prosecution. The usual practice was that a confessed
witch should not be executed, except in the event of the
confession being withdrawn. The effect of this in inducing
confessions from terrified and cowardly prisoners can
readily be imagined. We have seen the same happening
in persecutions other than at Salem.

At her own examination when she was arrested in April,
it may be noted, Deliverance Hobbs, after first denying all
knowledge of witchcraft, had later admitted that only
the night before she had signed a book brought her by
Goody Wildes, under threat of being torn to pieces. She
had also, she said, put pins into two images brought by
Goody Wildes and Goody Osborne, with whom was " a tall
black man with a high-crowned hat." There was no
mention of Burroughs here ; but when re-examined in
Salem gaol she introduced his name, telling the story of the
meeting in the pasture near Mr. Parris's, which we have
just heard. What happened in the gaol to quicken her
memory ?

Cotton Mather, in the section of *The Wonders of the
Invisible World* devoted to it, has much to tell of the trial
of " G. B." that amplifies the account in *Records of Salem
Witchcraft*. He says that not only was he accused by five or
six bewitched as the author of their miseries, but also by
eight of the confessing witches as " a head actor at some
time of their hellish rendezvouzes," who had the promise

---

[1] At Abigail's own trial, when she confessed herself a witch, there
was a quaint testimony by a girl of seventeen, who signed herself
" lidea Nichals." She wrote : " I asked abigaille hobs how she durst
lie out a nights in ye woods alone she told me she was not a fraid of
any thing for she told me she had sold herselfe boddy and soule to ye
old boy."

of being a king in Satan's kingdom. Altogether the testimonies brought against him "were enough to fix the character of a witch upon him, according to the rules of reasoning by the judicious Gaule[1] in that case directed."

Among the testimonies we may note those as to the alleged biting of the afflicted by the accused. "When they cried out," says Mather, "the print of his teeth would be seen on the flesh of the complainers ; and just such a set of teeth as G. B.'s would then appear upon them, which could be distinguished from those of some other men." There is a modern ring about this evidence from teeth ; except that here the teeth were not real, but "spectral"—to use the word commonly adopted in designating things apparitional at Salem.

As to the fits in court of many of the afflicted, which made them incapable of speech, Mather says that the chief judge asked the accused who he thought hindered them. G. B. answered that he supposed it was the Devil. "How comes the Devil so loth to have any testimony borne against you?" queried the judge ; which cast G. B. into very great confusion.

The ghosts of G. B.'s two previous wives are accepted by Mather, who declares that he had been infamous all the country over for his barbarous usage of them. People in court, and not merely one of the bewitched, were struck with horror at the apparition. But G. B., "though much appalled, utterly denied that he discerned anything of it, nor," adds Mather, "was it any part of his conviction."

Mather returns to the subject of the domestic life of Burroughs in the past. "Several testimonies . . . not only proved him a very ill man, but also confirmed the belief of the character which had been already fixed upon him." He kept his first and second wives in a strange kind of slavery. "He would pretend to tell when he came home the talk which any had with them. He brought them to the point of death by his harsh dealings, and then made people promise that, in case death should happen, they would say nothing of it. He used all means to make his wives write, sign, seal, and swear a covenant never to reveal any of his secrets." The wives privately complained to

[1] John Gaule, author of *Select Cases of Conscience* (1646).

neighbours about the frightful apparitions of evil spirits infesting the house, and many such things were whispered about the neighbourhood.[1]

Mather is apparently much impressed by the evidence of one Ruck, whose sister Burroughs had married. Ruck said that he went out one day with the two of them to gather strawberries. On the way back he and his sister rode slowly, Burroughs accompanying them on foot until he stepped aside into the bushes. They halted and "halloo'd" for him without response, and at last went homeward at a quickened pace. When near home, to their astonishment, they found him, still on foot, with a basket of strawberries. Burroughs fell to chiding his wife for what she had said of him to her brother on the way. When they expressed wonder, he said he knew their thoughts. "The Devil does not know so far," objected Ruck. "My God makes known your thoughts unto me," replied Burroughs—according to the witness.

To Ruck's evidence, Mather says, G. B. had nothing to answer that was worth considering, except that there had been a man with him when the two left him ; which Ruck said was untrue. "When the Court asked G. B. what the man's name was, his countenance was much altered, nor could he say who it was. But the Court began to think that he then stept aside only that by the assistance of the Black Man he might put on his invisibility and in that fascinating mist gratify his own jealous humour to hear what they said of him : which trick of rendering themselves invisible our witches do in their confessions pretend that they sometimes are masters of ; and it is the more credible because there is demonstration that they often make other things utterly invisible."

In this preposterous account Cotton Mather no doubt had the assistance of his father, who was present in court for the Burroughs trial.

Having related all the malicious gossip brought together against the man whom (out of respect for his cloth, we suppose) he will only call G. B., Cotton concludes : "Faltring, faulty, unconstant, and contrary answers upon

[1] It is curious to reflect that Cotton Mather himself had three wives, of whom the third became mentally unbalanced.

judicial and deliberate examination are counted some
unlucky symptoms of guilt in all crimes ; especially in
witchcrafts. Now there never was a prisoner more eminent
for them than G. B., both at his examination and on his
trial. His tergiversations, contradictions, and falsehoods
were very sensible ; he had little to say but that he had
heard something that he could not prove, touching the
reputation of some of the witnesses. Only he gave in a
paper to the jury, wherein, altho' he many times before
granted not only that there are witches, but also that the
present sufferings of the country are the effects of horrible
witchcrafts, yet he now goes to evince it that there neither
are, nor ever were, witches that, having made a compact
with the Divel, can send a Divel to torment other people
at a distance.''

The anonymous editor in 1862 of Mather's *Wonders of
the Invisible World* suggests that Burroughs's principal crime
was a disbelief in witchcraft itself. This attitude, even
when modified as in the prisoner's paper to the jury,
could not commend itself to the man who wrote in his
book published next year :

" The Devil, exhibiting himself ordinarily as a small
black man, has decoy'd a fearful knot of proud, froward,
ignorant, envious and malicious creatures to lift themselves
in his horrid service, by entring their names in a Book
tendered unto them. These witches, whereof a score have
now confessed and shown their deeds, and some are now
tormented by devils for confessing, have met in hellish
rendezvouzes, wherein the confessors do say they have
had their diabolical Sacraments, imitating the Baptism
and the Supper of our Lord. In these hellish meetings
these monsters have associated themselves to do not less
a thing then to destroy the Kingdom of our Lord in these
parts of the world ; and, in order hereunto, first they
each of them have their spectres or devils, commission'd by
them and representing them, to be the engines of their
malice.''

Concerning Martha Carrier, a memorandum made by
Cotton Mather is worth noting : " This rampant hag of
whom the confession of the witches, and of her own children
among the rest, agreed that the Devil had promised her she

should be Queen of Hell." Two of Martha's children, as we are about to hear, were subjected to torture before they confessed.

The result of the trials of Burroughs and those brought up with him was the same in every case, the condemnation which their enemies were bent on securing. Apart from Burroughs, John Proctor was the most prominent of the prisoners, being a respectable farmer with a number of friends who did their best to save him, but without avail. The principal accuser of him and his wife was their former maid Mary Warren, aged twenty, a girl of a most hysterical nature, to judge by her conduct in court. She had herself been charged with witchcraft, and had so many violent fits, before she could bring herself to confess, that she was twice removed from the dock. Also those whom she was alleged to have afflicted had fits of torture—which stopped, however, as soon as she had confessed—so that Salem Village meeting-house must have been a lively spot that day.

Mary Warren stated that her mistress had told her she was a witch and had put her hand to the book ; but that it was her master who had brought the book to her. Asked if she had signed, she said not unless putting her finger to it was signing. Did she see a spot where she had put her finger ? " Yes." What colour ? " Black." What did she dip her finger in when she made the mark ? " In nothing but my mouth."

It was after one fit that she suddenly cried " I will tell, I will tell. Thou wicked creature, it is you stopped my mouth, but I will confess the little I have to confess." (It was Samuel Parris who took down the note of this examination.) Of whom would she tell ? a magistrate asked. " Of Betty Proctor, it is she, it is she I lived with last. . . . It shall be known, thou wretch. Hast thou undone me body and soul ? " She added, " She wishes she had made me make a thorough league." According to Mary Warren's own accusers she was quite witch enough to afflict them effectually, for all that she had not made a thorough league.

After his condemnation John Proctor wrote a dignified letter from Salem gaol to the magistrates, protesting his innocence of the charges made against him. " Here are

five persons," he said, " who have lately confessed themselves to be witches, and do accuse some of us of being
along with them at a sacrament since we were committed
into close prison, which we know to be lies." Two of these
five, he said, were Martha Carrier's sons (she had four
children in prison with her), who only confessed after
torture ;[1] and his son was also tortured, being tied neck
and heels till the blood gushed out at his nose. " These
actions are very like the popish cruelties," he concluded.

But nothing availed to save the condemned from hanging,
except Elizabeth Proctor, who successfully pleaded that
she was pregnant. The other four, including the one
woman Martha Carrier, were taken in a cart through the
streets of Salem to execution on Gallows Hill on August
19th.

It must be admitted that George Burroughs, whatever
view we take of his character, died bravely and well, and
that he was treated with disgraceful indignity after death.
Calef, who writes very favourably concerning him, says
that upon the ladder at the gallows he made a speech for
the clearing of his innocence " with such solemn and
serious expressions as were to the admiration of all present."
His prayer was so affecting as to draw tears from many ;
and it seemed that some would hinder the execution. But,
" as soon as he was turned off, Mr. Cotton Mather, being
mounted upon a horse, addressed himself to the people,
partly to declare that he [Burroughs] was no ordained
minister, and partly to possess the people of his guilt, saying that the Devil has often been transformed into an
angel of light ; and this somewhat appeased the people,
and the executions went on."

There seems no doubt that Cotton Mather was at the
execution and acted as described. His father, Dr. Increase
—he received his D.D. degree this year—after he had
attended Burroughs's trial, wrote that had he been one of
his judges he could not have acquitted him " for several
persons did upon oath testify that they saw him do such
things as no man that had not a devil to be his familiar

[1] Richard Carrier is stated by Hutchinson in his *History of Massachusetts* to have said that he saw Mr. Burroughs at a witch-meeting in
the village administer the sacrament.

could perform." (Was this an allusion to the poor man's feats with the heavy gun and the barrel of molasses ?[1]) He was not at the execution. Cotton, by his own account, attended none of the witchcraft trials, but he had declared his opinion vigorously on the subject ; as in a sermon at Boston fifteen days before the execution, on the text from *Revelations*, " Woe to the inhabitants of the earth and of the sea ; for the Devil is come down unto you, having great wrath ; because he knoweth that he hath but a short time."[2] His argument to the crowd at Gallows Hill about the possibility of the Devil transforming himself into an angel of light is paralleled by what he says in *The Wonders of the Invisible World* about a discourse (? by himself) at " a meeting of some very pious and learned ministers " in Boston, which held that " the Devil may sometimes have a permission to represent an innocent person as tormenting such as are under diabolical manifestations." But he did not of course there mean to exonerate Burroughs as an innocent person !

When the body of Burroughs was cut down from the gallows, it was dragged by a halter to a hole, or grave, between the rocks on the hill, and, clad only in an old pair of trousers of one who had been executed, was put in the ground with Willard's and Martha Carrier's bodies, in such a way that Burroughs's chin and a hand, and a foot of one of the others, were left uncovered. So says Calef ; and, if he was not himself a witness of what went on at Salem, at least he obtained his information from the Brattle brothers, of Harvard and Boston, and from others keenly interested.

The Willard who was executed and buried with Burroughs was a man who had been employed in the arrest of many of those accused of witchcraft, and when in disgust he refused to arrest any more he was himself accused. He fled, but was captured, tried, and convicted.

In spite of the signs of some revulsion of feeling at the

---

[1] The younger Mather writes of " extraordinary lifting, and such feats of strength as could not be done without a diabolical assistance." He also says that G. B. was " a very puny man, yet he had often done things beyond the strength of a giant."

[2] This sermon is incorporated in *The Wonders of the Invisible World.*

execution of George Burroughs, the witch-hunting continued, with eight more kills on Gallows Hill on September 22nd, and another of peculiar atrocity elsewhere on the same date. The eight were Martha Cory, Mary Easty, and four more women, and two men. After their execution the Rev. Mr. Noyes, who was present, remarked, " What a sad thing it is to see eight firebrands of Hell hanging there ! "

Martha Cory and her husband Giles, an elderly farmer, who was the ninth now put to death, had both been incriminated, as we have heard, by Deliverance Hobbs, as having been at a Witches' Sabbat with Burroughs in April. The regular witnesses were forthcoming against them and the other accused as to various acts of witchcraft, tormenting of the afflicted, etc. Against Giles Cory evidence to which much attention was paid was that of Ann Putman,[1] who had had an apparition of a ghost in a winding-sheet, alleged to be that of a man whom Cory had killed while in his employ seventeen years before. Cory refused to accept trial by the grand jury, making no reply to the indictment, and so being held to remain " mute of malice," for which the ghastly punishment of being " pressed to death " was still on the English statute-book. This he accordingly underwent, the first example of the kind in New England. His reason for submitting to the prolonged torture was that, if he had taken his trial, with the practically inevitable conviction and execution for felony, his property would have been forfeited. He had willed it to his daughters' husbands, and by his attitude he secured the inheritance to them.

---

[1] Two more of the juvenile witnesses against Cory, though considerably older than Ann Putnam, were Elizabeth (18) and Alice Booth (younger), who were so illiterate as only to be able to put their marks to their depositions. Their evidence was as to a Witches' Sabbat at the widow Shaflin's house in Salem on September 12th, where " there appeared unto them a great company of witches, as near as they could tell about fifty, thirteen of which they knew, who did receive the Sacrament." Among these they saw Cory, " who brought to us bread and wine, urging us to partake thereof ; but because we refused he did most grievously afflict and torment us : and we believe in our hearts that Giles Cory is a wizard, and that he hath afflicted us and several others by acts of witchcraft."

It was put about, Calef states, that Cory had killed his
servant seventeen years ago by pressing him to death with
his feet—in order to palliate the dreadful sentence on the
farmer himself.

Another piece of testimony by the diabolical child Ann
Putman may be recorded as a relief after the horror of what
she brought upon Giles Cory. She charged one Thomas
Farrer with witchcraft. In May, she said, she had an
apparition of an old grey-headed man with a great nose,
who tortured her and almost choked her, and urged her
to write in his book. " I asked him what was his name and
from whence he came, for I would complain of him ;
and he told me he came from ' linne ' and people used to
call him ' old father Pharaoh,' and said he was my grandfather, for my father used to call him father. But I told him
I would not call him grandfather, for he was a wizard, and
I would complain of him. And ever since he has afflicted
me, by times beating me and pinching me and almost
choking me, and urging me continually to write in his
book."

Thomas Putman and another bore witness to having
heard Ann declare what she now said about Farrer's
apparition, and stated that they " perceived her hellish
temptations by her loud outcries, ' I will not write, old
Pharaoh, I will not write in your book.' "

No one else seemed to have made a charge against Farrer,
who escaped misfortune.

The malignants were not yet satisfied, however ; and
accusations were brought against a couple, Edward and
Sarah Bishop, whose son had married into the Putman
family. An evil feature of this case was that the son was
willing to accuse his parents, after, having been slow in
collecting testimonials as to their character, he had been
" quickly pursued with odd inconveniences." The older
Bishops were in prison, and the sheriff had seized their
farm, but allowed the branding of some of their cattle,
in case they should be acquitted. The son helped in the
branding, and while so doing felt something like a burning
brand clapped on his thigh, of which he could show the
mark. Calef says that it was a boil which had burst as he
strained at his work.

The Bishops fortunately made their escape from gaol, which perhaps argues less keenness at last in securing convictions at Salem. The mania, however, passed on to the neighbouring Andover, where there was a serious outbreak of witch charges, originally started by two " afflicted persons " imported from Salem, but spreading until more than fifty people were charged. " Here it was," Calef states, " that many accused themselves of riding on poles through the air ;[1] many parents believing their children to be witches, many husbands their wives, etc." The fits of the afflicted and the spectral sights that had been so common a feature at Salem were reproduced at Andover, fortunately without the same tragic results. A local justice of the peace named Dudley Bradstreet, after he had granted warrants for the arrest of some thirty or forty people, grew disgusted with his work (like Willard at Salem) and refused to issue any more warrants. Thereupon accusations of witchcraft were brought against him and his wife ; but they made their flight in time to avoid danger.

The Andover outbreak was ended by the imprudence of some of the witch-hunters, who made a charge against one who is described as a worthy gentleman of Boston. He, being a man of substance, issued a writ against his accusers, and claimed a thousand pounds damages for defamation of character. This damped the hunters' ardour, and the chase at Andover ceased without any kill ; for the only quarry from the place, Martha Carrier and two of those done to death on September 22nd, had been run down at Salem.

Another absurd accusation helped to discredit the search for fresh victims. John Hale, the minister at Beverly, had taken his share in upholding the prosecutions. Now his own wife, a lady of blameless and pious character, was charged

---

[1] For instance, Mary Osgood, a captain's wife, stated that she was taken in the company of others through the air to a meeting at Five-Mile Pond, near Andover, and brought back in the same manner ; she believed, upon a pole. And Goody Foster said that the Devil carried her, Martha Carrier, and others on a pole to a witch-meeting ; but, " the pole breaking and she hanging about Carrier's neck, they both fell down, and she then received a hurt by the fall, whereof she was not at this very time recovered."

with being a witch. Hale had the courage to change his attitude, and was supported by the people of Beverly, who treated the charges (brought, like the first at Salem, by children) for what they were worth. Some of Hale's fellow-ministers, too, were at least perturbed.

"And now," writes Calef, "nineteen persons having been hanged, and one prest to death, and eight more condemned, of which a third part were members of some of the churches in New-England, and more than half of them of a good conversation in general, and not one cleared; about fifty having confest themselves to be witches, of which none executed; above an hundred and fifty in prison, and above two hundred more accused; the special commission of oyer and terminer comes to an end, which has no other authority than the governor's commission."

Cotton Mather had the opportunity of showing what view he took of the same occurrences; for Sir William Phipps, who had found that his alliance with the Mathers brought him enemies as well as friends, and had aroused opposition not only by his partiality to the Congregationalists, but also by his unpolished manners and violent temper,[1] had grown alarmed at the turmoil over the witchcraft prosecutions, and asked Cotton to produce something in justification of them. The result was *The Wonders of the Invisible World*, first published in Boston towards the end of 1692, but evidently in preparation earlier.

Of the section of this work which deals with the Burroughs trial we have heard a good deal; and we have also had, on p. 116, what the author has to say of "the Army of Devils" broken in upon Massachusetts. He accepts without hesitation the confessions of "more than one twenty . . . that they have signed unto a Book which the Devil show'd them, and engaged in his hellish design of bewitching and ruining our land," but says in mitigation of the disgrace of this scandal that "the kingdoms of

[1] He is said to have once caned a naval officer who disputed his orders. When he had left Massachusetts, Cotton Mather produced an eulogy of him entitled *Pietas in Patriam : The Life of Sir William Phips, Knt.*, of which Calef made sport in a postscript to his *More Wonders of the Invisible World*.

Sweden, Denmark, Scotland, yea and England itself, as well as the province of New-England, have had their storms of witchcrafts breaking upon them, which have made the most lamentable devastations." He does not here, like his father Dr. Increase, argue that Protestants are less easily imposed on than Papists by the Devil.

He notes, with apparent satisfaction, in an addendum on " Matter omitted in the Trials," that nineteen witches had been executed in New England, one a minister, and two more ministers accused, while "there are a hundred witches more in prison and about two hundred more accused, some men of great estates in Boston."

Cotton Mather fortified his work with a letter from the lieutenant-governor, who signed himself " Your assured friend, William Stoughton "—thus giving the author " a shield, under the umbrage of which I dare walk abroad," he says.

And this was Rebecca Nurse's judge !

Whether inspired or not by the younger Mather's advocacy, the trials for witchcraft did not come to a complete end yet. There was a court at Salem at the beginning of January 1693, with Stoughton again as chief magistrate, and it had fifty-six cases before it, in twenty-six of which a true bill was returned. Three of the prisoners were found guilty and sentenced to death. It is notable that, when some of the jury enquired what account they ought to make of spectral evidence, they received the answer, " As much as of chips in wort." The tide had turned against testimony derived from apparitions.

The court moved on to Charlestown at the end of the month, and while it was sitting had word from Salem that seven persons lying in gaol there under sentence of death had been reprieved. " We were in a way," cried Stoughton indignantly, " to have cleared the land of these, &c. [sic]. Who it is obstructs the course of justice I know not. The Lord be merciful to the country ! " With this he left the bench and came no more to that court.

Stoughton presided, however, in April at the superior court in Boston, where witchcraft was again on the charge-list, a Captain John Aldin being acquitted. But now an order was issued for all prisoners in all gaols of

Massachusetts on this charge to be released.[1] Sir William
Phipps was about to proceed to England to answer certain
accusations made against him in his capacity of governor,
and took the opportunity of giving freedom to the class of
prisoner whom his first step on taking up office had been
to put into irons. Their freedom, however, cost them
about thirty shillings each to the King's Attorney, according
to Calef.

It is possible that we should not have had the invaluable
investigations of Robert Calef into the whole Salem business
if he had not been brought into direct opposition to Cotton
Mather in Boston in September 1693. Calef was a well-
to-do merchant of the town, and has this testimonial from
Thomas Hutchinson, a later governor of Massachusetts,
and a near relative of the Mathers—and a believer, it may
be added, in the real existence of witchcraft in New England
—that he was " a man of fair mind, who substantiated his
facts." Concerning witchcraft Calef was a thorough sceptic.

What brought him in collision with Cotton Mather was
the case of a Boston girl of seventeen, Margaret Rule, who,
on Sunday, September 10th, 1693, was seized with convulsive fits and claimed to see the shapes of people tormenting
her. She was the daughter of sober and honest parents,
according to Mather, whose parishioners the Rules
probably were, so that they would have had the advantage
of hearing his sermons against witchcraft. For about half
a year before her visitation, says Mather, Margaret Rule
was " observably improved in the symptoms of a new
creature . . . seriously concerned for the everlasting salva-
tion of her soul, and careful to avoid the snares of evil
company." But on this Sunday, " after some hours [!]
of previous disturbance in the public assembly," she fell
into odd fits, which caused her friends to carry her
home.

Some of the neighbours at once suspected " a miserable
old woman " in a house nearby, who had formerly been
imprisoned for witchcraft, and who had only the previous

---

[1] The release was not accompanied by a pardon. See the Reversal
of Attainder on pp. 159–60, where we read of some persons " lying still
under the sentence of the court, and liable to have the same executed
upon them."

evening " very bitterly treated and threatened " Margaret
Rule. As in the Goodwin case in 1688, Cotton Mather's
thirst to investigate was aroused. He was called in by
the Rules, and found Margaret " assaulted by eight cruel
spectres, whereof she imagined that she knew three or four."
On his advice she forbore blazing the names. " But," he
wrote in an account of the affair, " I will venture to say
this of them, that they are a sort of wretches who for these
many years have gone under as violent presumptions of
witchcraft as perhaps any creatures yet living upon earth."
Though he, too, forbore giving the names, there is no
doubt that Mather would have liked Salem treatment to
be applied to these people.

These accursed spectres, he goes on, brought Margaret
Rule a book about a cubit long, red and thick, but not very
broad, and demanded that she should set her hand to it,
as a sign of becoming a servant to the Devil. When she
refused they fell to " tormenting of her in a manner too
hellish to be described, in those torments confining her to
her bed for just six weeks together." Sometimes there
looked in upon her with the spectres " a short and a black
man, whom they called their master." (As the remains of
George Burroughs were on Gallows Hill at Salem, this
must have been the Old Boy himself!) For the first
nine days of her trouble Margaret kept an entire fast, the
sight of refreshment causing her teeth to set and throwing
her into tortures. But " once or twice or so in all this time
her tormentors permitted her to swallow a mouthful of
somewhat that might increase her miseries, whereof a
spoonful of rum was the most considerable."

Calef visited the Rules three days after Margaret's first
seizure, and found her in bed, speaking very little, and
then as if she were light-headed. The two Mathers came
while he was there, and altogether some thirty to forty
people were present. Cotton Mather sat on the bedside,
and began to question Margaret. Calef gives the following
report of questions and answers :

Q. " Margaret Rule, how do you do ? " No answer.
Q. " What, do there a great many witches sit upon you ? "
A. " Yes." *Q.* " Do you know that there is a hard master ? "
A fit followed, but on the girl's revival the question was

repeated. *A.* " Yes." *Q.* " Don't serve that hard master—
you know who." Thereupon followed another fit.

Cotton Mather asked the girl's attendant what she ate or
drank, to which the reply was that she did not eat at all,
but drank rum. Calef suggests, in a note upon this scene,
that the matter was nothing more than a bad case of
delirium tremens, comparing it with that of " the Surrey
demoniac, Richard Dugdale," in 1689, who was cured after
nine ministers had been engaged over him for many months
with prayer and fasting, until, as the patient had a terrible
fit and vomited, Satan finally departed, saying, " Now,
Dickey, I must leave thee, and must afflict thee no more ! "

Calef was perhaps not quite serious in his suggestion of
delirium tremens as the cause of Margaret Rule's affliction ;
though rum certainly was a curious remedy in the circumstances. Cotton Mather was very serious in his interpretation of the case, and chronicles its course in a way so
matter-of-fact as to render it positively ludicrous. He
moreover obtained a warrant against Calef, when he published his account in an open letter addressed to Mather,
and had him brought before a magistrate for scandalous
libel.

Calef's crushing retort was delayed until 1700, when he
published, in London, his *More Wonders of the Invisible World*,
reviewing the whole of the Massachusetts witchcraft
business, and including in the book Cotton Mather's
account of Margaret Rule's case, entitled *Another Brand
plukt out of the Burning*, which the author had only written
for private circulation.

" He sent this vile volume," wrote the younger Mather in
his diary concerning *More Wonders*, " to London to be published. . . . The books that I have sent over into England,
with a design to glorify the Lord Jesus Christ, are not
published, but strangely delayed ; and the books that
are sent over to vilify me—these are published." Dr.
Increase Mather, for his part, ordered *More Wonders* to
be burnt in the courtyard of Harvard.[1]

[1] In years to come Samuel Mather, Cotton's son, who compiled
his father's life, said that there was " a certain disbeliever in witchcraft"
who wrote against *The Wonders of the Invisible World :* " but, as the man
is dead, the book died with him." The verdict of posterity has not
been for Cotton's advocate.

The unprejudiced student, however, can only feel grateful to Calef for his industry in investigating the Massachusetts witch-hunting and his care in marshalling the facts. We may turn to a document which he reproduces, signed by six women of Andover who had taken their share, by their confessions of witchcraft, to keep the persecution alive. It throws considerable light upon the manner in which " evidence " was obtained.

The six miserable creatures, as Calef calls them, told how, when accused of witchcraft, though altogether innocent, and made prisoners and taken to Salem, they were " affrighted even out of their reason." Their relatives urged them to confess as the only way to save their lives. The confession they made " was no other than what was suggested to us by some gentlemen ; they telling us that we were witches, and they knew it, and we knew it, and they knew that we knew it, which made us think that it was so. . . . Also the hard measures they used with us rendered us uncapable of making our defence, but said any thing and every thing which they desired." They were told how Samuel Wardwell (one of the eight hanged on September 22nd, 1692), who had withdrawn a confession made, had been executed. Such, indeed, was the sure penalty for withdrawing a confession.

Besides the powerful argument of life if they confessed, adds Calef, there were the tedious examinations before private persons—among whom we may presume were a number of ministers—who took it in turn for many hours to question them until they were wearied out for want of sleep, etc. The questions were of the nature, " Were you at such a witch-meeting ? " or " Have you signed the Devil's book ? " ; and in the end they broke down and confessed, already under heavy pressure from their relatives with their escape from death in view.

Another document of great importance was the admission of error by one of the judges at the Salem trials, whose name is withheld. This was delayed until January 14th, 1697, a date which had been appointed by the lieutenant-governor, council, and assembly of Massachusetts as a day of prayer and fasting throughout the province, without any direct allusion to the subject of witchcraft. But the judge in a full meeting at the Fourth Church of Boston stood up while a paper that he had handed in was read, in which he desired the prayers of God's people for him and his. God having visited him and his family, he declared, he was apprehensive that he might have fallen into some errors in the matters at Salem, and he prayed that the guilt of such miscarriages might not be imputed either to the country in general, or to him or his family in particular.

Finally, there is an undated paper signed by twelve men who had served on several juries at Salem in 1692. They confessed that, for want of knowledge in themselves and of better information from others, they had accepted such evidence against the accused as on further consideration they were afraid was insufficient for taking the lives of any, " whereby they feared they might have brought on themselves and this people of the Lord the guilt of innocent blood." They now signified to all in general, and to the surviving sufferers in particular, their deep sense of sorrow for their errors, and declared that they justly feared they were sadly deluded, for which they begged God's forgiveness and that of all whom they had offended.

Thus we have admissions of wrong from confessed witch witnesses, from a judge, and from jurymen in the Salem trials. We may add, though it is not included in Calef's work, the retractation of Ann Putman, who was such a terrible weapon in the hands of the prosecution.

Ann Putman lost both her parents in 1699, by which time she was nineteen years of age. She fell ill and so remained for a long time, during which period she was perhaps convinced that she had drawn upon herself the visitation of God. Anyhow, she had a confession read out for her in the meeting-house at Salem—the scene of her many monstrous charges—in which she expressed contrition that " I, being then in my childhood, should be made an instrument for the accusing of several persons of a grievous crime, whereby their lives were taken away from them, whom now I have just grounds and good reasons to believe they were innocent persons." She added : " Though what was said or done by me against any person, I can truly and uprightly say, before God and man, I did it not out of any anger, malice, or ill-will to any person, for I had no such thing against one of them, but what I did was ignorantly, being deluded of Satan."

She expressed especial sorrow for having accused Goodwife Nurse and her two sisters.

Justice, if not adequate contrition, had overtaken the Rev. Samuel Parris much earlier. In April 1693[1] eight members of his congregation in Salem Village had issued a document entitled " Grounds of Complaint," in which they explained why they had withdrawn from communion —" because we esteem ourselves justly grieved and offended with the officer who does administer." Among the complaints were Parris's " easy faith " in the accusations of those who were called the afflicted ; his laying aside of charity towards his neighbours ; his approval and practice of unwarrantable methods for discovering what he wished to know concerning the bewitched persons ; his " unsafe and unaccountable oath against sundry of the accused," etc.

Parris was very slow in acknowledging the receipt of this document ; 1or his reply, " given to the dissenting brethren at their request," is dated November 26th, 1694, In that the Lord ordered the late horrid calamity to break out first in his family, he said, he could not but look on it as a very sore rebuke ; and that in his family were some of both parties, accusers and accused, he looked on as an aggravation of that rebuke. As to his oath he pleaded : " I never meant it, nor do I know how it can otherwise be construed, than as vulgarly, and everyone understood, yea, and upon enquiry it may be found worded also "—which is decidedly not lucid !

Parris appealed for an end of envy and strife, and that all from this day forward might be covered with the mantle of love.

On the matter being referred to the elders of the churches in Boston and representatives from elsewhere in the colony, a council which met at Salem on April 3rd, 1695, gave Parris a little satisfaction. This council included both the Mathers among its seventeen members. They found that he had taken " sundry unwarrantable and uncomfortable steps," but had, by the good hand of God, been brought

[1] The dates are as given by Calef.

to better things ; and they hoped that the distempers at Salem would not be so incurable that he could not with any comfort continue there.

This totally failed to heal the breach. A month later an address was presented to the council, signed by fifty-two householders and eighteen church members of Salem, which called for Parris's removal. He held on, while arbitrators were appointed at Boston between him and the people of Salem Village.

The attorneys for the villagers in July 1697 made a strong remonstrance to the arbitrators, in which they spoke of Parris's " oath against the lives of several, wherein he swears that the prisoners with their looks knock down those pretended sufferers," and contended that " he that swears to more than he is certain of is equally guilty of perjury with him that swears to what is false." They also referred to his partiality, in stifling the accusations of some and vigilantly promoting others, and denounced him as " the beginner and procurer of the sorest afflictions, not to this Village only, but to this whole country, that ever did befall them."

The arbitrators were convinced. They decided that, while Parris should have his arrears of stipend (withheld for some considerable period, it seems) and a sum to meet his expenditure on repairs of the ministerial house, he should be dismissed from his post at Salem Village.

Samuel Parris accordingly left the scene of his misdeeds. He did not fail to obtain other ministerial appointments in Massachusetts, first at Stowe and then at Dunstable, and finally died at Sudbury in 1720, aged sixty-seven.

With no undue haste, it will be agreed, came a public rehabilitation of the victims of the persecution, in the shape of an Act of the province of Massachusetts to reverse the attainders of George Burroughs and others for witch-craft.[1] This is dated October 17th, 1711, nineteen years after the hangings and imprisonments.

" Forasmuch," it begins, " as [in 1692] two several towns within this province were infested with a horrible Witchcraft or possession of devils ; and at a special court of

[1] See *Records of Salem Witchcraft* for the whole document and for the list of compensations paid under the Act.

oyer and terminer holden at Salem . . . [twenty-two names follow, five of men, the rest of women] were severally convicted and attainted of witchcraft, and some of them put to death, others lying still under the like sentence of the said court, and liable to have the same executed upon them

" The influence and energy of the evil spirits so great at that time acting in and upon those who were the principal accusers and witnesses proceeding so far as to cause a prosecution to be had of persons of known and good reputation . . .

" And some of the principal accusers and witnesses in those dark and severe prosecutions have since discovered themselves to be persons of profligate and vicious conversation.[1]

" Upon the humble petition and suit of several of the said persons and of the children of others of them whose parents were executed . . . it was enacted that the judgements and attainders against the named five men and seventeen women be and are hereby reversed, and that no penalties or forfeitures of goods or chattels be had or incurred."

Compensation was allotted to relatives of those who had been hanged, and to those who had suffered imprisonment during what Benjamin Nurse, one of the relatives, rightly speaks of as " the sorrowful times called the Witchcraft times." Fifty pounds were paid to Charles Burroughs, the dead minister's eldest son, as representative of his six brothers and sisters. In their petition it had been stated that their stepmother, who had married again, had taken what money, household goods, and books their father had left, so that they were without resources. It was a case, young Burroughs might well have quoted, of finding

Nil sibi legatum præter plorare suisque.

*　　*　　*　　*　　*

When we take the Salem affair as a whole certain aspects of it show forth prominently.

First as to the nature of the acts of witchcraft alleged

---

[1] It may be gathered from this that others besides the six confessed witches of Andover and Ann Putman had been found out for what they were.

against the accused. A charge that runs all through the testimonies is that of " tormenting," " afflicting," " torturing," by pinching, biting, and almost strangling ; these unpleasant afflictions coming from the hands (and teeth) of the bewitchers, not in their own bodies but in spectral " shape," but nevertheless leaving marks which, it was asserted, could be shown to other people. The tooth-impressions of George Burroughs and of little Dorothy Good are examples—though Calef ridicules the charge and cites an instance where the " biter " was toothless.

The alleged torments continued while afflicted and afflicters, otherwise accusers and accused, were in the court itself. We have heard of this at the examinations of Sarah Good and Martha Cory. At that of Bridget Bishop one of the magistrates went so far as to remark to the prisoner, " Why, you seem to act witchcraft before us by the motion of your body, which seems to have influence upon the afflicted ! " Edmund Gurney, as has been said, appears to accept this alleged phenomenon as no mere pretence, but as an illustration of hypnotic control by the witch, whose postures and gestures the " subjects " imitated, owing to the control over them. This is almost the same as allowing that the accused *were* witches, of a sort, even if the contemporary explanation of sorcery has not to be introduced.

The spectral appearances of living persons were another phenomenon constantly brought up, to the time when they were rejected with contempt at Salem in January 1693. Previously there is no indication in the records that testimony concerning them was regarded as otherwise than valid. They were more seriously treated than " ghosts before the Law " in England and Scotland.[1] These spectres were independent of the situation of the body of the persons they resembled, who might indeed be in prison while their shapes were about Salem Village working mischief. The confessed witches, too, were ready—or, at any rate, were induced—to allow that they did many things in spectral form, not merely tormenting, but also attending meetings of witches. But the subject of the

[1] See my *Historic British Ghosts*, pp. 93 *ff.*, 137–8.

" witch's " pretensions to the faculty of disembodiment has been dealt with elsewhere (see p. 41).

The seeming spectre of a person who was quite innocent of any wish to appear was a matter which sorely troubled the prosecutors and the ministers of Massachusetts. The accusations against Mrs. Hale, of Beverly, made the trouble acute. John Hale, willing to believe other people witches, was sure that his wife was not, and regarded charges of her " shape " tormenting people as lies. He had the sympathy of the ministers, but many of them were reluctant to reject testimonies from the afflicted, and so were driven to arguing that the Devil might assume the shape of an innocent person in order to afflict his victims. The help of Dr. Increase Mather was called in, and in 1693 he produced his *Cases of Conscience concerning Evil Spirits*, in which, with all the authority of the president of Harvard, he unhesitatingly pronounced that the Devil had the power imputed to him.

Other spectral appearances of the dead, as in the case of the first two wives of George Burroughs, have nothing to do with sorcery. What is akin to the matter of spectres of the living is that of the gift of invisibility, a regular witch attribute. The point arose, we have seen, in the Burroughs trial, whereon Cotton Mather commented that the trick of rendering themselves invisible claimed in some witches' confessions was the more credible *because there is demonstration that they often make other things utterly invisible*.

The most serious of the accusations, however, were those concerning the Witches' Sabbat and participation in the Black Mass—though that was not an expression used in New England, where " Mass " was a purely Popish word, of course. Could these charges be proved, it was felt that there was every justification of a strict enforcement of the scriptural injunction, " Thou shalt not suffer a witch to live." This was recognised by Cotton Mather in his fulminations against George Burroughs as head actor in the " hellish rendezvouzes " of the Salem witches. A number of the testimonies have been given in the preceding pages, their object being to show that Burroughs, a nominally Christian minister, conducted a parody of the Sacrament with bread and wine, both usually described as red. Moreover, there was a ceremony of baptism, involving renunciation of previous Christian baptism. And there was also the signing or putting the hand to the Devil's Book, that ever-recurring feature in the evidence ; the book so graphically described in the late Rule case as " about a cubit long, red and thick, but not very broad."

It is obvious that the importance to be attached to the testimonies depends on the view taken of the character of the witnesses, to which we shall come.

At the Sabbats the presence of the Black Man is often referred to, sometimes " a small black man," identified with Burroughs, sometimes a figure distinct from the minister. In his separate shape he is not always described as black, as for instance in Deliverance Hobbs's evidence, where he is merely " a man in a long-crowned, white hat," who sits at a table with Burroughs and pours out the wine —in tankards ! Another witness talks of a black man in a high-crowned hat ; but this was not at a Sabbat.

The Black Man, apart from attending the Sabbats, had also the diabolical effrontery to appear in court, according to the afflicted, to prompt his servant Martha Cory, for instance. One is tempted to echo the remark of Friedrich von Spee, in his *Cautio Criminalis* in 1632, that it does not enter the head to doubt the existence of witches until one studies the judicial evidence.

A point which is missing in the Massachusetts witchcraft trials is the charge against the female witches of carnal connection with the Devil, so prominent in some of the cases we have previously been examining. Perhaps in such a society as that of New England it was felt that it " wasn't done." Anyhow, it is not referred to, either in the court records or in the minister's writings.

To come to minor matters, there is not very much about broom- or pole-riding in Massachusetts. Tituba, we have seen, mounts to ride abroad with Goodwife Carrier " upon a poole," as they go to a witches' meeting, of which the account is tantalisingly missing. There is a little about the alleged practice at Andover. Elsewhere, when the initiated or their victims are conveyed to various places, there is no description of how they were conveyed thither.

Nor is there much about witch-marks. Burroughs was searched, and had none. Bridget Bishop was found to have a " teat," and there are a few other instances recorded of search. It would appear from what Calef says (see p. 175 that it was a fairly frequent practice.

As to " familiars," we have heard a few charges, but we do not get the imps as in the Lancashire and Essex trials. Sarah Good's and Martha Cory's yellow birds " suck between their fingers," but animal life among the Massachusetts witches does not seem to have been a regular institution. Widow Burt's cat and dog upon the road to Salem make but a brief and inconsequential appearance.

There is a certain amount about images and poppets, into which the witch always appeared anxious that the person tempted should stick pins or thorns rather than do so himself or herself.

We may turn to the subject of the characters of the witnesses who gave testimony in the Salem trials. These witnesses may be roughly divided into the two classes of children and adults ; the children including girls up to the age of eighteen or nineteen, if we follow the Salem practice. Frank Podmore, in his chapter on " Possession and Witchcraft " in *Modern Spiritualism*, remarks how in the Sixteenth and Seventeenth Centuries a prominent part in the initial stages of witch-persecution was played by malevolent or hysterical children. It is notable, too, that the children are usually girls. (Is this the incipient trait of feminine sadism ?) At Salem, the testifying children were all girls, most of whom we have mentioned by name, with their ages where they can be ascertained.

S. P. Fowler, who edited an edition of Calef's *More Wonders of the Invisible World* in 1861, observes that all the pretended spiritual manifestations of any note that have ever occurred in America had their origin with children and young persons ; and with regard to the Salem persecution he holds the charitable opinion—if it is really charitable—that it originated with children through their love of sport and mischief. He quotes the evidence of a woman at one of the Salem trials that she had heard one of the accusing girls cry out against Goody Parker (afterwards hanged) for sport. " The girls," she added, " must

have some sport !" She expressed without doubt, observes
Fowler, the feeling of the whole circle of those youthful
accusers. As a sport, as we have said, witch-hunting is
about on a par with fox-hunting. There is the additional
aggravation of malice, hardly imputable to the fox-hunter.

Calef himself is more to the point when he talks of " the
accusations of a parcel of possessed, distracted, or lying
wenches, accusing their innocent neighbours, pretending
they see their spectres, *i.e.* devils in their likeness, afflicting
of them."

A really charitable hypothesis, if it be tenable, is that of
hysteria, running in epidemic form through the young
girls of Salem. The testimonies given at the trials furnish
much strong support for the theory of hysteria. An instance
may be adduced of one of the confessing witches, though
she hardly comes within the children class. This was
Mary Warren, aged twenty, who was accused at the same
time as Bridget Bishop, Giles Cory, and others. She had
violent fits in court, but at first protested her innocence of
witchcraft. Then she seemed about to confess, wringing
her hands and crying out : " Oh, I am sorry for it, I am
sorry for it ! " Another fit came on, and lasted so long that
it was ordered she should be taken out of court. She was
later brought back and examined in private before the
magistrates and attendant ministers. Her words are
recorded : " I shall not speak a word ; but I will, I will
speak, Satan ! She [*i.e.* her mistress, Elizabeth Proctor]
saith she will kill me. Oh ! she saith she owes me a spite
and will claw me off. Avoid, Satan, for the name of God,
avoid ! " More fits followed, and the prisoner's lips were
so bitten that she could speak no more and was taken
away again.

Samuel Parris took the note of this, and adds that after
Mary Warren began to confess (in the open court) not one
of the " sufferers " was afflicted, though tormented before ;
the sufferers being the usual Ann Putman, etc.

If we could believe that such were the result of hysteria,
coupled with self-deception, it would be well. But, as
Podmore says, in such cases it is difficult to know where
self-deception ends and malevolent trickery begins. Take
those two precious children Ann Putman and Abigail

Williams, aged eleven and twelve respectively, who spread death with their testimonies. The most that can be said in their defence, apart from a plea of morbid dispositions, was that one was daughter of Thomas Putman, the other niece of Samuel Parris; both men revoltingly forward in pressing the cases against the witches, in fact huntsmen to the Salem Village pack of hounds.

For the adult witnesses it is hardly possible to make the slightest excuse. Malice is only too apparent; and the malice of a small community is, to use Cotton Mather's favourite adjective, hellish. Some pity may be felt for the confessing witches (since we know how they were made to confess) who proceeded to involve others in the guilt of which they accused themselves. They were nearly all women of a depth of ignorance such that their very " confessions " reveal where the promptings of their examiners have influenced their words, so different from the ordinary level of their thoughts. We may wonder how many names were suggested to them, by the pious Mr. Parris or others, as suitable subjects of accusation.

Even Sarah Good, who refused to admit herself a witch, gave the name of a tormentor of the children; but she was wearied under cross-examination, and only mentioned an old bedridden woman, who could scarcely be hanged. She herself went bravely and defiantly to death.

In the Act for Reversal of Attainder in 1711 there is a statement that some of the principal accusers and witnesses at Salem had since discovered themselves to be " persons of profligate and vicious conversation." Now besides Ann Putnam, who had admitted her sin, we do not know of any of the accusers and witnesses who came within the description in the Act; but we are prepared to believe it. It may be that some of the evil-hearted children of 1692 had so grown up. We cannot say.

Of those who were accusers, not in the sense that they made charges in court against the prisoners, but that they spoke and wrote about the guilt which they insisted was theirs, we need say no more about Samuel Parris. As to the Mathers, perhaps some readers may think that we have dealt with them in a hostile spirit. We were aware that they had been beatified, if not quite canonised, in New

England history. But it was necessary, nevertheless, to examine what share they took in the persecution, since they were leaders of opinion at the time. A few more words may be added here.

Their sincerity cannot be doubted. This is small palliation of their beliefs and the attitude resulting from them. Of Dr. Increase Kenneth B. Murdoch, in *The Dictionary of American Biography*, admits that by his writings on the reality of witchcraft he helped to make the Salem tragedy possible ; though " there is no evidence that he sought to accomplish what came to pass." It is allowed that he made no protest against the conduct of the trials until the autumn of 1692, when his *Cases of Conscience concerning Evils Spirits* was in private circulation, if not in print, in Boston, to be published in London next year with his *Further Account of the Trials*. In *Cases of Conscience* he expressed his disapproval of the " spectral evidence " at Salem (though he affirmed, as we have heard, that the Devil may assume the shape of innocent people for his wicked ends) ; and, according to his son, the book brought an end to the executions in Massachusetts. Also Sir William Phipps reported that it was Dr. Mather's opinion which influenced him in reprieving those of the condemned who had not already suffered. He held, unfortunately too late in many cases, that it was better for a guilty witch to escape than for an innocent person to die.

Cotton Mather was more responsible than his father for acts encouraging the persecution. Mr. Murdoch pleads in his behalf that " he was far from robust nervously ; he was a prey to a morbid love of introspection, and perhaps a victim of hallucinations." He was, however, very sure of the righteousness of his attitude with regard to the trials ; to show which we may quote a passage from the "Author's Defence " prefaced to his *Wonders of the Invisible World :*

" One of the least among the children of New England," he writes, " has done what is done. None but the Father who sees in secret knows the heart-breaking exercises wherewith I have composed what is now going to be exposed, lest I should in any one thing miss of doing my divine service for his glory and for his people ; but I am now somewhat comfortably assured of his favourable acceptance ; and *I will not fear ; what can a Satan do unto me !* ''[1]

He steadfastly adhered to his opinions in spite of all that happened at Salem, and when in 1723, after his father's death, he published an account of " Remarkables " (wonderful deliverances of the distressed, mercies to the godly, judgements on the wicked, apparitions, possessions, enchantments, etc.), which Dr. Increase had long designed, he repeated his views of Satan's work at Salem. He was disappointed of his ambition to become one day president of Harvard, a post which his father had resigned in 1701. Whether his share in the witch-persecution had any influence in this matter is uncertain.

We may now make a brief review of the Salem affair, attempting to see what there was behind it ; and we will begin by presenting the opinions of two modern writers who have shown a great interest in it.

The Rev. Montague Summers, author of *A History of Witchcraft and Demonology, The Geography of Witchcraft*, etc., has no doubt as to the real existence of the practice of witchcraft, with an organised coven, in New England. He writes emphatically in the second of the two books mentioned :

" It is *most certain* from the testimony of Deliverance Hobbs that she belonged to such a coven, of which the evidence against the Rev. George Burroughs, Bridget Bishop, and Martha Carrier *proves* them to have been members. There is a considerable amount of exaggeration, but when every allowance is made, very salient facts in regard to this Devil's Society are clear."

(The italics are ours, not the author's.)

" *There can be no doubt,*" Mr. Summers goes on, " that at Salem the traditional rites of the hideous black worship were precisely observed, allowing, of course, that it was a Protestant Communion and not Holy Mass which was the model of their hellish liturgy. These practices must have been carefully handed down and taught to the New England representatives of the witch-society. . . .

---

[1] I follow the punctuation of the author of 450 books. Richard Mather wrote a good deal ; Dr. Increase's name appears to about 130 publications ; but Cotton far surpassed them in number of writings.

" That a coven of witches did indeed exist in Salem is
proved beyond all doubt, and it is, I think, equally certain that
George Burroughs was the grand-master, Bridget Bishop
and Martha Carrier high officials.[1] . . . On the other hand,
it is plain that the majority at least of those who were
executed died upon a false charge, and that they had no
knowledge of all the sorceries so secretly practised in their
midst."

Mr. Summers further declares it *impossible* that the
several witnesses at the trials could have so exactly invented
the details of the old occult ceremonies and rites from their
own imaginations, and maintains that they *obviously* had
been more than once at a witch-coven.

So we, in turn, have no doubt what are this author's
views as to the guilt of some of the accused at Salem. His
assurance on the point would have pleased Cotton Mather.[2]

A very different standpoint is that taken up by Miss
Margaret Alice Murray in *The Witch-Cult in Western Europe*
and *The God of the Witches*. But the difference of standpoints
is not caused by a dispute over " facts " (which are really
not facts, but evidence as to alleged occurrences), but by
diverging interpretations. Miss Murray accepts the existence of witches at Salem, accepts the covens, accepts the
administration of a Sacrament, and does not deny the
complicity of George Burroughs and certain others of
the accused. Only she does not, so to speak, " impute
to them for sin." The Salem witches are not addicts
to hellish practices, parodists of Christian ceremonies,

---

[1] Why not also poor Giles Cory, on the evidence of the worthy
sisters Booth ? Was that too much for Mr. Summers to swallow ?

[2] Mr. Summers is equally positive about witches generally, in his
History of Witchcraft and Demonology. He sums up against them :
" I have endeavoured to show the witch as she really was—an evil
liver ; a social pest and parasite ; the devotee of a loathly and obscene
creed ; an adept at poisoning, blackmail, and other creeping crimes ;
a member of a powerful secret organisation inimical to Church and
State ; a blasphemer in word and deed ; swaying the villagers by
terror and superstition ; a charlatan and a quack sometimes ; a
bawd ; an abortionist ; a dark counsellor of lewd court ladies and
adulterous gallants ; a minister to vice and inconceivable corruption ;
battening upon the filth and foulest passions of the age."
So, in the vulgar phrase, that's that !

blasphemers ; but devotees of the Old Religion, to which she has given the name of the Dianic cult. In the two books mentioned out of her very extensive contributions to anthropology and kindred subjects she develops her theory with great earnestness and learned skill. It is certainly a more persuasive theory than that of the contenders for a degrading Satanism as the foundation of witchcraft.

Briefly Miss Murray's contention is that the evidence we have proves that, underlying the Christian religion in Western Europe, was a pre-Christian cult practised by many classes of the community, but chiefly by the more ignorant or those in less thickly inhabited parts of the country. Its ritual was analogous to many other ancient rituals, with the dates of its chief festivals May and November Eves, suggesting the religion of a race that had not reached the agricultural stage, Palæolithic and early Neolithic man in fact, but strove by fertility-rites to promote the increase of animals rather than of crops ; which explains the sexual element in the ritual of which the witch-persecutors made such a weapon of attack.

The god of the witches was the Horned God, typified by the bull, or more often the goat. In another form he was the man with two faces, the Latin Janus (Dianus) and had a feminine counterpart, Diana, who appears as the patroness of witches. (Possibly she was an original mother-goddess, worshipped by women, and was superseded by the male deity as the object of general worship.) The attribute of two-facedness has never been satisfactorily explained ; but it survived to modern times, as Miss Murray points out, in the Basses-Pyrénées region, where devotees would wear a mask on the back of the head or body, and in the English Midlands.

There is nothing to show that the ceremonies of this cult were copied from the Christian, though this was always a strong argument of the persecutors. With regard to the " Witches' Mass," Miss Murray is not the first to suggest that the borrowing may not have been by but from the old religion. The same opinion has been advanced, it may be recalled, with regard to the story of virgin birth. Where resemblances are found, the earlier Christian apologists at least maintained that the Devil

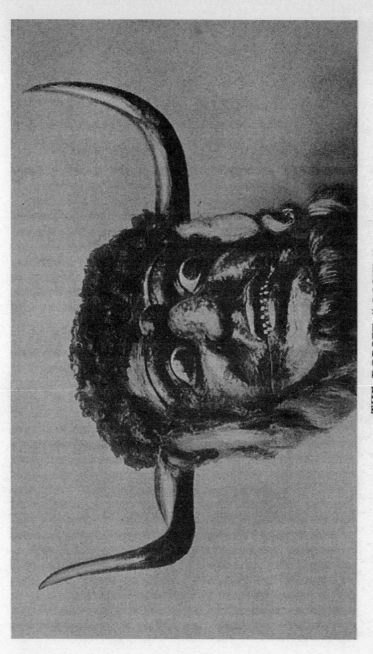

THE DORSET "OOSER"

From an ancient magic mask, formerly preserved in a Dorset family

THE WITCH AND HER FAMILIAR

From a sculpture in the Crypt, York Minster

had imitated. The *advocatus diaboli*, on the other hand, asked : Does the old imitate the new ?

The likeness of organisation of the worshippers is another point of contention. Cotton Mather remarks how like the witches' covens, though he does not use that word, were to the Congregational churches in this respect. The coven answers to the local body of elders, and the witch-leader or chief man, the representative of the god, to the minister. This resemblance is, indeed, more striking in a Protestant community such as that of Salem than in the days before the Reformation of the Christian Church.

Miss Murray holds that, on the evidence before him, Mather was justified in saying that the Salem witches " had a Baptism and a Supper and Officers among them abominably resembling those of our Lord." Moreover, she herself has no doubt that there were these witches in the Salem neighbourhood, and that they were organised in a society with George Burroughs at their head. " That Burroughs was a religious person," she says in *Witch-Cult*, " is no argument against his being the ' Devil ' of Salem. Apart from the well-known psychological fact that a certain form of religious feeling can exist at the same time as the propensity to and practice of sexual indulgence,[1] there is proof that many of the witches were outwardly religious according to the tenets of Christianity."

But, while so convinced of the reality of the Salem witch-belief, Miss Murray, we may repeat, does not condemn its devotees as blasphemous parodists of Christianity, but sees in them adherents of the Dianic cult. Burroughs is only a " devil " inasmuch as this was the name given by the Christians to the priest of the older religion ; as it was, and is to-day, among some of them, to the gods of all other creeds than their own. Thus she ingeniously links up the Salem witches with Joan of Arc, Gilles de Rais, William Rufus, and a host of other notable historic characters. She finds in the death of George Burroughs a welcome confirmation of her theory of the necessary sacrifice of the incarnate deity ; " consummate at the hands of the public

---

[1] But where is the evidence for this at Salem? The syllogism appears to be : Witches practice sexual license. —— There were witches at Salem. —— Therefore, etc.

executioner," adds Mr. Summers, in derision of a theory which he calls fantastic and absurd.

We may readily admit that *upon the evidence* there was a community of witches in Massachusetts, and that Burroughs was a leader. But what evidence ? So much of it is palpably absurd. So much of it was extracted by suggestion and by methods of torture, wherein the American Essex was not far behind the English Essex. So much of it is the routine evidence with which we have met so often before.

Miss Murray endeavours to combat the objection that the confessed witches' evidence at the trials is more or less uniform in character and must therefore be attributed to the publication by the Inquisitors (in what company does Cotton Mather find himself !) of a questionary for the judges, so that the evidence is worthless. No explanation, she says, is offered by the objectors how the Inquisitors arrived at their questionary ; and they also overlook the fact that the very uniformity of the confessions points to the reality of the alleged occurrences. If they had differed, it would be *prima facie* evidence that there was no well-defined religion—such as she is so anxious to show— underlying the witches' ritual.

This is a point well taken, we may admit. But the argument cannot be called conclusive. The suspicion still remains that the evidence which sent to the gallows a number of people, later admitted to be innocent, was manufactured evidence. The question is : Was it all manufactured, against all the accused ? Much centres upon the testimony of Deliverance Hobbs, the self-styled " Covenant Witch," whose confession did so much to secure the condemnation of the minister Burroughs.

This old woman stated on April 22nd, 1692, when she was first examined before the magistrates at Salem Village, that *on the previous day* she was at a meeting with Burroughs, the Proctors, the Cory couple, Goody Nurse, and Goody Bishop, when Burroughs administered the red sacrament to them. Was she, then, at liberty on April 21st ; or was she " present " at the meeting in disembodied form ? This is not revealed, though it is obviously a most important point. If she was still a free woman on April 21st, her arrest and examination must have followed immediately upon the witches' meeting ; and we should have supposed Burroughs to be at Wells, Maine, at that date. If, on the other hand, she was already under arrest on the 21st, her attendance at the sacrament in disembodied or "spectral" shape transcends the world of everyday existence even in the Seventeenth Century ! What is "most certain," "proved," "beyond all doubt," to Mr. Montague Summers, and accepted by Miss Murray, is (to say the least) devilishly difficult to some of us others. In fact, again we think of Friedrich von Spee's remark, quoted above. It is the judicial evidence that inspires the doubt. And there is nothing else to go upon, except theory.

Certainly Miss Murray's theory is attractive, if the Mather-Summers view is not. But they all profess to rely on evidence, particularly that of Deliverance Hobbs. It is a pity that we do not know any more about this woman after that by her confession of the sins of others she escaped the gallows ; whither had she gone, she might well have gained the epithet which the younger Mather bestowed on Martha Carrier, "this rampant hag."

Deliverance Hobbs's testimony was corroborated by other witnesses, of course. But we may ask, since we have heard so much of what they had to say, what certainty their evidence inspires. The word is indeed absurd in such a matter. All that we can feel sure of is that twenty people were done to death, and a few more condemned, but not executed, for the imputed crime of witchcraft. Their names remain a memory of what was discovered later to be a horrible miscarriage of justice, in the great majority of cases beyond all doubt.[1]

Where doubt is left, the solution is easy to Mr. Montague Summers, who in his *History of Witchcraft and Demonology* (p. 64), says that, when every allowance is made for fanaticism and hysteria in the accusations against witches,

---

[1] A friend, Mr. E. B. Osborn, of *The Morning Post*, tells me that he has seen slips of willow from Salem, inscribed with the names of the victims, who are wrongly stated to have been burnt. In New England, unlike as in Scotland and in France, for instance, but as in the country from which New England was colonised, witches died by hanging, not by burning at the stake.

" there remain innumerable and important cases which are not covered by any ordinary explanation, which fall within no normal category." There are present in these cases underlying and provocative phenomena, for which " there is no other way of accounting save by acknowledging the reality of Witchcraft and diabolic contacts."

In his introduction to the facsimile edition in 1929 of *The Trial of the Lancashire Witches*, Mr. G. B. Harrison divides the three possible attitudes of mind toward the subject of witchcraft as follows :

(1) To admit the evidence and, in part, its diabolic explanation ;

(2) To deny both, and explain the accusations by hysteria, gross credulity, etc. ;

(3) To rationalise, accepting the evidence but denying the supernatural explanation.

Mr. Summers and the Mathers illustrate the first attitude, Robert Calef the second, Miss Murray may be said to illustrate the third ; for she refuses to range herself with the sceptics, whose only weapon, she says, is the appeal to common sense and sentiment combined, and their only method a flat denial of every statement seeming to point to supernatural powers.

That Calef, however, is not to be dismissed as a pure sceptic is shown by a passage in the Postscript he appends to his *More Wonders of the Invisible World*, in which he exhibits no anti-Christian spirit, it will be admitted, whatever may be the extent of his quarrel with the Massachusetts Calvinists. It appears to us that a good part of this passage merits reproduction. It runs :

" As long as Christians do acknowledge the law of God to be imperfect, as not describing that crime that it requires to be punished by death : . . .

" As long as the Devil shall be believed to have a natural power to act above and against the course of nature :

" As long as the witches shall be believed to have a power to commission him :[1]

---

[1] We may compare George Gifford's argument a century earlier than Calef, that if a witch can control the Devil to work for her she is more powerful than the Devil ; which is contrary to Scripture, since only God can control Satan.

" As long as the Devil's testimony, by the pretended afflicted, shall be received as more valid to condemn [the accused] than their plea of not guilty to acquit :

" As long as the accused shall have their lives and liberties confirmed and restored to them upon their confessing themselves guilty :

" As long as the accused shall be forced to undergo hardships and torments for their not confessing :

" As long as teats for the Devil to suck are searched for upon the bodies of the accused as a token of guilt : . . .

" So long it may be expected that innocents will suffer as witches :

" So long God will be daily dishonoured, and so long His judgements must be expected to continue."

We venture to say that this is a far more Christian document—as it is certainly far humaner—than many of the statements of Dr. Increase Mather and his son concerning the Salem witches. Yet it is not Calef who is honoured among the New England protagonists of this period, but the reverend gentlemen whom he so earnestly and painstakingly opposed.

Note.—Concerning the Dorset " Ooser," of which an illustration faces p. 170, Miss Margaret Murray says that it was " stolen from its Dorsetshire owners within the last thirty years ". A painted wooden mask, worn over the head of a man wrapt in an ox-skin, it represents " the last remains of that most ancient of all recorded religions, the worship of the Horned God " (*The God of the Witches,* p. 31).

CHAPTER IV

MODERN INSTANCES

THE series of events with which we have been dealing in the three preceding chapters may appear almost incredibly remote from the life of the world as we know it to-day. Amid such surroundings, in thought, we may seem to be in some imaginary realm, the creation of a storyteller with a taste for the grotesque and the horrible. Even if we are driven, by the force of evidence, to accept the events recorded as having actually occurred, we may be tempted to think that they belong to a long-dead past, having no parallel in modern times.

But there we should be entirely wrong. The continuity of the belief in witchcraft, and of the existence of something that we may still call witchcraft, has not been broken, it has merely been obscured by the increased complexity of life. There is so much less time to spare for the consideration of matters that to our ancestors appealed as deserving of serious attention. Be it granted that if we did attend to them we should probably attempt to interpret them far otherwise than our ancestors. But the attention is not given. The item of news is buried in the mass. " There are strange things lost and forgotten," says Mr. Arthur Machen in the opening sentence of *The Great Return*, " in obscure corners of the newspaper." Often, too, even that obscure vision is denied. The papers ignore the curious happening, which has no " publicity value." Only in the magazine of some small society may its record appear ; or perhaps in the pages of *Notes and Queries*, or some other periodical hardly to be called popular reading-matter.

For some reason, in the 'nineties of last century—so often nowadays given an adjective little suggesting the occult— there was quite a considerable number of reports showing

the survival of at least a faith in the reality of witchcraft.
We may take a few cases.

The first is from Ireland, in 1895, and this did succeed
in gaining the notice of the newspapers, because it involved
the death of a human being by violence. At Baltyvadhen in
Tipperary a married woman, Bridget C., was put on her
kitchen-fire and burnt as a witch. Her own family were
the perpetrators of the act. Their excuse was that what
they burnt was not a woman but a *clurichaune*, substituted
by the fairies, and that when these snatched the changeling
from the flames the real wife would be restored to her
husband.[1]

Somerset furnished a number of stories about the same
period ; not so tragic in reality, but some of them showing
that a firm belief in the possibility of death by bewitchment
and in the justification of meeting magic by counter-
measures. One instance is from an unnamed place in the
county in 1894, and is vouched for by the editor, as well
as by a writer, in *Somerset and Dorset Notes and Queries* for
December of that year. Abbreviated, it is as follows :

A poor woman, with a large family, had for two years a
series of misfortunes. Her husband was ill, two children
met with accidents, and all were laid up by a prevailing
epidemic. She came to the conclusion that there must be
some evil influence at work, that she had been " overlooked." Her husband and children fell in with the idea,
and soon were saying that they saw little black objects
at night, which would try to pull them out of bed by their
feet.

The woman went to consult a " wise man " who lived at
Wells. He agreed that she had been bewitched, and said
that if he knew the name of the witch he could be of help
against her. The woman went through the list of names
of her female acquaintances until at last she reached one
whom the wise man accepted as the culprit. He could
break the charm, he said, but it would take a lot of prayer
and work. He directed her to sit with her husband in

[1] I read a reference in a recent newspaper to a case just twenty years
earlier than that at Baltyvadhen, when at Long Compton, in
Staffordshire, a man killed an old woman whom he believed to be a
witch.

front of their fire about midnight, burning salt and speaking no words for an hour except the following lines :

> This is not the thing I wish to burn
> But Mrs. ——'s heart, of ——, to turn.
> Wishing thee neither to eat, sleep, drink, nor rest
> Until thou dost come to me and do my request ;
> Or else the wrath of God may fall on thee
> And cause thee to be consumed in a moment. Amen.

When they had done with this incantation before the fire, the husband and wife were to go out of the room backwards, mount the stair backwards, and repeat the Lord's Prayer backwards, using no other speech until they were in bed. The result is not recorded.

Now in *The Spectator*, earlier in the same year, H. S. has a similar tale from the Mendip district, with the difference that it was a pig, not a human being, that " took bad." The woman who owned it applied to a white witch, who directed that a sheep's heart should be stuck full of pins and roasted before the fire, salt being sprinkled on the flames from time to time, while the following charm was sung :

> It is not this heart I mean to burn,
> But the person's heart I mean to turn,
> Wishing them neither rest nor peace
> Till they are dead and gone.

H. S. states that after this had gone on for some time " the inevitable black cat jumped out from somewhere and was pronounced to be the fiend which had been exorcised." But surely this is a false conclusion. Whatever the black cat has to do with the matter, the charm is not an exorcism, but an example of counter-magic, to harm the person who had injured the pig.

In the before-quoted *Somerset and Dorset Notes and Queries*, again in 1894, the Rev. W. F. Rose gives two incidents that obviously belong to the same story, and may therefore be amalgamated. They date from 1875, but apparently did not appear in print until nineteen years later.

At Worle, near Weston-super-Mare, a man lost a " varth o' paigs " (a farrow of pigs), and sent for a wise man from Taunton to advise him what to do. The white witch accused four women of the village, whom he promised to make cry for mercy. By his direction, the heart of one of the dead pigs was stuck full of pins and burnt, the consultant and his wife sitting by fire in expectation of the bewitcher coming to them to ask why they were hurting her.[1] No one came ; but soon after one of the suspected women fell on her fire and was burnt to death. On the day after, the harriers were out on a hill near her house and lost the hare among some stone walls. The following day a man picked up a dead hare on the spot, and took it to his master ; whereon the maids fled in terror from the house, declaring that the hare was old Mrs. ——, the burnt witch.

Mr. F. T. Elworthy, who in *The Evil Eye* (1895) brought together so many tales of " overlooking," in his own county of Somerset as well as elsewhere, notes the fact that in England the pig is the commonest victim ; due to the number of peasant-owners here, as well as to the well-known difficulty of physicking pigs. It is certainly the case that the bewitchment of these animals was one of the most frequent of charges against persons accused of evil powers. In the St. Osyth prosecution of 1582 a man named Thomas Death alleged against the witch Cicely Celles that through her " he had presently after severall swine which did skippe and leape about the yarde, in a most strange force, and then died." A vast number of similar instances could be adduced.

To revert to Mr. Elworthy and more recent times, he shows how regular was the appeal to the white witch, *i.e.* the witch-finder, whether it were pigs, cattle, or children that were afflicted. Failing the antidote of a magic character, a child was " safe to die " ; and if he did, the mother, having scorned recourse to ꭤ doctor, would merely say :

---

[1] A parallel to this is shown by something I omitted to mention in connection with the Malden witch, Ellen Smith, on p. 100. When the man she had cursed had burnt the rat-toad in his fire, Ellen Smith, in great pain, came to his house and enquired how all there were. " Well, I thank God," he replied. " I thought you had not been well," she said, " and so I came to see how you did "—and so went her way.

" Oh, I know'd very well he wouldn't never get no better ! 'Tidn no good vor to go agin it."

" This is no fancy or isolated case," declares Mr. Elworthy, " but here in the last decade of the Nineteenth Century one of the commonest of everyday facts." He adds in a footnote that in October, 1894, two persons were dying in Wellington parish who firmly believed themselves, and were firmly believed, to be suffering solely from " overlooking." He gives the case of a girl dying in hospital, concerning whom her mother asserted that she *knew* who had overlooked her ; naming an old woman who certainly bore no good character.

In the old days, remarks Mr. Elworthy, the accused woman would have been hanged as a witch. But we may add that the white witch, too, would have had no better fate in the Seventeenth Century if John Stearne had had his way. " But yet I say all Witches to be bad, and ought to suffer alike, being in league with the Devill."

The belief in the blighting power of the witch's evil eye is therefore brought down to a comparatively late period in England, and could no doubt be brought down to to-day. If we go abroad, to Central Europe, the instances might be multiplied indefinitely. One may be cited as recent as December, 1935, when the Vienna correspondent of the *Daily Telegraph* reported a witch-trial just ended in that city. A sixty-year-old woman, Ida Markus, was acquitted on the charge of having caused grievous bodily harm to another woman through making her collapse, paralysed, at the Schafberg bathing-pool in 1934, by means of " mysterious hypnotic passes."

It was not denied that the alleged victim, Frau Prinz, was still paralysed at the time of the trial. What was most astonishing was the accused woman's defence. Her eyes had been opened, she asserted, since 1928, enabling her to watch all the activities of the spirit-world, on which she had published fifteen books. All pure-minded persons had their guardian angels, who were opposed by demoniacal spirits. She could see both. " The air round Frau Prinz at the pool," she said, " was so thick with demons trying to paralyse her that I made mystic passes to banish them, but was not strong enough." She told the judge that he was surrounded with guardian angels, "all creatures of light, who are telling you to find me not guilty."

The doctors, however, contributed to the acquittal by testifying that Frau Markus held her beliefs honestly and that there was no proof of her having hypnotised Frau Prinz.

No mention of white witchcraft is reported in the trial. But the connection between witchcraft, aiming at either bad or good, and hypnotic suggestion has engaged some attention among modern writers on psychological subjects.[1]

This Viennese case presents a woman as having reputedly the power of " fascination," even if hypnotic passes take the place of the evil eye. Now the author of the book named after the latter says that while it was anciently believed that women have the power more than men (explained by Varro *quia irascendi et concupiscendi animi vim adeo effrenatam habent*, " because so unbridled is the force of their irascible and desirous spirit ") in modern times it is more common to attribute the evil eye to men than to women. But is this a fact ? Admittedly it would be a very difficult task to furnish statistics, and without them it is impossible to prove the matter. Some indication, however, is given by the almost purely feminine character given now to the term " witch " in common language. " Old witches " still abound, though the name may be usually mere vulgar abuse ; while " magicians " are rare, and " conjurers " (greater than witches, poor George Burroughs was alleged to have boasted) have now no sinister implication about them.

The gipsy, nearly always a woman of the tribe, still conveys to the popular mind an idea of magic powers. Only as recently as in the May of the current year a judge, addressing the jury at the Cambridgeshire Assizes, suggested to them that it might have passed through their minds whether they were sitting in a jury-box in 1936 or had been transported back to the Middle Ages when some matter of witchcraft was being discussed at a trial.

The case under review was certainly reminiscent of the days of old. A gipsy woman, aged forty, was charged

[1] See, for instance, Gurney's *Phantasms of the Living*, I, pp. 182–3.

with demanding money and groceries with menaces
from a Cambridgeshire tradesman. She had, it appeared,
visited his shop about a year previously, when she told his
fortune, and advised him that he had an enemy, whose
curses and spells she could counteract for him. In March
this year she called again with a demand for money, etc.,
threatening otherwise to put a curse upon him and cause
him to be sent to an asylum. The grocer gave her £2 10s.;
but when she came again with a further demand he had
taken the precaution to have a policeman concealed on
his premises, who overheard what she said, and further
found upon her some marked money just given to her
by the grocer. Though the gipsy denied at the Assizes
that she had made any threats, and said that she had
received the money for telling the grocer he would have
good health, she was found guilty ; but, having no previous
conviction against her, and being the mother of several
children, she was merely bound over for twelve months.

There is, of course, no exercise of witchcraft here, merely
first an offer and then a threat to exercise it ; the gipsy
appearing in turn as a white and a black witch.

While the present book was still being written, a murder-
case was tried in London, in connection with which strange
tales of black magic, of curses that had disastrous effect,
of fatal hypnotic powers, were published ; not indeed at
the Old Bailey, where the trial took place, but in a place
where publicity is none the less readily secured, on the
front page of at least one daily newspaper. No doubt,
therefore, the tales went round the world. The matter is
so recent that no names need be mentioned. It is enough
to remark that it was given to be understood that witchcraft, of the kind that causes death, still flourishes among us.

But perhaps we need not feel astonished at this—at the
allegation, that is to say. Do we not see the announcements
of " Europe's greatest astrologer," and regular series of
articles upon what the stars foretell ? *Populus vult decipi* . . .
we may suppose. Some of the directors of the Press, at
least, so interpret the case, and hasten to gratify the wish.

PART III

WARLOCKS WEIRD

CHAPTER I

MAGICIAN IN SPITE OF HIMSELF

SOME old writer speaks disrespectfully of " Wizards," who he thinks should rather be called " Dizzards " ; and this expressive word, though nowadays out of use in speech, conveyed well what opinion the writer held of them. They were fools. It does not matter much whether the implication was of a professional, a " motley fool," in his robes of office, or of the man who was a fool because he could not help it, a natural, in fact.

Meric Casaubon, the editor-biographer of Doctor John Dee, puts the case much more politely when he writes : " Some men come into the world with *Cabalistical Brains ;* their heads are full of the mysteries ; they see nothing, they read nothing, but their brain is on work to pick somewhat out of it that is not ordinary ; and, out of the very ABC that children are taught, rather than fail they will fetch all the secrets of God's wisdom, tell you how the world was created, how governed, and what will be the end of all things. Reason and sense that other men go by they think the acorns that the old world fed upon ; fools and children may be content with them, but they see things by another *Light. . . .*"

It is clear whom Casaubon esteems the fools ; not those whom the cabalistically-brained considered such, but those who affected superiority over them.

In writing of Doctor Dee's life Casaubon is at pains to show the difference between him and the man whose name was chiefly associated with his in wizardry, Edward Kelly. Dee is " a very free and sincere Christian "—like Casaubon himself—" his only (but great and dreadful) error being that he mistook false lying spirits for angels of light, the Divel of Hell (as we commonly term him) for the God of

Heaven." Kelly is "a cunning man," "a vile and diabolical man." Dee's case is "altogether inexcusable, that,
knowing the man to be such a one, he would have to do
with him, and expected good by his ministeries." Yet
Casaubon will not allow more blame against the Doctor
than that "his faith and his intellectuals were so much in
the power of his spirits that they might persuade him to
anything."

On the whole, Casaubon's judgement, except in the matter
of the nature of the spirits which Kelly summoned and Dee
accepted as real, has been endorsed by posterity. One
remarkable theory has been put forward, that Dee used
his dealings with the spirits as a cloak for his activities as a
political spy ; but this had been rejected, leaving him in
the character of a simple-minded scholar and philosopher,
easily gullible as such men are prone to be. As for Kelly,
it is doubtful whether anyone has made a plausible attempt
to vindicate him, though some few have applied themselves
to the task of interpreting his "revelations" for modern
readers.

We may now turn to the story of these two notable
wizards, as opposed to witches ; of whom one indignantly
refused the name, while the other gloried in it, and made
a living by it.

* * * * *

John Dee, born in London on July 13th, 1527, was the
son of Rowland and Jane Dee, and grandson of "the
illustrious Bedo Dee, who was standard-bearer to the Lord
de Ferrers at the siege of Tournai." That illustrious one,
about whom history has not preserved much except his
name and his office, was not the founder of his family.
Very proud of his lineage, John Dee drew up a pedigree
(which is still among the Cottonian MSS. at the British
Museum) showing that he was directly descended from
"Roderick the Great, Prince of Wales." The antiquarian
Dr. John David Rhys, in 1592, states that he was of the
ancient family of the Dees of Nant-y-groes, Radnorshire ;
and Dee in his diaries frequently mentions relatives from
Wales, including Radnorshire.[1]

[1] *E.g.* John Blayney of Over Kingesham, in that county (*Private
Diary*, June 29th, 1595).

Rowland Dee had obtained the post of gentleman-sewer, or superintendent at the royal table, to Henry VIII ; but he was not happy in his office, and for some unknown reason he was imprisoned in the Tower in 1553. For this indifferent treatment of him, we are told, Henry's descendants felt it right to make up. Certainly John Dee enjoyed the favour of Edward VI, and then, after being under a cloud in Mary's reign, very markedly of Elizabeth.

At the age of ten the boy was sent to the Chantry School at Chelmsford, where he remained for five years before proceeding to St. John's College, Cambridge. He made a name rapidly—by " vehement study," he says himself, allowing only four hours for sleep and two for meals and recreation daily—and after taking his B.A. degree in 1545 was chosen as a Fellow of St. John's. Then, when Henry at the end of 1546 founded Trinity College, he was made one of the original Fellows, and was also, in his own words, "assigned there to be the under-reader of the Greek tongue."

Dee is the authority for another of his achievements at Cambridge, anticipating the A.D.C. " I did sett forth," he writes, " a Greek comedy of Aristophanes named in Greek Εἰρήνη, in Latin Pax ; with the performance of the Scarabæus his flying up to Jupiter's palace, with a man and his basket of victuals on her back : whereat was great wondring, and many vain reports abroad of the means how that was affected."

This feat of stage-management was in a way disastrous to Dee ; for it seems that among " the many vain reports " was one that he had used supernatural means ! It is hard to believe ; but so it is said. There were grave drawbacks to living in the Tudor era with an ingenious mind—even if one were under-reader in Greek.

In the spring of 1547 Dee, who had already taken an interest in astronomy, among many other subjects which attracted his catholic attention, went on a holiday to the Netherlands, making Louvain his headquarters and devoting much time to astronomical subjects. He acquired some instruments devised for the study of the stars by Regnier Gemma, the Dutch mathematician patronised by the Emperor Charles V, and also two of Gerard Mercator's globes, all of which he later gave to Trinity College,

Cambridge. With Mercator he formed a personal friendship ; and he was so pleased with the atmosphere of Louvain that he resolved to become a student of the famous University. He returned to Cambridge and took his M.A. degree, and then, armed with testimonials as to scholarship and personal character, in the summer of 1548 he gained admittance to it.

Here he increased his range of learning, adding to mathematics and natural philosophy the more occult studies of astrology (which in those days was so closely connected with astronomy) and alchemy. As Louvain had long been the home of the late Cornelius Agrippa, librarian to Margaret of Parma, Governess of the Netherlands, it was almost inevitable that Dee should steep himself in the works of that eminent alchemist, author of the book *De Occulta Philosophia*, and be profoundly influenced by his doctrine that magic was one of the lawful means of attaining to knowledge of God and Nature.

At Louvain University Dee remained two years, and may have taken a degree entitling him to call himself doctor, though this has never been proved. He was certainly known as " Doctor Dee " for the greater part of his life ; but it has been suggested, in the absence of records, that the title was merely honorary. In his old age, as Warden of Manchester College, he only signed himself in the college-register as M.A.

He was still but twenty-three when he left Louvain, but, with his reputation for deep learning and the good looks for which he was always noted, he had made a circle of admiring friends, and had attracted numerous visitors from the Court of the Emperor Charles at Brussels. When on his way home he broke the journey at Paris, he found that his fame had preceded him, and was able to give a course of lectures on Euclid at the Collège de Rheims, treating his subject, he says, in its mathematical, physical, and Pythagorean aspects. With a free entry, crowds came to hear him (even with that condition, crowds in the times of the New Learning must have been differently minded from those of to-day !) ; and at the end of his course he was offered a royal professorship of Mathematics at the College, with an annual stipend of two hundred crowns. This, however, as well as an invitation to accompany a French embassy extraordinary to Turkey, he refused, preferring rather to return to England. He had made friendships with many notable people, which he was able, by correspondence, to keep up for long years to come ; and he had won a name both among scholars and, what he by no means despised, among their patrons. For the moment he desired to see his own country again.

Dee was back in England before the end of 1551, and lost no time in obtaining an introduction to the boy-king Edward VI, through his tutor John Cheke. He had approached Cheke by means of two books which he had dedicated to Edward, and of which he had perhaps submitted the manuscripts. His reception was favourable, and he was granted an annual pension of a hundred crowns. This he unwisely commuted a little later for the rectorship of Upton-on-Severn, Worcestershire. Even when he was made in addition rector of Long Leadenham, Lincolnshire, he found that his bargain was bad.

Although he now and later held ecclesiastical posts, Dee never seems to have qualified by ordination to perform the full duties, which were carried out for him by curates. He is not known to have visited Upton-on-Severn ; and it is only surmised from an inscription that he went to Long Leadenham in 1565. At no time did he preach ; and, in spite of his piety, he was already under suspicion through his attraction to the occult.

The reputation which made Camden afterwards hail him as *nobilis mathematicus* was unaffected by this suspicion ; and in 1554 he had an invitation from Oxford to become a lecturer on mathematics, with an adequate stipend. Again, as in Paris, he refused. He aspired to something better ; but he came for the time into grave danger of losing all chance of preferment, if not his life as well.

Queen Mary had succeeded her brother on the throne in 1553 ; and two years later a great sensation was caused by some arrests on a serious charge of conspiracy against the Queen and her husband. Among the State Papers of the reign is a letter from a correspondent to Edward Courtenay, Earl of Devon, dated June 8th, 1555. The writer announces the apprehension of four who "did calculate the natyvytee" of the King (Philip of Spain), the Queen, and the Lady Elizabeth ; naming "Dee and Cary and Butler and one other of my Lady Elizabeth's." They were charged also with having a familiar spirit, which was the more suspected because one of the accusers, George Ferrys, alleged that immediately after the charge both his children were stricken, one with death, the other with blindness.

Ferrys had an associate, Prideaux ; and between them they seem to have added another count against the accused, of designing to compass the Queen's death by either poison or magic. Further, the orthodoxy of Dee's religious views was called in question.

The real fact appears to have been that, whoever made the first approach, Dee had been in communication with some of the Princess Elizabeth's servants on the subject of casting horoscopes—which would interest Elizabeth as showing if and when she might expect to come to the throne. Coupled with some of the other allegations, the indictment was one of high treason. Dee was arrested and thrown into gaol, while his London lodgings were searched. He was examined in turn before Sir John Bourne, Secretary of State, the Privy Council, and the Lord Chief Justice, and then tried by the Court of Star Chamber. He was found innocent of treason. His religious views were left to be tested by Bishop Bonner ; but that he succeeded in satisfying him is shown by his release at the end of August, after entering into recognisances for his good behaviour.

In spite of the fortunate issue, this affair was scarcely calculated to recommend Dee to Mary's favour. But he did not hesitate to propose for her approval a grand scheme for the recovery of lost books and manuscripts, and the erection of a large royal library. He undertook himself to procure copies of famous manuscripts from the Vatican, Vienna, and other great libraries on the Continent, provided that the mere cost of making copies and transporting them to England were guaranteed. The scheme unfortunately did not attract Mary ; and Dee had to content himself with being a private collector, spending, it was said, about three thousand pounds upon the library he ultimately left behind him ; which partly explains his constant struggle with debt, so vividly shown by his diaries.

Mary's death inspired him with new hope of some good post that would enable him to lead a peaceful life of study and research in library and laboratory. The horoscope-casting, which had so nearly brought him to grief in 1555, now in 1558 seemed likely to advance him well. Elizabeth and her advisers decided to have astrological aid in the selection of an auspicious day for her coronation, which Dee found for them in Sunday, January 15th. He was also personally introduced to the Queen by Sir Robert Dudley and the Earl of Pembroke, to whom she made the remark that "where her brother had given Dee a crown she would give him a noble."

John Eglington Bailey, editor in 1880 of the *Diary of Dr. John Dee, Warden of Manchester*, is not quite just when he says that this was the first of the large number of royal promises never fulfilled. It appears from Dee's earlier diaries that, if Elizabeth was slow to give him a substantial post, she was at least in the habit of making him presents of money by no means niggardly. And, if he wearied of waiting for the good post, he could not, and does not, complain that she did not show him marked personal friendship. His good looks no doubt appealed to her ; his learning attracted her. It may be wondered if she were amused at his claim to the same high ancestry as the Tudors. It is well known that she did not care for claims to near relationship, though that was chiefly where her mother's family, the Boleyns, were concerned.

Early in the reign the friendship between Queen and subject did not ripen fast. Dee had some legitimate ground for grievance that Elizabeth seemed to him to promise that he should have the governorship, when vacant, of the hospital of St. Katharine-by-the-Tower, and then, as he writes : " Dr. Wilson politickly prevented me "—it was given to Thomas Wilson, LL.D. In his disappointment, Dee went on a visit to Antwerp before the end of 1562.

It was not, however, mere pique that influenced his departure. He had been engaged for some time on a work which he entitled *Monas Hieroglyphica*, dealing with the mathematical and magic properties of a certain mysterious symbol, for the publication which he thought Antwerp more suitable than London ; and perhaps he had authorities whom he wished to consult before finishing the book. At any rate, he succeeded in finding an Antwerp publisher for it.

His discontent with the position of affairs in England for students like himself is shown in a letter which he wrote to Sir William Cecil, in the February after his arrival in Antwerp. The English Universities, he complained, lacked men competent in manifold sorts of wonderful sciences, such as those concerned with formal numbers, mystic weights, and divine measurements, whereof knowledge had fallen to him after long search and study, great cost and travail. He asked Cecil whether he should return to England or continue his study in Antwerp.

The Secretary of State replied, surely not to Dee's entire satisfaction, with a certificate testifying that his time abroad was well spent.

Pursuing his regular course of trying to make friends of princes, Dee in the autumn visited Pressburg, to present a manuscript or advance copy of his *Monas Hieroglyphica* to the new Emperor Maximilian, to whom he had dedicated it. That this was not a wasted piece of flattery was afterwards proved. Then, after more travels, including a trip to Venice to meet the scholar Thomas Ravenna, who had written on the means of prolonging human life to a hundred and twenty years (without recourse to glands, it may be noted), he made his way home.

It is not certain whether it was now that Dee first took up his abode in his mother's house near the Thames-side at Mortlake, where he spent so many years of the rest of his life and ultimately died. He came there now, destined to discover that even such a country place as Mortlake then was provided no peaceful retreat for a man with the reputation of being a magician.

He did not contemplate settling down yet to existence on such small means as he had. Without dissipation, in the ordinary sense of the term, he always found that his expenditure exceeded his income, and we cannot suppose that his constant borrowing of money began only in the days when his *Private Diary* shows him applying for aid to innumerable friends and acquaintances. For the present he had great expectations from Queen Elizabeth. He obtained an interview with her at Greenwich Palace in June, 1664, and explained to her some of the secret import of his *Monas Hieroglyphica*. It is said that she now became his pupil. Well, Elizabeth was a pupil of many men, of whom not many derived much personal benefit from their teaching of her.[1] By the end of the year, however, there did seem a good hope for Dee. The deanery of Gloucester was held out to him. When he tried to grasp it, he was forestalled by the Warden of Merton, Oxford, John Man ; perhaps " politickly," as in the case of Dr. Wilson and the hospital governorship.

It may be urged in Elizabeth's defence that Dee himself was the chief obstacle in the way of his obtaining ecclesiastical positions. He was terrified, by his own account, at the idea of taking one which involved his acceptance of a " cure of souls." He knew that his undesired notoriety in the matter of magic would lead to trouble.

He did not feel the same difficulty when there appeared a chance of the reversion of the provostship of Eton ; but unfortunately for him the actual provost continued to live.

At the beginning of 1568 Dee made another attempt to reach the Queen through the medium of a book of his. Cecil suggested this, and the Earl of Pembroke agreed to present a copy of a new edition of his *Propædeumata Aphoristica* on his behalf. Her Majesty was graciously pleased to accept it, and in February invited the author to have a talk with her in the gallery at Westminster Palace. But, though he spoke of some great secret to be revealed to her, she remained untouched—perhaps the last word should be in inverted commas ; for, while Pembroke made a donation of twenty pounds to the author for a copy, Elizabeth went no further than gracious acceptance.

Dee's literary activity was not to be checked by any disappointments, and early in 1570 he was ready with a new appeal to the reading public, contributing " a fruitfull

---

[1] But Dee does say of Elizabeth that " she vouchsafed to account herself my schollar in my book." She had seen it while he was abroad, and had sent for him, on his return, to expound it to her.

Preface " to Henry Billington's translation of the works
of Euclid, which was no ordinary preface, but an example
in his best style of treatment of his beloved mathematics.
His complaint in this of the injustice done him by his
countrymen when they condemned a modest Christian
philosopher like him as " a companion of helhounds, and a
caller and a conjuror of wicked and damned spirits,"
shows how far his reputation as a dealer in magic had
already grown.[1]

In 1571, following a visit to Lorraine, a serious illness
overtook him, which had some consolation in that Elizabeth
sent two of her own doctors to attend him, and also Philip
Sidney, conveying kind messages and " rarities to eat."
The patient made a good recovery, and in the next year
gave a demonstration of his astronomical ability by the
discovery of a new star.

Still no suitable recompense of his merits came to him ;
and in October, 1574, he wrote a remarkable letter to the
former William Cecil, now Lord Burghley, suggesting that
twenty years of hard study had entitled him to reward,
if it were only a sufficiency of two or three hundred pounds
a year for the pursuit of science with some ease. He
proudly boasted that, " in zeale to the best lerning and
knowledg, and in incredible toyle of body and mynde, very
many yeres," this land had never bred any man whose
account could be proved greater than his. He offered to
discover a gold or silver mine for the Queen in her
dominions, in return for a right to all treasure trove in those
dominions ; and Burghley might have half his profit.

The Lord Treasurer made no immediate reply to this
proposed use of the diviner's wand, not having so much
faith in the Doctor as his royal mistress had.

In spite of his necessities, Dee in this same year, 1574,
made up his mind to take a wife. He was already forty-
seven, and his first experience of marriage was unfortunate.
He took the wise precaution of informing the Queen

---

[1] " O my unkind countrymen," he also exclaims, " O unnatural
countrymen, O unthankful countrymen, O brainsicke, rashe, spitefull
and disdainfull countrymen ! Why oppress you me thus violently
with your slaundering of me, contrary to veritie, and contrary to your
own conscience ? "

before the event, having doubtless observed that those who neglected to do so always aroused Elizabeth's anger.

It is curious that nothing, not even her original name, is known of the first Mrs. Dee. She died very soon after the marriage ; and Elizabeth, who had planned to call on Dee and look at his library, reached Mortlake on March 10th, 1575, to find that he had only buried his wife four hours before. She declined therefore to enter the house, though allowing him to bring out and show her one of his treasures, a convex mirror on a stand, to which magic properties were attributed, though not by the Doctor himself.

He was, indeed, except when " the spirits " began to enter actively into his life, singularly free, for his times, from vulgar delusions. When a comet appeared in 1577 and spread much alarm, on being sent for by Elizabeth he was able to spend three days with her at Windsor explaining the natural cause of the supposed portent. And when a wax image of the Queen was discovered in Lincoln's Inn Fields, with pins stuck in it, he satisfied her that such a charm could do her no hurt.

In such matters he was eminently practical. His unpracticality was shown when he neglected to secure the attachment of the Great Seal to the charter which Elizabeth had directed the Archbishop of Canterbury to give him for the holding of his two country rectories for life ; thereby losing, he afterwards calculated, a thousand pounds. The reason for his neglect was that he was deeply interested at the time—it was in 1576—in a scheme of his to improve on Pope Gregory's reformation of the calendar.

Less than two years later he showed his practical side again, when on February 5th, 1578, he took a second wife, in the person of Jane, daughter of Bartholomew Fromonds (as he nearly always spells the name), of East Cheam, Surrey. Aged twenty-two, she proved herself on the whole an admirable woman in the difficult part of wife of a man of genius ; and she bore him a large family, which was perhaps not an unmixed blessing in the straitened life they were all compelled for the most part to live. But without such a companion as her it is difficult to see how Doctor John Dee could have battled with circumstances, pursued his studies, and poured forth his stream of writings to the end. She is herself called by one who met her abroad, Francis Pucci, a very well-read woman. She had, previous to her marriage, been lady-in-waiting to the wife of Lord Howard of Effingham, the great Admiral.

Shortly before his marriage Dee had begun to keep a private diary, which is quite distinct from *The Compendious Rehearsall*, of which we shall hear when we come to the year 1592, and is of a far more intimate and entertaining character. It has been twice printed, once as a whole and once in part,[1] from Dee's manuscript in the Ashmolean Museum library at Oxford. Dee wrote it on the margins and in the blank spaces of three old quarto *Ephemerides*, or almanacs, published at Louvain, in a hand very difficult to decipher, and where he wished particularly to keep a private note used Greek characters. Without this work we should lack the more intimate knowledge of his character.

Apart from a few notes on dates of nativities, for the purpose of casting horoscopes, *The Private Diary* begins in January, 1577 (new style), on the 16th of which month the Earl of Leicester, Sir Philip Sidney, and others paid a call upon the writer, followed on the 22nd by the Earl of Bedford. Throughout we find the house at Mortlake the constant scene of visits by noted persons, both English and foreign ; as for instance, on March 24th of this year, by " Simon the Ninivite," who promised his host his services into Persia, which may imply a dream of Dee's to travel to that country.

As early as June, 1577, Dee is seen borrowing money freely ; £40 from John Hilton of Fulham, £27 from Bartholomew Newsam, and £27 from someone unnamed upon a chain of gold. In November another £30 is borrowed from a Mortlake neighbour, Edward Hynde, to be repaid at Hallowtide next year.

In November three visits to the Queen are recorded, on

---

[1] *The Private Diary of Dr. John Dee*, edited for the Camden Society by James Orchard Halliwell (1842) ; and *Diary for* 1595–1601 *of Dr. John Dee, Warden of Manchester*, edited by James Eglington Bailey (privately printed, 1880).

the third of which Dee declared to her " her title to
Greenland, Estetiland, and Friseland." Geography was
one of Dee's hobbies, which he kept up-to-date by a wide
acquaintance with celebrated navigators ; and with the
Queen he delighted in showing what new countries might
be added to her dominions.

It is possible that Dee's borrowings and one of his visits
to Elizabeth were connected with the event of February
5th, 1578, which he briefly records as " *sponsalia cum Jana
Fromonds.*" Money for the wedding and the Queen's
permission were both desirable.

In June of the following year his mother, Jane Dee,[1]
surrendered what he calls the Mortlake houses and land
to him to the end of his life. This turned out to be no
figure of speech ; he died in the house twenty-nine years
later.

On July 13th, 1559, Dee records the birth of his first
child Arthur, at 4 a.m. To the caster of horoscopes the
hour was important. Unfortunately at 10 p.m. the same
day his father-in-law was lying speechless ; and the next
day he was dead, which marred the rejoicings over the
birth. However, on the 16th Arthur was duly christened,
his godfather being Master Dr. Lewys, judge of the
Admiralty, and his godmother Dee's cousin, Mistress
Blanche Parry, of the Privy Chamber, for whom another
cousin, Mistress Aubrey, was deputy. In spite of financial
troubles—and soon Sir Lionel Ducket was sending an
" unkend letter for mony "—Dee always managed to get
good names when an occasion had to be celebrated.

Towards the end of 1578 Dee was sent on a special
mission to Frankfurt-on-Oder, of which the only reason
given is that he had been asked to consult some eminent
physicians about the Queen's health. But there was at
least a suspicion that both now and on some other occasions
he was engaged in secret diplomatic work for the English
Government. It cannot be said that anything in the vast
mass of his writings bears this out. The extreme limit of
this theory is alluded to in a manuscript note in a copy of

[1] She was originally Jane Wild. Owing to the identity of the
two married names, Dee continues at first to call his wife Jane
Fromonds.

Meric Casaubon's *True and Faithfull Relation*,[1] transcribed
and edited, with an introduction, from Dee's multi-
voluminous *Liber Mysteriorum*, in which all the Doctor's
researches into the spirit-world were recorded. This copy
of the book, in the British Museum Library, was once the
property of Edmund Wyndham, in whose hand the note
perhaps is. It states that " this book made a great noise
upon its first publication, and many years after the character of it was scored by Dr. Hooke, who believed that
Casaubon, Archbishop Usher and other learned men were
mistaken in their notions about it, and that in reality the
author never fell under such delusions, but being a man
of great Art and intrigue, made use of this strange method of
writing to conceal things of a political nature, and instead
of a pretended enthusiast was a real spy, but that supposition is not received for very solid reasons which are shewn
in his life."

Only a Baconian, it might be said, would attempt to
discover a cypher in Dee's Book of Mysteries ! But even in
later days some writers have assumed that Dee and his
associate Kelly were both intelligencers for Lord Burghley.

The *Private Diary* is reticent as to the trip to Frankfurt.
It does not tell of any interviews with Elizabeth until
September 17th, 1780, when she drives over to Mortlake
from Richmond, and asks Dee, standing at her coach-side,
to resort to her Court, and to " give her to wete " when he
comes. It is known that she had enquired of him concerning her title to new countries recently discovered, and that
he drew up for her two rolls describing the geography and
hydrography of these countries, which he took to her on
October 3rd, to be informed a week later of Lord
Burghley's approval.

Elizabeth herself drove over again to Mortlake to tell
Dee, and found him in sad trouble. It was October 10th,
and early that morning Jane Dee the elder had died, at

[1] *A True and Faithfull Relation of what passed for many Yeers between
Dr. John Dee . . . and some Spirits* (London, 1659). The pages are
headed throughout *A true Relation of Dr. John Dee his Actions with
Spirits, &c.*, by which title, or variations thereof, the book is sometimes
quoted. The catalogue-reference in the British Museum Library is
31 g. 8.

the age of seventy-seven. Elizabeth arrived in the evening,
and at Dee's door exhorted him to bear his loss patiently.
She reminded him how on his first wife's death it was
likewise her fortune to call upon him.

Three entries in the *Private Diary* give an inkling of a
change that was coming about in Dee's life. They are
meagre, but sufficient to furnish a clue. The first, on
February 26th, 1580, states that " this night the fyre all
in flame cam into my maydens' chamber agayne, between
an 11 and 12 of the cloke ; continued half an hour terribly,
so it did a yere before to the same maydens." This odd
phenomenon, which Dee notes in quite different way from
his common remarks on storms, great winds, etc., was
followed in the next year by another manifestation in his
own part of the house. On March 8th, 1581, between
10 and 11 p.m., there was " the strange noyse in my chamber of knocking ; and the voyce, ten times repeated,
somewhat like the schrich of an owle, but more longly
drawn, and more softly, as it were in my chamber."

From the reference to " the noyse " and " the voyce " it
seems as if this was not the first occasion of their being
heard. Was the Mortlake house really beginning to be
haunted, as doubtless the neighbours had long been
saying it was ?

The third entry is more momentous. On May 25th,
1581, Dee briefly states that he had sight in a crystal
(which he writes in Greek) offered to him ; " and I saw."
Truly a concise way of announcing the opening of a new
phase in the diarist's experience !

CHAPTER II

THE CONJURERS AND THE CRYSTAL

JOHN DEE had, as we have seen, in his Cambridge days been very unjustly accused of recourse to supernatural means to produce an ingenious stage-effect. Gradually, with no desire thereto, he had gathered about himself the reputation of a magician, and deplored it. Not that he had not studied magic and held with his master Cornelius Agrippa that it was a lawful way to the higher knowledge. But he was well aware of the common opinion of its dangerous and evil character. *Omne ignotum pro horrifico* was the vulgar attitude. He knew better, and pursued his studies, paying the price because it must be paid.

Unfortunately, in the occult, the path is so obscure that the traveller is often impelled to look about for a guide ; and one may come forward, comforting because a living being, to answer an immediate question, not a book which in general terms shows the difficulty of the road.

Such was Dee's case. The romance of alchemy had called him on a certain way, and he wished to go further, to get in direct touch with the spiritual beings that were alleged to exist beyond the veil of the ordinarily visible world. And, so craving, he unfortunately came upon men who professed to be able to lead him towards his goal.

He had read, of course, of the method of seeing apparitions of a spiritual nature by means of crystalomancy, gazing into a polished crystal or stone, and so " skrying." He had his convex mirror, to which the ignorant attributed magic powers, though he was well enough advanced in the science of optics to understand its real properties. But with the crystal he had apparently not experimented until he was about fifty-four years of age, when, as he says in his Book of Mysteries, he heard of a man who was accounted

DOCTOR JOHN DEE

From an engraving by Cooper, after the painting by an
unknown artist in the Ashmolean Museum

EDWARD KELLY AND PAUL WARING AT
WALTON-LE-DALE

From an engraving by Ames, after Sibley's picture

a good seer and skryer, a master of arts, and a preacher of
the Word. This reputation for magic and piety combined
attracted him to Barnabas Saul, as the man was named.
He welcomed him to his house, where he was wont to have
various students and helpers in his laboratory. Barnabas
Saul was ready with promises of what he could do, and
Doctor Dee resolved to try what might come to him through
the crystal.

It is not certain what exactly Dee meant by the entry
quoted at the end of last chapter about the sight offered
him in a crystal on May 25th, 1581, when he *saw*. He
was at no time able to " skry " himself. He does not
mention Saul's name in connection with this vision. It
may be that Saul was the person who offered him the
sight, and that Dee attempted crystal-gazing, with some
result, through his eyes, on his brain. The first séance of
which he gave any account in the Book of Mysteries was on
December 12th, 1581. Dee calls it *Actio Saulina*, " actions "
being the word by which he denotes séances. It was not
very significant. Saul announced, after preliminary
prayers, that the angel Annael had appeared ; and questions were put to him and answered. Before this, in August,
there had been two nights of very strange knocking and
rapping in Dee's chamber ; while on October 9th
" Barnabas Saul, lying in the hall, was strangely troubled
by a spirituall creature abowt mydnight." It seemed
as though the seer were fulfilling his promise to produce
results. Suddenly there came disillusionment. Saul was
arrested on some charge, and tried at Westminster. He
was acquitted ; but the falseness of his pretensions was
revealed. On March 6th he confessed to Dee that he had
had no vision of any spiritual creature in the hall. He
did not apparently say that his skrying was an imposture,
but his character as an occultist was ruined, and he left
Mortlake. Some months later he called on Dee again, and
was chidden for his manifold untrue reports. The Doctor
had come to the conclusion that evil spirits had come to
Saul, and was terrified at the idea.

In the interval someone else had visited Dee and offered
to display the real method of contact with the spirits. And
so enters into Dee's life-story that very remarkable person

Edward Kelly ; a complete conjurer in the sense of the word as it was used then, and one who almost succeeded in branding the name also on his dupe.

Of Edward Kelly's early days not very much is known. He was a native of Worcester ; and from Dee's notes of dates for the purpose of working out schemes of nativity, at the beginning of his *Private Diary*, the day of his birth is fixed as August 1st, 1555.[1] His surname was originally Talbot, by which Dee first knew him in 1582. He was generally said to have been apprenticed in boyhood to a chemist in Worcester ; and it is clear from his story that he had considerable chemical knowledge. He must, however, have received a wider education if he went to Gloucester Hall, Oxford, at the age of seventeen. (Thomas Seccombe, who write the article on him in *The Dictionary of National Biography*, says that there were three Talbots in Gloucester Hall in 1573, but no Kelly.) He left Oxford after a year, without matriculating.

He is supposed to have gone next to London and worked as a scrivener, or professional penman, and attorney. He did not find this paying, for he wandered from London up to Lancashire, where two exploits of his brought him into prominence, which first is uncertain. When he was twenty-four or twenty-five he was arrested, and was condemned to stand in the pillory at Lancaster and to have his ears cropped. " For manifest fraud," says Dr. Thomas Smith in his life of Dee in 1707. One version was that his offence was forgery of old title-deeds ; another that it was base-coining. His later career shows that neither charge was improbable. As to the loss of his ears, the legend was that he ever afterwards wore a close-fitting black cap to hide his loss. But supposed portraits of him do not represent him in any but an ordinary cap of the period ; nor do Dee's writings show that he had knowledge of his constant associate for so long being without ears.[2]

The other Lancashire exploit is vouched for by John Weever in his *Ancient Funerall Monuments* (London, 1631).

[1] " At the fourth hour after noon, as his father recorded," states Dee, who presumably had something to base his note upon.

[2] The illustration in this book, it will be noticed, shows Kelly earless.

Weever, writing of Kelly, " that famous English alchymist of our times," in his character of necromancer, tells the story thus :

" This Diabolical questioning of the dead, for the knowledge of future accidents, was put in practice by the said Kelley, who upon a certain night, in the Park of Walton in le dale, in the County of Lancaster, with one Paul Waring (his fellow companion in such deeds of darkness) invocated some of the Infernal Regiment, to know certain passages in the life, as also what might be known by the Divel's foresight of the manner and time of the death of a noble young gentleman, as then in wardship. The black ceremonies of the night being ended, Kelley demanded of one of the gentleman's servants what corse was the last buried in Law churchyard, a church thereunto adjoyning, who told him of a poor man that was buryed there but the same day. He and the said Waring intreated this foresaid servant to go with them to the grave of the man so lately interred, which he did ; and withal did help them to dig up the carcase of the poor catiff, whom by their incantations they made him (or rather some evil spirit through his organs) to speak, who delivered strange predictions concerning the said gentleman. I was told thus much by the said serving-man, a secondary actor in that dismal abhorred business ; and divers gentlemen and others are now living in Lancashire to whom he hath related this story. And the gentleman himself (whose memory I am bound to honor) told me a little before his death of this conjuration by Kelley, as he had it by relation from his said servant and tenant, onely some circumstances excepted, which he thought not fitting to come to his master's knowledge."

Weever thus puts forward as near as we have to first-hand evidence about Talbot, *alias* Kelly, in the days before he met Dee. Vaguely the young man is stated to have retired from Lancashire into Wales as an itinerant astrologer, and to have come across in his wanderings a person who was willing to sell cheaply an old manuscript and two bottles, one broken, containing respectively a red and a white powder, which had been found in the tomb of a bishop. According to one tale, the discovery was made at Glastonbury Abbey. As the tale must have been originally

Kelly's, not much attention need be paid to conflicting versions. A manuscript and some powder he certainly had, however acquired ; and he was able to make good use of them later.

Kelly's first appearance in Dee's *Private Diary* is in March, 1582. On the 3rd, " Mr. Clerkson and his frende came to my house." The next day Mr. Clerkson and Mr. Talbot dined with the Doctor. It was just after Barnabas Saul's downfall ; and the visitors " declared a great deale," writes Dee, " of Barnabas nowghty dealing toward me." Barnabas had told Clerkson that Dee would make his friend (*i.e.* Talbot) as weary as he himself was of him ; also that he would so flatter his friend (whom he now calls " the learned man ") that he might borrow money of him. As for Talbot, he informed Dee, before his wife and Clerkson, that " a spirituall creature " had told him that Barnabas had censured both Clerkson and Dee, and had done the latter great injuries in divers ways.

It is clear that on his first introduction to Dee, Talbot had set himself to prevent Saul's return to his employer, and had designs of profiting by his absence. The Book of Mysteries makes this clearer still. On March 10th Talbot was again at the house, and expressed a wish that his host should show him something in spiritual practice. Dee at once disclaimed all magic skill. " I truely excused myself therein," he writes, " as not in the vulgarly accounted Magik neyther studied once or exercised." But he brought out his stone in a frame, which was given him by a friend, and said that he was credibly informed that certain good angels were answerable to it. Also, he said, he was once willed by a skryer to call for the good angel Annael to appear in the stone in his own sight. He desired Talbot now to call Annael " and if he would Anachor and Anilos likewise, accounted good angels." (These must have been two more of Saul's spirits.) He was not prepared to do this himself. A séance followed, which is thus described :

" He [Talbot] settled himself to the Action, and on his knees at my desk, setting the stone before him, fell to prayer and entreaty, &c. In the meane space D. in my Oratory did pray and make motion to God and his good creatures for the furdering of this Action. And within a quarter of an hour or less he had sight of one in the stone."

This was Uriel, the Spirit of Light, who vouchsafed the information that the two enquirers should *jointly* have knowledge of the good angels, forty-nine in number, who were answerable to their call. He gave instructions for the making of a "Holy Table" and a "Seal of God" to enable them to carry on their work properly, and also counselled that a spirit named Lundrumguffa, who designed Dee's ruin, should be driven away ; which may be a hit at Barnabas Saul.

Dee was so pleased with this result that he continued the Actions daily, Talbot skrying and he recording. The angel Michael appeared one day, and gave Dee a tangible present, in the shape of a seal-ring. Talbot on March 21st became dizzy and was obliged to take a rest,[1] and it was agreed that on the next day he should be allowed to go to Leicester to fetch some books of Lord Monteagle's, which he said would otherwise perish.

In the *Private Diary* there is a very curious entry, or rather set of entries, for the date March 22nd. Dee wrote : " Mr. Talbot went to London to take his jornay." Above this is written in another hand : " You that rede this underwritten assure yourselfe that it is a shameful lye, for Talbot neither studied for any such thinge nor shewed himselfe dishonest in anythinge." Dee again writes the comment : " This is Mr. Talbot, or that lerned man, his own writing in my boke, very unduely as he cam by it."

As Halliwell, first editor of this diary, states that there are in it various notices of Talbot erased, probably by him, we may suppose that there is something missing here. If so, it is a pity, for Dee's early impression of the young man would have been welcome.

Later in their intercourse Kelly admitted that he, as Talbot, had originally been sent to Mortlake to entrap Dee into confessing to dealings with the Devil, but perceived that it would be more to his advantage to play upon his credulity. It is plain, however, that Kelly had genuine ability as a skryer, whatever that may ultimately imply.

[1] It has been denied by modern skryers that the practice has any injurious effects, provided the skryer is not in ill-health.

The doub' is as to whether he actually thought he saw or heard all that he described to the recording Dee. " Crystal-vision," says Podmore in *Modern Spiritualism,* " is not of course necessarily associated with moral excellence ; but it is clearly impossible, with such a *dossier* [as Dee's records] to have much confidence in Kelly's good faith."[1]

It is not until nearly four months after the first series of Actions that Mr. Talbot's name appears again in the *Private Diary.* He came to Mortlake on the afternoon of July 13th, and there were some words of unkindness between him and Dee ; but they parted friendly. Talbot promised to bring some books, a sure way to Dee's heart. After this we hear no more of Talbot, but only of E. K. or Kelly spelt in various ways. The old name had evidently been shed.

However, the Actions had not been suspended during this interval in the diary, and the Table and the Seal had been fashioned according to Uriel's directions, and, of course, at Dee's expense. Another item of the apparatus came on November 21st, in a miraculous way—so he believed. Towards sunset a child-angel appeared in Dee's room, holding in hand something " most bright, most clere and glorius, of the bigness of an egg." Michael, too, was there with his flaming sword, and bade Dee, " Go forward, take it up, and let no mortal hand touch it but thine own." As he directed that Dee and Kelly should be united as one man in the holy work, it seems that the prohibition against touching did not apply to Kelly. After all, he was the skryer.

This gift to the enquirers was what Dee usually calls his " shew-stone." It is claimed by some that it is the identical stone which is on view in the British Museum as having belonged to Dr. Dee ; but that hardly corresponds to the description given by Casaubon. " The form of it was round," he says, " and it seems to have been of a pretty

[1] " But after all," he continues, " the interest of the revelations does not depend on the seer's veracity. It is enough for our present purpose that they apparently reflect with fair accuracy the ideas of the time. They form indeed a valuable link in the historical series, for while generally they appear, as Kelly himself on one occasion points out, to be founded on earlier mystical writings, they in many respects foreshadow with singular fidelity the utterances of later clairvoyants."

bigness . . . most like unto a crystal, as it is called sometimes." There were other stones, he adds, which Doctor
Dee considered sacred. " Observe *Principal Stone ;* and
this other Stone ; and *first Sanctified Stone, usual Shew-stone,*
and *Holy-stone.*" There is no doubt that Dee at different
times used various stones or crystals ; but that brought by
the child-angel and Michael was the most valued by him.

Now properly equipped, Dee and Kelly proceeded with
their Actions, of which Dee patiently took down his report,
extending to many volumes of bound manuscripts, still
existing under the name of the Sloane MSS. in the British
Museum. Moreover, an industrious scholar-student came
upon them, who rated them sufficiently highly to copy out
the contents of the last thirteen volumes and have them
published in one large book, with a preface by himself.

Dee was fortunate in his transcriber and editor. Meric
Casaubon, who was nine when Dee died, was sufficiently
close to him in time to be able to interpret him sympathetic-
ally, if critically, and sufficiently scholarly to penetrate into
his obscurities. He understood, too, the dangers to which
Dee had subjected himself by the suspicion of being a
student of black magic ; for his own father had suffered
a like fate, with far less reason than Dee. The charge was
a great falsehood, says the son.

Isaac Casaubon, a Huguenot of a family driven from
France to Geneva to escape persecution, came to England
in 1610, and joining the Church of England, was favoured
by James I and made a prebend of Canterbury Cathedral.
But the Puritans, looking on him as a renegade, and distort-
ing his learning, particularly in theology, accused him of
dabbling with magic, stoned him in the street, and broke
the windows of his house in London. He lived but four
years after his arrival in England.

Meric Casaubon, born at Geneva in 1599, and by his
father brought to England and sent to Eton, went thence
to Christ Church, Oxford, taking his M.A. degree in 1621.
After a rectorship in Somerset he became a prebend of
Canterbury, and later a D.D. of Oxford. Patronised in
turn by James I and Charles I, he was after the Rebellion
deprived of all his preferments, fined, and put to prison.
The Restoration brought back prosperity to him, and he

lived another eleven years, writing indefatigably to the end.

His edition of some of Dee's manuscript remains, however, was published in the year before the Restoration.

In his Preface Casaubon says of his first acquaintance with Dee's " book " that it was communicated to him by Sir Thomas Cotton, " that right worthy gentleman who is very studious to purchase and procure such records and monuments as may advantage the truth of God and the honour of this land, following therein the example of his worthy progenitor, Sir Robert Cotton, known to all the learned as far as Europe extendeth"—and a personal friend of Dee's, it may be added.

He continues : " I read it cursorily because I was quickly convinced in myself that it could be no counterfeit imaginerie businesse, and was very desirous to see the end, so far as the book did go. Afterwards, when I understood that the said worthy gentleman . . . was willing it should be published, and that he had committed the whole business to me, I read it over very exactly, and took notes of the most remarkable passages, as they appeared to me. Truly I was so much confirmed in this first opinion by my second reading that I shall not be afraid to profess that I never gave more credit to any Humane History of former times."

Sir Thomas Cotton had been influenced by the opinion of the Archbishop of Armagh, who, says Casaubon, reading the book before his death, " wished it printed." Owing to Casaubon's industry, under Cotton's patronage, it was printed, fifty-one years after the death of the man who wrote it and so much more, the rest of which may never see the light except in the form of extracts made by the curious in such things as occupied part of Dee's " vehemently " studious life. The derelict mine, in truth, is likely to attract very few. As an example of what may be brought up from it, it perhaps suffices to mention one of " the seven names of God, which not even the angels can pronounce "—so Kelly told Dee—SAAI $\frac{21}{8}$ EME.

Modern writers, however, have maintained that these " Actions " have some real value. We have heard what Podmore has said about them ; and Miss C. Fell-Smith, who published her study *John Dee* in 1909, has called his

notes the earliest record of mediumistic transactions, a sort
of Proceedings of the Society for Psychical Research in the
Sixteenth Century.

Mr. Theodor Besterman, in his *Crystal-Gazing* (1924),
points out that Kelly's description of what first appeared
to him in the crystal is remarkably like the descriptions of
later skryers. We may take three examples :

(1). E. K. announces : " In the middest of the Stone
seemeth to stand a little round thing like a spark of fire, and
it increaseth, and seemeth to be as bigge as a globe of
20 inches diameter, or thereabout " (*True and Faithfull
Relation*).

(2). " Before visions appear in the crystal, it becomes exceedingly bright, as if it were illuminated by an effulgence
pervading its interior, in the midst of which the vision
appears " (" Gamma," an early modern writer on the
subject, in *The Zoist*, London, 1849).

(3). " After a minute or two I seem to see a very bright
light in it, which disappears after a few seconds, and then
the surface appears cloudy and thick. This mist clears away.
. . . They only last for a few seconds, or sometimes minutes,
and between each new picture I see the same light and
mist " (" Miss A," in F. W. H. Myers's *Subliminal Consciousness*).

So far as Dee is concerned, we cannot doubt his absolute
good faith. He could not see nor hear the " spirits "
himself, though he often writes as if the actual perceptions
came to him. He took down all Kelly's statements as
skryer.[1] Occasionally he allowed his hesitation to accept
them to appear ; as when he notes once, " Of this K. I doubt
yet." And he detected in him some " abominable lyes,"
though here he may refer to Kelly in his ordinary life, not
when acting as a medium.

It is strange how Kelly at times blended the two phases
of his existence, not always to his advantage. One revelation

---

[1] One odd story told by Kelly was to the effect that, trying once
to consult the spirits on his own account, without Dee present, he
wrote some questions and put them " in the window." Then he took
the crystal and a spirit Nalvage appeared to him, who told him that the
Devil had taken the questions away. Looking to see if they had gone,
Kelly found that they had.

from the angel Michael, as early as April 1582, was that Kelly was to take a wife. He told Dee that he was not inclined to do so. But Michael insisted, and Kelly married a girl of nineteen, Joan Cooper, who lived with her mother at Chipping Norton. She did not come to join him at once in London. Kelly had from Dee a promise to give him fifty pounds a year as his skryer, which, perhaps, he could not at first make good. But Kelly spent much of his time at Mortlake, not apparently to Mrs. Dee's satisfaction. One of the erased entries in the *Private Diary*, for May 6th, 1582, can be made out to refer to " a merveylous rage " of Jane from eight o'clock one night until eight the next morning. The words " that came to me only honest and lerned men " are also legible ; and it would seem that Jane did not include Kelly in that class. As a man of her own age, who had such an influence over her much older and famous husband, he no doubt was looked upon by her as an interloper, and even an impostor. Yet she had to consent in time to the arrival of Joan 'Kelly in her house, which did not lead to greater harmony. On the contrary, Kelly once told Dee, "I cannot abide my wife, I love her not, nay I abhor her," and complained that at Mortlake he was misliked because he did not favour Joan better.

With this new disturbing element to vex his peace the poor philosopher must have been unhappy. In 1583 however there came promise of relief from financial troubles at least. On March 18th Dee had " receyved salutation from Alaski, Palatine in Poland " ; and soon arrived in London a man who was to bring about a remarkable change in Dee's life.

Albert Laski was a nephew of the celebrated Polish religious reformer, John Laski, or a Lasco, who had been Archbishop Cranmer's guest in England, and was credited with considerable influence at the court of Edward VI. The nephew was one of those of his family who had returned to the Church of Rome. He held the position of Prince or Duke Palatine, of Siradz, in Bohemia, was passably rich, and a man of varied interests. Apart from the fact of his uncle's visit to England some thirty years earlier, he claimed a connection with the country as a descendant of

Henry de Lacy, third Earl of Lincoln, Edward I's chief adviser and the founder of Whalley Abbey.[1]

Laski had come to London on a visit to Queen Elizabeth, was received with great pomp, and was lodged at Winchester House. One of his hopes in coming to England had been to make the acquaintance of the great Doctor Dee, of whom he had heard much ; and on May 13th the two were introduced in the Earl of Leicester's chamber at Greenwich Palace. Five days later Laski called on Dee at Mortlake, without ceremony, and " tarryed supper," says the *Private Diary*, which gives no particulars of the conversation. Two probable topics of this were Laski's English descent and the crystal, as soon appears. On May 28th Dee and Kelly had an Action at Mortlake, which is the first in Casaubon's *True and Faithfull Relation*, and also introduces a new spirit seen by Kelly, differing much from Uriel, Michael, Gabriel, and others that had previously come through the crystal. It is worth while to look at this record in detail, as a very good example of what Kelly in his medium-state announced, and Dee took down from his lips. It will be noted that Dee's description might, in places, be taken as of things perceived by himself.

The following is the account, somewhat abbreviated :

" As J. and E. K. sate discoursing of the noble Polonian Albertus Lasci . . . suddenly there seemed to come out of my Oratory a spirituall creature, like a pretty girle of 7 or 9 yeares of age, attired on her head with her hair rowled up before, and hanging down very long behind, with a gown of Sey, changeable green and red, and with a train she seemed to play up and down . . . and seemed to go in and out behind my books . . ."

Casaubon here evidently found Dee's manuscript illegible or defective, for the next four lines do not give consecutive sense. We come, however, to " the diverse reports which E. K. made unto me of this pretty maiden " :

" I said, ' Whose maiden are you ? '

" Sh[e] : ' Whose man are you ? '

" ' I am the servant of God both by my bound duty, and also (I hope) by his adoption.'

[1] In the present year 1936 the tomb has been found, among the Abbey ruins, of a descendant of the founder ; the name being given as de Lascy in *The Manchester Guardian* last April.

" A voyce : ' You shall be beaten if you tell.'

" ' Am I not a fine maiden ? Give me leave to play in
your house, my mother told me she would come and dwell
here.'

" She went up and down with most lively gestures of a
young girle, playing by her selfe, and diverse times another
spake to me from the corner of my study by a great
perspective-glasse, but none was seen beside her selfe.

" ' Shall I ? I will ' (Now she seemed to answer one in
the foresaid corner of the study) . . .

" ' Tell me who you are.'

" ' I pray you let me play with you a little, and I will
tell you who I am.'

" ' In the name of Jesus then, tell me.'

" ' I rejoyce in the name of Jesus, and I am a poor little
maiden, Madini.¹ I am the last but one of my mother's
children, I have little baby-children at home.'

" ' Where is your home ? '

" Ma. : ' I dare not tell you where I dwell, I shall be
beaten.' "

A little later E. K. reports : " She smileth, one calls her,
saying, ' Come away, maiden,' to which she answers ' I
will read over my Gentlewoemen first. My Master Dee
will teach me if I say amisse.'

" ' I have Gentlemen and Gentlewoemen,' she continues,
' look you here.' " She then brings a little book out of her
pocket, and points to various pictures in it, giving the
names of historical characters : Edward Duke of York,
Richard Plantagenet, the Duke and Duchess of Clarence,
and so on.

Questioned about the pedigree of Albert Laski, Madini
says : " Alas, I cannot tell what's done in other countries,"
but promises that one of her sisters will shortly come and
tell them.

Finally E. K. observes, " There seemeth someone to
call her, whom I hear now." Madini answers, " I come,"
takes up her book, and departs, saying, " This may stand
you in some stead "—this being a by no means clear

¹ Later the name appears as Madimi ; but in the earlier mentions
it has an N, not an M. Casaubon had difficulty in deciphering Dee's
script. Madinia is the name of one of Dee's daughters.

genealogical tree of the Laski family, connecting it with Richard (Plantagenet), Edward Duke of York, and other people to whom she had referred before the question was asked her about Albert Laski.

After this Action Madini played a great part in Kelly's revelations ; and what may be considered evidence that he was truly in a state of trance is that the girl-spirit did not hesitate to rebuke him. He loved not God, she told him once ; he had not faith, hope, and charity, but hate. " Dost thou love silver and gold ? " she asked. " The one is a thief, the other is a murderer. But thou hast a just God that loveth thee, just and virtuous men that love thee. Therefore be thou virtuous ! " Again Madini called forth the evil spirits which had possessed Kelly, whereon he exclaimed, " Methinks I am lighter than I was, and I seem to be empty, and to have returned from a great amazing." " Thou are eased of a great burden," replied Madini. " Love God, love thy friends, love thy wife."

Nevertheless, in his normal state Kelly showed little sign of repentance, as in June 1583, he went away from Mortlake, leaving his wife without her husband and Dee without his skryer.

During June Dee had two visits from Laski. The first was when the Pole, who had been to see Oxford, was rowed down the river in a barge with the Queen's boatmen, and had with him Lord Russell, Sir Philip Sidney, and others. " He can of purpose to do me honor," wrote Dee, " for which God be praised ! " On the second occasion Laski stayed all night at Dee's house. Yet Dee was at the time so hard pressed for money that when, in July, he heard that Laski would dine with him, he let it be known he would not be able to prepare a " convenient " dinner without selling some of his plate or pewter. Within an hour forty gold angels arrived from the Queen.

Kelly's return to Mortlake enabled the Actions to begin again. The only note in the *Private Diary* records on August 7th, a great tempest of wind at midnight, and also, in Latin, great wrath of E. K. with his wife. But from the other sources of information we know that Laski now attended séances at Mortlake, where he learnt that he had a good angel or governor named Jubanladec, and that he

was spiritually advised to take Dee and Kelly with him
to Poland. The Prince was so interested in the experience
he had obtained of the crystal, and also in talk which he
heard of alchemy at Mortlake, that he invited the two men,
with their wives, Dee's young children, and some servants,
all to come back with him. They accepted ; and on September 21st the party set out for Gravesend, where two
ships were waiting to convey them to Holland.

According to Dee's own account his original intention
was to be abroad only a year and eight months. He let
his house temporarily to his brother-in-law, Nicholas
Fromonds. The arrangement turned out ill. Hardly had
Dee left England when a mob broke into his house, and
destroyed or looted his furniture, books, and some of his
chemical apparatus valued at about two hundred pounds.
With the wizard away his enemies did not fear to play havoc
with his belongings.

Kelly's object in leaving England need not have been,
as often stated, to escape justice for some crime. He saw
in Laski a heaven-sent patron, one who could afford to
provide the chemicals and the paraphernalia for the
experiments he was anxious to make in the transformation
of other metals into gold. Though a skryer, he was more
interested in alchemy than in the crystal.

Laski's large party of English guests, after over four
months of travel across the Continent, at length arrived
at their host's estate of Laskoe, near Cracow, on February
3rd, 1584. Dee's *Private Diary* is unfortunately missing
for this period, and does not begin again until near the
end of 1586. But we know that the Actions proceeded,
and that Laski heard much about how he was to become
the ruler of two kingdoms, was to restore the city of Jerusa-
lem, and to be a mighty influence throughout the world.
His name was in the Book of Life, Madini declared.

Laski was impressed ; and he also showed himself willing
to provide the necessary money for the alchemical experiments. Now Kelly had told Dee long ago of his old manuscript and two bottles of powder, acquired by him in
Wales or at Glastonbury, and had boasted of their extreme
value. The time had come, he thought, to give practical
proof of his assertions. Laski, hoping that something like

the philosopher's stone or the elixir of life was about
to be produced on his estate, went on pouring out his
money in answer to Kelly's requests, until at last his purse
was nearly exhausted, and no remarkable result had been
achieved. Kelly did once propose to raise an evil spirit
for a proof of his art ; but, says Casaubon, " Doctor Dee
would not suffer him to do it in his house." He would
never consent to traffic with spirits not certified as good.

As Dee was anxious to meet the Emperor Rudolph II,
whose predecessors, Charles, Maximilian, and Ferdinand,
had all taken notice of him, it was arranged that a visit
should be paid to Prague in August. Rudolph, however,
showed little interest, and refused Dee a second interview
with him. Returning to Poland, Dee obtained from Laski
an introduction to King Stephen Bathory. On him, too,
Dee failed to make an impression, and an Action by Kelly
was declared by him to be an imposture.

Dee and Kelly were now reduced to the position of
adventurers. They went back to Prague, where they found
things even less favourable to them than before. The
ecclesiastical arm had stirred against these visitors dealing
in magic, and the Papal nuncio, the Bishop of Piacenza,
induced Rudolph to issue a decree banishing them from
his dominions within six days, as being " notorious magicians." Kelly's wits here proved useful. He had succeeded
in making a friend of one who is called " the Lord Rosenberg "—William Ursinus Count Rosenberg, the Emperor's
viceroy in Bohemia ; and, after they had wandered about
for over two months in Thuringia and Hesse-Cassel, in
August 1586 the decree of banishment against them was
partly revoked. They might reside in any castle or town
belonging to Rosenberg. On September 14th Dee starts
his *Private Diary* again with the words, *Trebonam venimus*,
we came to Tribau—a castle in Southern Bohemia.

Peace seemed again attainable. Dee received in September a flattering offer from " the Emperor of Moschovia "
to come to his court, where he promised him a pension
of £2000 a year and equal treatment with the best of his
subjects. Dee was flattered by the invitation, but did not
accept it. He had overstayed the length of time that he was
meant to spend abroad, and wished to return home if he could.

For the present, however, Rosenberg was a good patron. He sent to Mistress Dee from Prague a chain and a jewel estimated to be worth three hundred ducats. For Kelly he showed much liking, and ultimately secured even the favour of the Emperor. It was perhaps Kelly's gold-making claims that commended him here, as they did later to Queen Elizabeth. To her, indeed, Kelly had already made an advance. With some of his mysterious powder from Wales or Glastonbury he made a projection of one grain of it upon one minim of mercury, and " produced " nearly an ounce of gold. Then, with a frying-pan, he cut a piece of metal out of the bottom, transmuted it into a gold ingot, and there was a gift to be sent to Elizabeth—frying-pan and all. Later there were tales of Kelly making pieces of gold for little Arthur Dee to play quoits with ; while later still the astrologer Lilly told how Kelly's sister, living at Worcester, showed him some of the gold her brother had produced.

His success in alchemy, however attained, disinclined Kelly to continue with his skrying. The Actions had indeed recommenced at Tribau, but soon there was trouble. Kelly did not wish to proceed, and perhaps suggested Arthur Dee as a substitute. Anyhow, the boy was tried on April 15th, 1587, but failed as a skryer.[1] Kelly was prevailed upon to return to his work, with a result which no one anticipated—unless he did.

The account of this affair is indeed strange ; and Casaubon cites as a particular example of Dee's simplicity and sincerity his " large and punctual relation of that sad abominable story of their *promiscuous, carnal copulation*, under the pretence of obedience to God."

What Dee has to say about the matter is that on April 18th, 1587, Kelly told him (at a séance) that Madini had spoken to him to the effect that " we two had our wives in such sort as we might use them in common." An enquiry whether Madini referred to carnal use or spiritual love was answered by the production of a scroll, described as like the edge of a carpet, on which was written " *De utroque*

---

[1] As it was usual to insist on having a pure boy, or at least a virgin, to perform divination by the crystal, it is odd that Doctor Dee employed first Barnabas Saul and then Edward Kelly as skryers !

loquor." At this both men, according to Dee, were in great amazement and grief of mind. Madini on this occasion, it appears, discarded her previous maiden modesty, and all clothing.

It remained to acquaint the ladies with the spirit's command. At dinner that day, when all four were together, Dee " found means to make some declaration of our great grief (mine chiefly) now occasioned, either to try us, or really to be executed, in the common or indifferent use of matrimonial amongst any couple of us four ; which thing was strange unto the women, and they hoped of some more comfortable issue of the cause.

Kelly, however, was determined that there should be but one issue. With the aid of the crystal he told Dee that another spirit, announcing itself as " William, the son of Ursine," brought this message to him from the Lord : " As unto thee, barrenness dwelleth with thee, because thou didst neglect me and take a wife unto thyself [at Mortlake four years previously], contrary to my commandments. . . . Therefore thou shalt have the womb which thou hast barren and fruitless unto thee, because thou hast transgressed that which I commanded thee." Addressing both men, the spirit bade them, " Lay your hands to work, and your bodies unto labour, and participate one with another, as is commanded you."

Dee took down the words of the spirit at Kelly's dictation, and the two at last agreed to perform the command. But Jane Dee and Joan Kelly were not so easily convinced. Kelly himself describes their attitude in a statement which Casaubon included in his edition of Dee : " The women disliked utterly this last doctrine, and consulting amongst themselves gave us this answer : the former actions did nothing offend them, but much comforted them, and therefore this last, not agreeing with the rest, maketh them to fear, because it expressly is contrary to the commandment of God. And thereupon, desiring God not to be offended with their ignorance, required another action for better information herein ; in the meantime vowing, fasting, and praying."

Presumably Edward Kelly was ready with another " action " ; for on Sunday, May 3rd, 1587, a document was signed by both couples, which Dee recorded in his *True and Faithfull Relation* : " I John Dee, Edward Kelly, and our two wives covenanted with God, and subscribed the same, for indissoluble and inviolate unities, charity and friendship keeping between us four, and all things between us to be common, as God by sundry means willed us to do."

So Kelly, through Madini and William, the son of Ursine, had accomplished his design, though we hear no more about the " cross-matching," as Dee calls it. We do, however, read in the *Private Diary* for the date May 1st an entry, in Latin, to the effect : " I have seen, by my doctor's demonstration [so-and-so]. Praise be to God and to my doctor E. K. ! " It is clear that Casaubon exagger- ates but little when he asserts that Dr. Dee was so much in the power and government of his spirits that they might persuade him to anything under colour of doing service to God—" yea, had it been to cut his own father's throat, as we see in the *Relation* that they persuaded him to lie with another man's wife, and prostitute his own to a vile and, by himself believed, Diabolical man."

Dee has a simple comment on the matter : " If it offend not God, it offended not me, and I pray God it did not offend him."

The affairs of the household in the castle of Tribau were certainly complicated at this period. Edward Kelly's younger brother Thomas had appeared at Cracow, and was now at Tribau, where he was married on June 16th. Jane Dee and Joan Kelly were evidently not living entirely in charity and friendship, as on July 19th Dee writes of " a certayn kind of recommendation between our wives," while " next day saw relenting of E. K. also by my Lord [Rosenberg]'s entreaty."

Kelly's relenting did not mean that he skryed any more. The last Action with him had been on May 23rd, when Madini made some unimportant revelations. With that Kelly closed his five year's of mediumship for Doctor Dee, who now abandoned the use of the crystal until near the end of his life.

We do not know what was the cause of a " terrible expostulation, accusation, &c." at Tribau one afternoon in December. Kelly was likely to have been concerned in

it, as he was in most of the quarrels. Nor did the year
1588 open well. First " Mistres Lidde K. [Thomas Kelly's
wife, Lydia] had an abortion of a girle of 5 or 6 months,"
Dee assisting her after giving her myrrh in warm wine.
Then Mistress E. K. revealed to Dee how untrue some of
his accounted friends were. One of these seems to have
been Francis Pucci, an Italian who had first been in trade
at Lyons, then turned Protestant and gone to Oxford, where
he took his M.A. degree ; later appeared in Cracow as an
enemy of the Jesuits ; and finally became once more
Roman Catholic. He had been admitted by Dee and
Kelly to some of the Actions, but was now their enemy.

Joan Kelly was formally reconciled to the Dees when in
May 1588, after receiving the Sacrament, she gave her
hand to the Doctor and his wife in charity ; " and we
rushed not from her," he writes.

Edmund Cooper, Joan's brother, arrived at Tribau in
August, and an endeavour was made to have an all-
round reconciliation. As far as the amiable Doctor was
concerned he was always ready for peace. On the 28th
of the month Edward Kelly gave him a demonstration of
the *divina aqua*, some magic fluid which he made prepared ;
and Dee writes of " the magnificent master and my incom-
parable friend, Master Ed. Kelly." Not long after he
presents Kelly with " my Glass, so long esteemed of our
Quene and of the Emperor " ; while in return great
friendship is promised for many, " and two ounces of the
thing," and soon Kelly actually gives him " the water,
erth, and all." Dee purposely leaves obscure in his
Private Diary matters pertaining to magic ; and obscure
they remain.

Meanwhile the intrigues at Rudolph's court against the
foreign " magicians " had continued, and the news that
reached the English Government seemed to make advisable
their recall home. An order was accordingly sent to them.

Even without this the household at Tribau was on the
point of breaking up, very largely through Edward
Kelly's self-seeking character and disregard for his fellow-
student of the occult. Dee does not refer in the diary to
any final quarrel, but merely records on February 4th,
1589, that he gave K. the powder (that used in the trans-

mutation of metals), the books, and the bone (whatever
that may have been) for the Lord Rosensberg ; and " he
thereupon gave me dischardg in writing of his own hand,
subscribed and sealed." Their association was at an end,
and on the 16th Kelly and some others of the household
rode away to Prague. Kelly was assured of employment
with Count Rosenberg, and through him with the Emperor.
At first, indeed, all seemed going well for him. Rudolph
created him an *eques auratus*, and when Dee refers to him
again in his diary it is usually as " Sir Edward Kelly."[1]

Dee left Tribau with his family on March 16th, and made
his way leisurely across Europe, so that it was not until
December 2nd that he landed at Gravesend, having spent
no less than six hundred pounds on the journey, he records.
He presented himself to the Queen on the 19th, and was
graciously received. He was not able to move into his house
at Mortlake until Christmas Day, having been away six
years, instead of the original twenty months that he had
contemplated.

Dee's first task was to try to get some of the property
which he had lost when his house was attacked by the mob,
and he succeeded in recovering about three-quarters of his
library. But owing to his extravagance on his journey to
England he was very short of money ; and, Thomas
Kelly calling on him on January 23rd with news of his
brother, Dee borrowed ten pounds from him. With Edward
Kelly he was keeping up a correspondence, and he still
hoped that his old associate would join him again in
England. It was a blow to him when in June there came,
as he curtly notes, " terrible yll newes of Edward Kelly
against me."[2]

---

[1] As Sir Edward Kelly he appears frequently in English literature ;
but it must be remembered that his title was a foreign one.

[2] Since his return, on the other hand, Dee had been trying to do
what services he could for Kelly ; hoping, no doubt, to secure his
return to England. He had commended him to Lord Burghley as
a man of high intellect, and a master of Greek, Hebrew, Latin, French,
and Italian. In his friendship the Doctor exaggerated somewhat.
It is said elsewhere that Kelly had not Greek, or very little.

As to the bad errors of language in the Actions, Casaubon points
out that " Kelley, for the most part, when he made report to Dr. Dee,
of voices and speeches . . . did not know what he said himself, and
so might the easier mistake." In a trance does the grammar go ?

A domestic event early in 1590 was the birth of a daughter, who was christened Madinia, after the girl-spirit of the Actions. Dee secured as godparents Sir George Cary, Lady Cobham, and Lady Walsingham. The chief picture presented by the *Private Diary* in this year, however, is of worries by creditors. In November Dee called on the Archbishop of Canterbury, and obtained from him five pounds in " ryalls and angels " ; while near the end of the month Queen Elizabeth summoned him to Richmond and promised to give him something wherewith to keep Christmas. She renewed the promise by a messenger, who spoke of a hundred angels and brought half that sum ; and on December 4th she called at Dee's door as she passed. He came out to her at the East Sheen Gate, he says ; when she " graciously, putting down her mask, did say with mery chere, ' I thank thee, Dee ; there never was a promise made but it was broken or kept ! ' " Twelve days later she sent the balance of her Christmas present, together with a " warrant by word of mouth to assure me to do what I would in philosophie and alchemie, and non[e] shold che[c]k, control or molest me." Dee must have asked about this in the interview at the East Sheen Gate.

His favour with Elizabeth did not éscape hostile comment ; and someone ventured to call him in print, as he afterwards complained, " the Conjuror of the Queen's Privy Council."

Still the tale of loans and bills continues. Over the payment of a sum of ten pounds to his brother-in-law, probably in connection with the surrender of the house, there was trouble ; for Dee says that Nicholas Fromonds " most abhominably reviled me." It has been calculated that in the space of three years he borrowed about five hundred pounds from friends, and raised over three hundred more by pawning his jewelry and plate (of which he seems to have had a good stock) or by recourse to money-lenders. He felt acutely his neglect in 1576 to secure his revenues from Upton-on-Severn and Long Leadenham. Nor did a pension which he had been told he might expect from Count Rosenberg reach him. Perhaps the " yll newes " of Kelly concerned this.

Before 1592 ended Dee, who this year put his son Arthur

to school at Westminster, was so straitened that he addressed
a petition to the Queen for assistance. She replied by
sending Sir John Walley, of the Privy Council, and Sir
Thomas Gorges, of her Wardrobe, to look into his affairs.
For them he had had ready the manuscript *Compendious
Rehearsall of John Dee*, substantiated by documents and by
names of witnesses still living, as well as copies of his eight
printed books and his thirty-six works in manuscript.

For the moment Dee only got a hundred marks from
Sir Thomas Gorges ; but his request for the Mastership of
the Hospital of St. Cross, near Winchester, of which the
present holder was an expectant bishop, was favourably
received. Elizabeth promised the reversion, and also
(though it is not certain whether this promise was broken
or kept) a temporary allowance from the revenues of the
vacant see of Oxford.

Dee's household at this time numbered seventeen ;
himself and his wife, seven children, including Arthur at
Westminster, and the rest servants. In March, 1593, he
obtained some relief by taking as a pupil a Francis Nichols,
to whom he was to teach " the conclusion of fixing and
teyming the moon, &c."—astronomy with astrology, it
seems. For this Nichols was to pay three hundred pounds
in instalments by July.

Dee had suggested, as an alternative for the Mastership
of St. Cross, that he should have the Wardenship of Manchester College ; and this became vacant first. On April
18th, 1595, Elizabeth was actually able to sign the bill
for Dee's appointment. His installation could not take
place until the next year ; but at least he had, after so
many years of waiting, a substantial post in view—or what
appeared so.

By a curious irony he shortly afterwards had an offer from
the Emperor Rudolph to return to his dominions and enter
his service. It was conveyed in a letter from Edward
Kelly, and was therefore perhaps not too sure an offer.
Kelly himself had had a precarious time with the capricious
Emperor since he left Dee in early 1589. At first his
alchemical work seemed likely to make his position secure ;
and when Lord Burghley, in May 1591, wrote to him
urging his return to England, in order to bestow the gifts

God had given him on his own Prince and country rather
than on strangers, Kelly preferred to stay where he was.
He suspected that as a conjurer he would be in considerable
danger in England ; to say nothing of his other past
record there. Burghley still urged him, since the idea of his
making gold for the Queen's Navy was attractive. But
Kelly would not come ; and suddenly it was taken out of
his power to move. The Emperor threw him into prison.

Casaubon says that it was " for a notable Chymical
cheat that he had put upon him." Other accounts state
that the numerous enemies of Kelly, as a foreigner drawing
Imperial pay, accused him of speaking against Rudolph
and of trying to poison him. At any rate, he was confined
in the castle of Pirglitz, near Prague, where he remained
for two years, until on Queen Elizabeth's intervention he
was released. On October 4th, 1593, Dee notes in his
diary, " Sir Edward Kelly set free by the Emperor." After
this Dee heard from him at least twice, the second time in
August 1595, conveying the offer from Rudolph. Then,
on November 25th, Dee's diary has a laconic entry as to
news that Sir Edward Kelly was " slayne."

Somehow Kelly had offended the Emperor again, and
was in danger of rearrest. Casaubon relates his end thus.
Elizabeth had sent very secretly Captain Peter Gwynne,
and other agents, " to persuade him to return back to his
own native land, which he was willing to do ; and thinking
to escape away in the night by stealth, as he was clammer-
ing over a wall in his own house in Prague (which bears
his name to this day, and sometimes was an old sanctuary),
he fell down from the battlements, broke his leggs, and
bruised his body, of which hurts within a while after he
departed this world."

So died, at the age of only forty, Edward Kelly, who was
certainly much more truly a " conjurer " than John Dee.
What else he was, except a very successful skryer, it is difficult to say. Casaubon moralises upon his end. " All men,"
he writes, " may take warning by this example, how they
put themselves out of the protection of Almighty God,
either by presumptuous unlawful wishes and desires, or
by seeking not unto Divels onely directly (which Dr. Dee
certainly never did, but abhorred the thought of it in his

heart) but unto them that have next relation unto Divels,
as Witches, Wizzards, Conjurers, Astrologers, Fortune-
tellers, and the like, yea and all books of that subject, which
I doubt were a great occasion of Dr. Dee's delusion. That
men are commonly cheated by such is sure enough ;
and those that are not very fools would take heed how they
deal with them, and avoid them, to avoid the imputation
of fools ; but those that are wise much more if they can
more than cheat ; for the more they can do the more
they know they have of the Divel in them."

" It is a great sign," concludes Casaubon, " that God is
very angry with them when he doth suffer them to thrive
by means which Himself hath cursed."

It cannot be said that Kelly throve particularly well.
Lilly's story of his once giving away, after a mysterious
visitant had brought him a new elixir, rings worth four
thousand pounds at the wedding of a maidservant seems,
like so many of Lilly's stories, apocryphal, even if others
also had heard the report.

Among his many accomplishments Kelly had acquired
a certain facility in writing verse ; and he left behind him a
Metrical Treatise on Alchemy, which may have been composed
while he was Rudolph's prisoner. In this, addressing " all
you who faine philosophers would be," he writes :

> The more you worke, the more you loose and spoile.
> To you I say, how learned so e'er you be,
> Go burn your bookes, and come and learn from me.

Of his prose works Kelly's chief was *De Lapide Philoso-
phorum*, in which he expressed his hope that his name and
character would become so well known to posterity that
he might be counted among those who have suffered much
in the cause of truth. It is to be feared that his fate has
been far different.

* * * * *

In the year that Kelly died, Dee wrote to the Archbishop
of Canterbury a letter in which he shows how different is
his attitude from his one-time associate's with regard to
the claim to occult knowledge. No one can say that Dee,
with all his humility in face of his conception of God, was

unduly modest in his pretensions to ability in attaining to
the higher knowledge, whether by sheer mental effort or
by magic. But he, unlike Kelly, fervently disclaimed all
dealings with aught that was not good in the spiritual
world ; and that was an accusation which dogged him
throughout life.

" The great losses and dammages," he said to the Archbishop, " which in sundry sorts I have sustained do not
so much grieve my heart as the rash, lewde, fond, and untrue fables and reports of me and my studies philosophicall
have done, and yet do ; which commonly, after their first
hatching and devilish devising, immediately with great
speed are generally all the realme overspread, and to some
seem true ; to other they are doubtfull ; and to onely
the wise, modest, discreet, godly, and charitable (and
chiefly to such as have acquaintance with me) they appear
and are known to be fables, untruths, and utterly false
reports and slanders."

It is at this period of his life, before his departure for
Manchester, that we have the well-known painting of him
by an unknown artist in the Ashmolean Museum at Oxford,
having come into the possession of Elias Ashmole through
John Dee's grandson Rowland, a London merchant. It
brings out well the man as described by John Aubrey
(his " yong coosen," as Dee calls him) with " a very fair,
clear, sanguine complexion, a long beard as white as
milke ; a very handsome man."

Dee went to Manchester in February 1596, and was
installed Warden of the College on the 20th. He soon
found that the post was not at all the peaceful one that he
had hoped it would be. In the first place, his interpretation
of Christianity was very divergent from what J. E. Bailey,
editor of the Manchester portion of his *Private Diary*, calls
the " sturdy Protestantism " of the Fellows of the College.
His predecessor, Dr. Chadderton, now Bishop of Lincoln,
had been a bigoted Puritan. Dee met with opposition,
notably from Oliver Carter, senior Fellow and Bursar,
and a man of much influence. As he was not qualified to
preach, he had to employ a curate ; and the curate chosen
was not to his liking. Then again there was trouble as to
his stipend as Warden ; it seems as if he never got it in full.

The college finances were in an involved state. He had only been two years in Manchester when he was obliged to go to London in the matter, and it is supposed from a gap of over two years in his diary that he was absent all that time. In October 1600, an arbitrator was appointed. At the end of that year he was borrowing ten pounds from " Mr. Edmund Chetham the scholemaster," upon security of some plate ; and next month five pounds from another man, as well as five pounds on a double-gilt silver salt, with cover, weighing fourteen ounces. Even food for himself and his family seems to have run short.

Owing to his vexed life at Manchester, at a period when he particularly needed quiet—for he was in the seventies—the entries in Dee's diary become very meagre, until they cease entirely on June 9th, 1601. There are a few other sources of information as to his fortunes ; but there is not much to be told.

In his first year as Warden there was an attempt to interest him in a case of alleged witchcraft in the neighbourhood ; but, as will be told in the next chapter, he cautiously kept out of it, though he lent a local justice of the peace who was dealing with the case a number of books on witchcraft.

He resumed at Manchester his Actions through the crystal, but could not find a skryer comparable with Kelly. He had recourse to Bartholomew Hickman, who in his youth had been a servant or assistant in the laboratory at Mortlake, and who now paid several visits to Manchester, for which Dee paid him a few pounds in the course of the year. Hickman's skrying came to an abrupt end on July 11th, 1600, as the diary narrates. Dee begins by recording an intermittent beating of his pulse, for the first time in his life, but explains that he had been somewhat disturbed by the disagreement of his two seers as to the things which they saw. It appears that Dee was now employing both Hickman and Francis Nichols, his former pupil in astronomy or astrology, to skry for him, and that there was a quarrel. On July 14th both went home. On September 29th comes the entry : " I burned, before Mr. Nichols, his brother, and Mr. Wortly, all Bartholomew Hikman his untrue actions, &c."

Hickman's Actions in Manchester do not appear among Dee's records of the crystal. He went back to Dee for a short time in 1607, but produced nothing of importance.[1] Nor did Nichols.

As his diary ended before her death, Dee does not comment on the passing of his patron for so many years, Queen Elizabeth. Early in the new reign, on June 5th, 1604, we find Dee petitioning James I at Greenwich, that he may be tried and cleared of the horrible slander that he is, or has been, " a conjurer or caller or invocator of divels." He offers to submit to the death penalty if the accusation can be proved.

Seeing that James's reign began with increased severity in the law against witchcraft, and that the Earl of Salisbury, when consulted by the King, expressed no favourable opinion as to the character of the Doctor's studies, it was perhaps as well for Dee that James refused his petition.

In November 1604, Dee retired from his ungrateful post at Manchester. He was ailing in health, he had saved no money, and he had no prospects of assistance from the new King. His wife died at Manchester, aged fifty, during an epidemic—plague, it is said—through which she had nursed some of her children. Dee was back in his Mortlake house without her. Arthur Dee, though he was to attain to a good position at Court in the next reign, was too young at present to do much for his father, who was compelled to relieve his poverty by selling some of his treasured books.[2] He was still cherishing hope that he would be able to take another journey to the Emperor's dominions, as the spirits in the crystal seemed to tell him he might. But in December 1608, death put an end to hopes and fears ; and he was buried in the churchyard at Mortlake, close to the house where he had lived so long.

[1] According to Miss Fell-Smith, Bartholomew Hickman exhibited " slight mediumistic powers."
[2] When he wrote to the Archbishop of Canterbury in 1595 he spoke of 48 books, printed or unprinted, written by himself, and of his library of about 4000 works, including 700 ancient MSS., Greek, Latin, and Hebrew.

CHAPTER III

"THE KISSING WITCH"

IN connection with the later life of Doctor Dee, when he was Warden of Manchester College, we have had reference to an attempt made to get him to intervene in a matter of witchcraft. The case is one of considerable interest, and introduces a variety of male witch, or conjurer, different from those whom we have seen hitherto. It also brings before us two enemies of witchcraft, who made war upon it on more legitimate lines, according to their own accounts, than those of the persecutors whom we have seen in action in Part II of this book. It is on these two that we have chiefly to rely for our acquaintance with what happened at Cleworth, Lancashire, in 1596–7 ; for Dee is very reticent about an affair in which he had no desire to be involved. Fortunately what Darrell and More wrote about the subject,[1] vindicating the parts they played, seems on internal evidence as credible as any documents of the period relating to cases of possession. We may reject much, but we cannot dismiss the whole as a tissue of falsehoods.

At Cleworth Hall, in the parish of Leigh, there were living in early 1594 Nicholas Starkie, his wife, and two children, John aged ten and Anne aged nine. The wife, More says, was an heiress, of whose kindred some were Papists ; and they, for the sake of the inheritance " wished

[1] *A True Narrative of the Strange and Grevous Vexation by the Devil of 7 persons in Lancashire*, by John Darrell, Minister of the Word of God (? London, 1600).

A True Discourse concerning the certaine Possession and Dispossession of 7 persons in one familie in Lancashire, by George More, Minister and Preacher of the Worde of God (? London, 1600).

In quotations from these works I have not followed too closely the authors' eccentric and very inconsistent spelling. Darrell usually, and More often, write of the Starkie family as the Starchies.

and vowed still to pray for the perishing of her issue."
Her four eldest-born children indeed died, pining away in
most strange manner. She made over her estate to her
husband and his heirs, and subsequently bore two more
children, John and Anne, who prospered well until
February 1594. Then trouble came upon them. First Anne,
in Darrell's words, was " taken with a dumpish and heavie
countenance, and with a certaine fearfull starting and
pulling together of her body." The next week the boy was
also affected. On his way to school he felt compelled to
shout, and could not stop himself ; and he grew worse
and worse, " falling into often and extreame fits."

The Starkies had also with them at Cleworth three young
girls, of whom Nicholas had the education, together with
their portions, committed to him by their parents ;
Margaret and Elinor Hardman (or Hurdman), aged
fourteen and ten, and Ellen Holland, aged twelve. These
three were not at first affected.

As his own children's malady continued, Nicholas
Starkie sought about for someone to cure them. He went
first to " a Seminarie priest, who could do no good because
(forsooth) he had not then his books," More says. Hearing
at last that there was in the neighbourhood a travelling
" conjurer," Edmund Hartley, he went to him and begged
him to deal with the case.

Hartley came to Cleworth ; and to continue the story
from Darrell, with whom More is in fairly close agreement, " after he had used certaine popish charmes and
hearbes, by degrees the children were at quiet." For
about a year and a half they continued well, so long as
Hartley paid periodical visits. When, however, he
announced his intention of leaving the country, John was
at once taken ill, " falling of bleedinge," and, had not
Hartley arrived in time to staunch the flow, would have
died—or so Hartley declared.[1]

---

[1] More says that about January 4th, 1597, John was reading
a book, when something gave him such a thump that he fell down with
a most horrible " skrike," and said Satan had broken his neck. He
lay pitifully tormented for the space of two hours. More frequently
mentions, though not here, a vomiting of blood during the sufferers'
fits.

In order to retain the conjurer's services, Starkie offered him his board at Cleworth. He came ; but, on being further offered forty shilling a year as a fee, he stood out for a house and some ground, which Starkie refused. Hartley, " in a fume," threatened to make such a trouble as never was at Cleworth. It appeared, too, as if he had the power to carry out his threat. That very afternoon, and again in the evening, " seven of them sent forth such a strange, supernaturall, and fearefull noyse, or loud whapping, as the like was never heard at Cleworth."

More only mentions the children as being afflicted yet. But Darrell includes two adult women as well ; Margaret Byrom, aged thirty-three, a poor kinswoman of Mrs. Starkie, over on a visit from Salford, and a servant-maid, Jane Ashton, aged thirty.

The next step was that Hartley accompanied Nicholas Starkie on a visit to his father's house in Whalley parish. The object of the journey is not stated ; but on the next day, after he himself had been " tormented " all night, Hartley went with Starkie to a little wood. Here he described a circle about a yard and a half across, divided it into four parts, with a cross at every division, and desired Starkie to tread out the circle. " I may not tread it out myself," he said, " and further I will meet with them that went about my death."

The importance of this circle-drawing to the magician's fate will appear very soon. It was not such as he can have expected at the time.

It is clear that Darrell derived this part of his story directly from Starkie ; who now, he says, when he saw this " wretched dealing " of Hartley's, and his children still molested, " waxed wearie of him, but knew not how to rid his hands honestly of him."

John being the worst of the sufferers, his father consulted first a Manchester physician, who could discover nothing wrong with him, and then approached Doctor Dee. If he was hoping for magical aid from the old Warden he was disappointed. Dee " utterly refused, saying he would not meddle, and advised him that, setting aside all other help, he should call for some godlye preachers, with whom he should consult concerning a publicke or private Fast."

Dee consented, however, to have Hartley before him, and so sharply reproved him that for three weeks the children had more ease. But on New Year's Day, 1597, they went over to Manchester to visit relations ; and Hartley accompanied them as overseer. They had promised to call on Doctor Dee as they went back. Hartley objected, and, when they went in spite of him, told them angrily that it would have been better for them not to have changed an old friend for a new. He went on ahead of them all the way to Cleworth, in a rage. In three days' time serious troubles broke out again among the children.

John was the first affected. He leapt out of bed with a loud cry, tumbling about, acting like a mad dog, biting everyone, including his mother, and hurling pillows, bed-staves, etc., either at people or into the fire. His sister was the next to be troubled, and the other girls followed. Hartley himself was tormented the same night, and also the next day, when a remarkable scene occurred. Hartley was so violent that " many "—the grown-up members of the party, we may suppose—held on to him. Among them was Margaret Byrom, who was told to sit down and hold him from behind, which she did. When he came out of his fit she tried to rise, but was so giddy that she could not stand, " and was senseless and very unruly." Hartley said he feared he had done her harm. Then she, the poor relation over on a visit from Salford to " make merry," began to call those present by nicknames and to taunt them. She " wist not what she said, nor knew or saw any of them save Hartley only, whom she both knew and said she saw, albeit her eyes were shut close."

The recognition of Hartley was not to his advantage, for she railed at him and " angerly smote." When her fit was over he approached her and tried to comfort her. He " pretended to bear a loving affection towards her," Darrell says, " and it was thought he had kissed her."

This is the first mention in the narrative of the habit that gained Hartley the name appearing at the head of this chapter. Darrell goes on to explain :

" Now they judged in the house that, whomsoever he kissed, on them he breathed the divell. He often kissed

John for love (as he said), he kissed the little wenches in jest, he promised Margaret Hardman a thrave of kisses. He wrastled with one Johan Smyth, a maid-servant in the house, to kiss her, but he failed of his purpose ; whereupon Elinor [Hardman] in a fit said if he had kissed her three men could not have held her. When he came to comfort Margaret [Byrom], she could not abide his company. He demanded of her why. She said for that she thought he had bewitched her. He asked the reason why she thought so ; she answered, ' For thou art ever in mine eyes, absent and present.' "[1]

Still this extraordinary household continued to live together. It was nine days later when, the five children being in their fits, one of them began to bark and howl, the others joining in, until they were " like a ring of five bells for order and time, and so continued almost a quarter of an hour." At the end they became " speechlessly senseless and as dead."

As for Margaret Byrom, her first fit occurred when one day, as she was sitting by the kitchen fire, she was suddenly thrown forward right against the bars and took about half an hour to recover. This happened several times again. From the description she was able to give of her sensations, they were chiefly stomachic ! Not unnaturally, towards the end of January she thought it would be best for her to go home to Salford. Hartley insisted on escorting her, which he did with another man. On the road she had ten fits, and on recovery, asking Hartley how she might be helped, was merely told that she and the rest were past his hands. It was too great a work for any one man ; there must be two or three at least with fervent and hearty prayer.

[1] More's account of the kissing is as follows. " His manner was, when he meant them a mischiefe, then he would kisse them if he could, and therewith breathe the Devil into their bodies. . . . He struggled much with Joan Smith to have kissed her, but with much adoe she escaped his hands, so that of all the maide servants she only was preserved and not once troubled at all."

He says that Hartley offered Jane Ashton large promises in the way of marriage, and had kissed her. " The like loving affection he some-times showed to Margaret Byrom, as she confessed, and had kissed her also as it was thought."

This touch is given by More, and perhaps we may doubt whether Hartley actually used the words attributed to him. When, at home in Salford, Margaret Byrom the next morning had yet another fit, Hartley himself came alone to pray over her.

But at last Nemesis was close upon the magician's heels, appearing in the form of Matthew Palmer, Doctor Dee's curate. Where Dee had feared to tread Palmer rushed in. Seeing Hartley, he asked him what he was doing. " Praying," was the reply. " Thou pray ! " said Palmer, " thou canst not pray. What prayer canst thou say ? " " None but the Lord's Prayer." " Say it," Palmer insisted.

Apparently Hartley broke down. Palmer took charge of the case, and examined him in private, after which he had him brought before two justices of the peace, one of them being Edmund Hopwood, who knew Doctor Dee. The justices seem to have accepted Palmer's ministrations in the affair, as it was by their direction that he had Hartley confronted by Margaret Byrom, to hear what she could say against him. But as soon as she saw him she was speechless and was cast down backwards. This happened a second time ; and altogether on five occasions she was dumb when Hartley came in front of her.

At last she was able to find her tongue, when it was evident that the Puritan minister had helped her to find it. She told how, on the morning of her fit at Salford, when she went to the fireplace a great black dog with a monstrous tail appeared, coming at her open-mouthed, and running by her left side cast her on her face hard by the fire. A little after came a big black cat, staring fearfully, and running by her left side. Later still came something like a big mouse, which leapt upon her left knee, and also cast her backwards. The insistence on the left is noteworthy.

Upon Margaret Byrom's accusations and other testimonies, Hartley was sent by the justices to Lancaster gaol. On his way, on February 2nd, he was allowed to call at Cleworth to get his clothes. In his absence the children had all been well ; but now, More relates, they fell into very violent and outrageous fits. " They made at him all at once offering to strike him ; it was much adoe for two strong men to hold the least of them, and if they had not been forcibly restrained the witch would have been in great danger, for they were so fierce and furious against him, as if they would have pulled him in peaces."

Edmund Hopwood seems to have made an effort to give Hartley a fair chance under the charges made against him ; for he sent to Doctor Dee to borrow some books concerning witchcraft. Dee's *Private Diary* shows that he lent Hopwood John Wier's *De Præstigiis Dæmonum,* and the two works, *Flagellum Dæmonum* and *Fustis Dæmonum,* by the monk Hieronymus Menghi. The first-named of these was at least a plea for mercy towards alleged witches, as persons with distempered brains.

It was one of Hopwood's tasks to take the evidence of the children at Cleworth against Hartley, and here again he was met by the same strange manifestations as in Margaret Byrom's case. Their recent behaviour had been very odd. They " fleed " from all company, calling them devils with horns, crept under the beds, and when Mrs. Starkie questioned them talked of being led by an angel like a dove, whom they must follow to Heaven. Before Hopwood they became speechless, and would fall down on their way from one room to another. When they found voice, all they could say was that Edmund would not suffer them to speak against him.

Jane Ashton, the maidservant, was also a difficult witness. When asked what she had to say about Hartley, she began to bark and howl. It is stated that this was only the second time she had been troubled ; the previous occasion being almost a year before, when " it took her in the throat like a pin sticking there," and she brought up blood and was very sick. She was said then to have gone into Hartley's room and looked into his chest—was this a " magician's cabinet " ? When she was now afflicted, one of the young girls, also in a fit, exclaimed, " Ah Edmund, dost thou trouble her now when she should testify against thee ? "

In spite of the difficulties in marshalling the evidence, there was no chance for Hartley when the case came up to the Lancaster Assizes on March 6th. As a witch he was convicted and hanged. Darrel says that " the making of his circle was chiefly his overthrow." He denied what

Nicholas Starkie said about this,[1] " but, breaking the rope, he after confessed it." The first attempt to hang him failed. The second did not.

The witch might be dead, but the six sufferers at Cleworth still remained under " possession," as also did Margaret Byrom. In a statement made by the last (whether it was used against the prisoner or not is uncertain), two nights in succession the Devil had appeared to her in Hartley's likeness, bidding her take heed what she said and speak the truth, for the time was come. He promised her silver and gold ; but she answered that she had already spoken the truth, and would not favour him for silver or gold. The second night he had departed, saying, " Do as thou wilt ! "

The day before his execution, according to Darrell, was a sore one to her. When she went to church " it took her about the middest of the sermon, in heaving up her shoulders, depriving her of her senses ; after the recovery of her senses it would away the use of her leggs ; and thus it molested her in the church, to the admiration of the people, about an hower and halfe." However, though she went daily to morning prayer, she was never again troubled in church. But at night she would lie quaking and trembling, until she came to Cleworth again. Here, too, for a whole day and night, she was troubled by a terrible vision, " like a fowle black dwarfe with halfe a face, longe shagged haire, blacke broad hands, and blacke cloven feet."

This is More's account of how she described what she saw ; and he goes on at considerable length about the black man with half a face, who apparently continued his visits at night, first throwing his victim backwards as she was going to bed, then sitting on her head in bed, and finally, when he took his leave, giving her " a great thump upon the hinder part of her head, insomuch that with those thumps she felt her head sore a good while after." Sometimes, too, she saw six spirits, five of them black, marvellous ugly to behold, which kept " shoveing and thrusting into her great nayles to torment her." The sixth spirit, however,

---

[1] More states that " they could find no law to hang him, whereupon M. Starkie called to mind the making of the circle, which being delivered upon his oath was received."

was like a very fair little child, as fine and comely as ever might be seen, which she said sat ever next her, and would say unto her, " Fear not, for thou shalt have no harm."

As for the possessed children, More has many marvels to relate, such as how they could rest in no one place, but would leap up from the floor to a bed, and down from the bed to the floor, " hopping so up and down as lightly like frogs, and so continued for the space of seven hours at the least."

Nicholas Starkie was at his wits' end what to do about his afflicted household. He procured first one preacher, then another, to see the victims ; but they were unable to do anything for them. Then he heard from Doctor Dee's butler at the College how his uncle's son, a boy named Thomas Darling, had recovered from a like grievous afflic- tion upon advice given by John Darrell, a professed exor- cist. Starkie therefore procured a letter from Doctor Dee, and sent it with his own to Darrell, who, with some show of reluctance, and, " craving first the advice of many of my brethren in the ministry," yielded at last to Starkie's request and went to Cleworth.

The man who now comes personally into the story is worth some attention. He is one of those who made a living, or part of a living, out of witchcraft ; not by prac- tising it but by preying on its practisers—yet not in the odious way in which Matthew Hopkins and John Stearne preyed. His approach was by way of exorcism of the evil spirits that " possessed " the bewitched ; and this was not in itself a despicable profession, provided that he sincerely believed in his own powers and refrained from manufactur- ing evidence to convince other people of them. To this he soon descended ; but he did not start like Hopkins and Stearne, or some African witch-doctor, as a professional " smeller-out " of witches, ready to sacrifice lives for the sake of gain. However, we can best show what he was by a glance at his career before he took up the Cleworth case.

John Darrell was born at Mansfield, Nottinghamshire, about 1562, and, after taking his B.A. degree at Cambridge and beginning a study of the Law, decided to become in- stead a preacher. Presumably he had been ordained when he added to his practice the exorcism of evil spirits. He was brought into prominence in 1586 by a case which ended none too fortunately for his reputation. Being called on to drive a "devil" out of a girl of seventeen, named Katherine Wright, he appeared to do so. The girl was then re-possessed by eight devils, which he likewise expelled. But when the patient accused a woman, Margaret Roper, of having bewitched her, the magistrate, George Foljambe, was so dissatisfied with the case that he reproved Darrell, and told him that if he so demeaned himself any more he would send him to gaol. Still, imposture on Darrell's part was not proved.

He may, however, have found his connection with the case unpleasantly notorious, for, whether or not he continued to preach, it was ten years before he again came into notice. Then, when living at Ashby-de-la-Zouch, he figures in a story that takes us back to a type of case with which we are already familiar, the persecution of an elderly woman reputed by her neighbours to be a witch, credited with a "familiar," and found on search to have a witch-mark. In fact, we have two witches, mother and daughter, of whom the younger was sixty years of age.

The incident that brought the witches into trouble was as follows. In February 1596, a boy of fourteen, Thomas Darling, of Burton-on-Trent, went out hare-hunting with his uncle, Robert Toone, but lost his way and returned home alone, when he began to be sick. The next day he was worse, having fits, and seeing green angels and a green cat. A doctor and a Bible-reading neighbour, who were brought in to see him, suggested that he had been bewitched. Eventually he told a tale of how, after parting company with his uncle, he had met in a wood a little old woman, in a grey gown and a broad-brimmed hat, with three warts upon her face. He did not know her name, but had seen her before at the door. Neighbours who were present at once suggested that this must have been either the witch of Stapenhill, Elizabeth Wright, or her daughter, Alse (Alice) Gooderidge.[1] The boy admitted that unseemly words had passed between him and the old woman.

---

[1] The contemporary pamphlet is entitled *The most wonderfull and true storie of a certaine Witch named Alse Gooderige* (London, 1597). Its author seems to have been one Jesse Bee, of Burton.

As fits continued, early in April Alice Gooderidge was summoned to the house. Thomas Darling immediately had another fit ; but she declared that she did not know him. When someone in the room urged him to scratch her, he did so, on both face and hands. According to the superstition, a familiar should have appeared, to suck the witch's blood ; but nothing of the kind occurred. Nevertheless, two days later both Alice and her mother were arrested and examined before a justice of the peace, to whom all Alice would allow at present was that she had met a boy in the wood, and that, taking him to be " Sherat's boy," who had once broken her basket of eggs, she had used words to him for which she was sorry if they had caused any harm.

Four days after a further examination was held at Toone's house, the local justice of the peace being assisted by the presence of Sir Humphry Ferrers, an important man in the neighbourhood. A regular witch-trial was developing. All Alice's family were involved, her mother, her husband, and her son. The two women were searched for marks. The mother had a thing like a cow's udder behind her right shoulder. On the daughter's stomach was a hole " fresh and bloody," which she said had been caused by a knife when she slipped down a ladder. A surgeon thought it seemed to show evidence of having been sucked by a familiar.

Apart from the charge of bewitching Thomas Darling, there was another of the bewitchment of a cow belonging to one Michael. The cow, said Michael, after its seizure had broken all fastenings put upon it, and had made its escape to Alice Gooderidge's house, scraping at the door and the window to be let in. The story is now not quite clear. But one of the women agreed to cure the cow, if she might have a penny to bestow upon her god. Then, going to Michael's house, she knelt before the cow, crossed its forehead with a stick, and prayed to her god—since when the cow had continued well.

Alice Gooderidge was committed to Derby gaol for trial at the assizes. As is usual, examinations in gaol made her more communicative. She ultimately gave her story in connected form, beginning with the meeting with the

boy in the wood, when he called her the witch of Stapenhill. " Every boy doth call me witch," she had answered,
" but did I ever make thy a— to itch ? " She stooped to the
ground, and the Devil appeared to her, like a little red and
white dog. (Later she said that this familiar had been given
to her by mother.) To this she said, " Minny, seeing
that every boy calleth me witch, therefore go thy ways
and torment this boy in every part of his body at thine
own pleasure."

The dog had followed the boy to Burton, and when
she met it again the same evening told her that it had
fulfilled her request. Since then it had been with her divers
times, in gaol and out, and " continually he scratcheth at
my head, and scrapeth in the straw."

She had been brought from Derby to Burton Hall,
perhaps for further questioning by Sir Humphry Ferrers ;
and she was again confronted by her alleged victim, who
went off into *thirty-seven* fits ! She did not now deny that
she had caused them. " He will not mend except you seek
for help," she said. " You may have help enough."
Then, as she would have spoken further, something
stopped her throat, and she could only utter, " Come out,
thou foul serpent ! "

Such was the early part of the story ; all, it is to be noted,
before the arrival in Burton of Darrell the exorcist.

Alice Gooderidge was duly tried and condemned, and,
says the pamphlet on the case, she should have been
executed, except that her spirit killed her in the prison.
Miss Margaret Murray, who does not overlook the support
which this affair gives to her theory of the Dianic cult,
suggests that what really happened is that the condemned
woman was strangled by one of her witch-associates. It
is certainly easier, however, to suppose that she had some
throat-trouble, which choked her at Burton Hall and caused
her death at Derby.

Thomas Darling, not having been helped by Alice
Gooderidge, still awaited cure ; and his family sent for
Darrell, who was able to claim that he " dispossessed "
him—though what others alleged afterwards we shall
hear in due course. This did not apparently leave Thomas
an estimable character, for after he had gone up to Merton

College, Oxford, he was in 1603 found guilty of a libel upon the Vice-Chancellor of the University, for which the Star Chamber sentenced him to be whipt and to lose his ears. It looks as if Doctor Dee's butler had a not very reputable cousin.

Nicholas Starkie, however, had occasion to be grateful to the butler for the introduction of Darrell to his household, since, by what may perhaps be looked on as a faith-cure he succeeded in ending the victims' possession.

Darrell arrived at Cleworth in the company of another minister, George More, from Calke, near Ashby-de-la-Zouch; whence it comes that we have two parallel accounts of the cure. It is amusing to note that in each of the accounts the author attempts to give more credit to himself than to his partner; Darrell rather ignoring More's part in the proceedings, while More, whose story is the fuller, claims for himself the chief share where the children are concerned.

The two ministers came to the house on March 16th, and were received by Nicholas Starkie, who told them that John had now been well for a fortnight, Anne for several days, and the other girls had begun to mend since the hanging of Hartley. After the receipt of Darrell's letter saying that he was coming, however, the younger girls had been heard talking together in this strain : " Thou naughty lad, thou makest us sick, for thou knowest the preachers will come shortly." The sickness was genuine, and they said that their " lads " (familiars) would not let them eat or drink, nor suffer them to speak, except among themselves or to the lads.

In spite of Starkie's account of general improvement in the victims' health, the ministers " suspected greatly Satan's lurking in them " ; and their opinion was soon confirmed. When Starkie's wards were introduced, Margaret Hardman immediately had a fit, rearing backward in a chair, with her body stretched out and as stiff as iron. The other two immediately followed her example, and for a quarter of an hour they all lay senseless. Then they stood up, and one of them asked—" jocondly," writes Darrell—" Do they think they could hang the Divel ? I wis no ; they might hang Edmund, but they could not

THE TRISKELION

A charm against the Evil Eye, from a relief at Palermo

TWO ABYSSINIAN MAGIC CHARMS

hang the Divel. No marvel though the rope brake, for they were two, Edmund and the Divel ! "

Then they began to rail and revile, and to strike out with their hands and feet, until removed to an upper room. Nor did they cease from speaking and doing much evil from 2 p.m. on the first day till 6 p.m. on the second, " when it pleased God to deliver them and the rest."

The ministers' advice to Starkie was that there should be a course of fasting and prayer ; and it was agreed that they should be joined by Mr. Dickoms or Dickons, the minister at Starkie's parish church in Leigh. Before his arrival all the sufferers were gathered together, including Margaret Byrom and Jane Ashton. The latter had not been troublesome until March 16th, but upon Darrell's and More's appearance she showed strange symptoms. She was swollen, as with child ; and coupling this with a statement of Darrell's about Hartley's " kisses before, with a promise of marriage," we might suppose that it was not a matter of demoniacal possession with her, but something much more simple. But she also struck out and howled.

The children, however, engaged most attention. Starkie held John, Mrs. Starkie Anne, in their arms, while the three wards lay on beds, and Darrell began to exhort them all. The two little Starkies presently " cryed out mightily, with such outrageous roaring and belling [sic] that they could not of a long time be restrained." John was especially tormented. The three girls on the beds mocked Darrell's words with laughter, cries of " Bible-babble ! Bible-babble ! He will never have done prating. Prittle-prattle ! " and " sundry also filthy scurrilous speeches."

Darrell and More were much discouraged, but when Dickoms came, and divers honest neighbours also, they continued with prayers and exhortations until nearly midnight. By that time the afflicted had fallen into a great calm. (Perhaps some of them had gone to sleep, but we are not told so.) At seven the next morning the performance recommenced, in the large parlour of Cleworth, into which couches and pallets had been brought ; and for eight hours the ministers carried on in turn.

Dickoms delivered the first exhortation or sermon, in the midst of which Margaret Hardman was heard to say :

" I must be gone—whither shall I go ?—I will not die."
More was approaching the end of his sermon at 3 p.m.,
when the same girl exclaimed : " I cannot tarry, I am too
hot, let me go ! " Then all broke out " roaring and
belling," and it was with difficulty that they could be
restrained.

The ministers judged Satan to be ready to depart. In
More's words, " there was such struggling and striving
between us and those seven devils, crying out so loud with
such violence and extention of voice, labouring who
should be loudest, till our voices were spent and no
strength almost left in us."

This astounding drama of exorcism by prayer was at
length approaching its end. Jane Ashton, the strongest
and now the worst of the afflicted, was led aside by
Darrell and Dickoms to a large window in the parlour,
away from the rest, while More remained with the other
six, who had fallen from their pallets and were all lying
stretched out by the fireplace. Suddenly they began to
rise, Margaret Byrom recovering first. She had been full
of pain and vomiting blood, lying for half an hour as if
dead. Now she " started up most joyfully magnifying
God, with such a cheerful countenance and voice that we
all rejoiced with her." Next John Starkie, after gushing
with blood from mouth and nose, and seeming to be dead,
also started up and praised God " in most cheerful and
comfortable manner." The four girls followed in turn.

So says Darrell. More claims that Darrell, standing by
the window with Jane Ashton, neither saw nor heard of
the deliverance of the six until they were all perfectly
restored, leaping, and dancing, and praising God, while
the onlookers testified their joy by shouting and clapping
of hands, so that the whole house was filled with the
sound thereof.

The servant-maid still resisted treatment, and it was not
till 1 p.m. the next day that she was dispossessed. Even
then it was not a perfect cure. " A good space after,"
according to Darrell, " she, leaving Master Starkie's
house, went and dwelt in a place of ignorance and among
papists, and became popish herself, as I have heard, for
which opportunities and advantage the Devill watching

and no doubt compassing, he then reconquered her and now dwelleth there, whose last estate . . . shall be worse than their first."

More adds the information that Jane, when she left the Starkies, went to dwell with a papist uncle in the furthest part of Lancashire, and " there resorted unto her certain Seminarie priests, by whose conjurations and magical enchantments (as it is reported) the evil spirit was brought into her again, since which time she hath been exceedingly tormented, and so still continueth."

The Puritan ministers professed no doubt as to the close connection between popery and witchcraft !¹

So ends the remarkable Cleworth dispossession story. What is known of the two exorcists' careers after the affair is of some interest in so far as it may affect the credibility of anything that they wrote about the subject ; but it may be dismissed briefly. In November, 1597, Darrell was invited to Nottingham to dispossess an apprentice named William Somers. This he appeared to do success-fully ; and when Somers was re-possessed it only added to Darrell's fame, for he was able to cast out the evil spirit again, making him a notable figure in Nottingham. A ballad of the day refers to the affair thus :

> But when that M[aster] Darrell came
> The Devil was vexed with the same :
> His limbs he rack't, he rent and tore,
> Far worser than he did before.

Emboldened by his success, particularly among the " wives " of Nottingham, Darrell suggested as a subject for exorcism one Mary Cooper, a married sister of Somers. But opposition had now risen up against him, and tales

---

¹ However, Samuel Harsnett, the future Archbishop of York, who was decidedly not a Puritan, is equally positive. " Jane," he writes, " is since fallen into the hands of certaine Seminarie priests, and hath been carried by them up and down that country to sundry recusants' houses (as certain idle men were wont to carry puppets) and by her cunning counterfeiting of certain fits and staying of herself by the secret directions of the said priests, she hath gotten God knows what ; they by such lewdness have won great credit, but Her Majesty's subjects have in the mean time been shamefully abused " (*Discovery of the fraudulent practises of John Darrel*).

began to get about that his practices with Somers were a fraud. The matter came to the ears of the Archbishop of Canterbury, who appointed a commission of enquiry. Witnesses were examined at Nottingham, where feeling ran very high. "The pulpits," we are told, "rang of nothing but devils and witches; wherewith men, women, and children were so affrighted as many of them durst not stir in the night, nor so much as a servant almost go into his master's cellar about his business without company."[1] By the credulous every sick person was thought to be possessed.

But now Somers turned against the exorcist, saying that his possession, dispossession, re-possession, and ultimate cure were all a pretence. For the benefit of the mayor and aldermen of Nottingham he showed how he had acted all his former fits, and revealed how he had received his instructions from Darrell.

The next step was the transference of the matter to a special ecclesiastical court at Lambeth, where sat the Archbishop of Canterbury, assisted by the Bishop of London, the Lords Chief Justice of Her Majesty's Bench and the Common Pleas, etc. Present also was Samuel Harsnett, at this time chaplain to the Bishop of London and prebendary at St. Paul's. After hearing the confessions from the witnesses at Nottingham the court, in May, 1599, condemned Darrell as an impostor; and with George More (who, says Harsnett, took upon himself to justify Darrell, and otherwise greatly misbehaved himself) was deposed from the ministry and committed to prison in the Gatehouse. Here they seem to have remained a year.

The Church had exerted her authority; but controversy was by no means killed by the degradation of the two ministers. Darrell's friends, in particular, were very angry, and are said even to have threatened the Bishop of London with action on the part of " great persons " on his behalf. Dr. Bancroft, however, had a stalwart supporter in his chaplain, who, stirred to protest by an account of the Cleworth affair by Dickoms, the minister at Leigh, brought out in the year of the trial his book *A Discovery of the fraudulent practises of John Darrel, Bacheler of Arts.* No

---

[1] S. Harsnett, *Discovery of the fraudulent practises*, etc.

author's name appears on the title-page, but the " Epistle to the Reader " is signed S. H., and no doubt the authorship was well known. Harsnett's attack is very vigorous, and he fairly establishes that in all his cures of possessed people, except in Lancashire, what was done between Darrell and the alleged sufferers was " merely counterfeited."

Harsnett deals with each case—Katherine Wright, Thomas Darling, William Somers, Mary Cooper—and, leaving the Cleworth affair out, charges Darrell with having been a suborner of evidence concerning his power over evil spirits. In the matter of Thomas Darling, he reproduces his confession to the court at Lambeth, of which the main sentences are as follows :

" I do voluntarily of myself confess that, whatsoever Maister Darrel did say about my supposed possession, or about prayer for my dispossession, or about my fits before or after my dispossession, I did all either of ignorance or to get myself a glory thereby. . . . As for all and singular, the fits mentioned in the book [by Jesse Bee] and the dialogues with Satan . . . as also all those supposed apparitions of a cat, a dragon, a bear, lightnings, thundering, a lamb, a dove, a woman, and so all the several visions and torments set down in the printed book, I confess they be all untruths, and no credit to be given to any of them."

Speaking of exorcists in general, Harsnett says that " they make choice of such boys or wenches as they think are fit for their purpose, whom they procure by many promises and allurements to keep their counsel and to be (as they term it) advised by them. . . . When they have any of these in hand, they do instruct them so perfectly as when they come to exorcise them they are in a manner secure, their scholars knowing as well what to do as their false masters themselves."

Darrell and More both wrote vindications of themselves, possibly begun while they were in the Gatehouse, which they published in 1600.[1] More designed his book partly as a reply to Harsnett's, adding after the title the words

---

[1] See p. 228, footnote. Darrell wrote, as well as his *True narrative*, a pamphlet called *A Detection of that Sinful, Shameful, Lying and Ridiculous Discours of Samuel Harsnett.*

" which also may serve as part of an Answere to a fayned
and false *Discoverie*, which speaketh very much evill, as
well of this as of the rest of those great and mightie workes
of God which be of the like excellent nature." It has been
noted that each of the ministers took the chief credit for
the Cleworth dispossessions to himself. More in so doing
made a pretext of wishing to clear Darrell's character from
charges brought against him. He was ready to take his
full share of responsibility for what happened at Cleworth,
although in his prefatory address " to the Christian
reader " he makes his complaint against " that *Discoverie*,
fraught with so many fraudulent accusations . . . specially
charging these seven persons to be all counterfaits, and that
M[aster] Darrell had taught them that deceitfull trade,
coupling mee equallie in that craftie juglinge, making us
bewitching mates and joynt companions, working together
in that cousinage."

There is no admission on the part of either Darrell or
More of fraud. But their careers in the Church were
ruined, and after their condemnation they disappeared
from view, except that we still find Darrell as a writer on
religious subjects in the early Seventeenth Century. Five
years after the Lambeth trial the Canons resulting from the
Hampton Court Conference were drawn up ; the 72nd
of which enjoined that no minister must without license
from his bishop attempt to cast out devils, " under pain
of the imputation of imposture or cozenage and deposition
from the ministry." Perhaps therefore it may be considered
that Darrell's and More's conduct was not entirely without
benefit to the Church.

Of all the people concerned in the Cleworth affair,
however, Edmund Hartley is the most provocative and
most puzzling. It would have been welcome to have had
an idea of his looks and his age ; but we have none. When
he makes his entrance upon the scene, it is as a travelling
conjurer. He disappears as a witch on the gallows. Apart
from the matter of witchcraft he might be taken to have
been a professional faith-healer ; and his first contact with
the young Starkies produced a good effect upon their
disordered nerves. Darrell's assertion that he used popish
charms and herbs—whatever a popish herb may be !—

need not be taken too seriously. He certainly acquired an
influence over the children. When the astonishing Mr.
Starkie set him up as a regular member of his household,
his influence increased, and extended itself not only to
the three young girls in Starkie's charge, but also to Mrs.
Starkie's kinswoman, who was thirty-three, and to the
servant-maid, who was thirty. With both these women he
was on terms which suggest that he was at least a philan-
derer. Then there is his magic practice with the circle in
Whalley parish, which told heavily against him at his
trial. It is said to have helped to disgust Starkie with
him. Yet Starkie, after getting Doctor Dee to administer
a sharp reproof to him, sent the children under his care to
Manchester on New Year's Day, 1597, and allowed him to
share in the merry-making that ended in such an extraordinary scene at Cleworth four days later, where first we
get the allusion to Hartley's kissing performances. Darrell,
it may be remarked, does not give the opinion that,
" whomsoever he kissed, on them he breathed the divell,"
as his own, but as that of the household at Cleworth.

A very difficult point is the nature of the " possession "
which afflicted the household. It began before Hartley's
arrival, though the first symptoms, in Anne and John
Starkie, might be looked on as some sort of nervous dis-
temper, to the origin of which we have no clue. After
Hartley's appearance the sufferers increase gradually to
seven ; and Hartley himself is several times mentioned as
being " tormented." Now all the early history of the
case, including the scenes in January, 1597, is long antecedent to Darrell's arrival at Cleworth, so that we cannot
accuse him of manufacturing the evidence here.[1] He no
doubt derived it from Nicholas Starkie and his wife.

Nor have we here an instance of malicious children
inventing tales out of mischief, as so notably at Salem.
The young Starkies and their companions were more than
reluctant to talk against " Edmund."

More gives one especially remarkable tale of the possession
of the girl Margaret Hardman, who in a trance lasting
three hours could talk of nothing but dress, in the spirit

[1] We have heard that Harsnett did not include the Lancashire
case among Darrell's " fraudulent practises."

of " the proud women of our times." Speaking to the devil or familiar at her side, she went on for what occupies two pages and a half of More's book. A sample may suffice.

" Come on, my lad," she said, " I will have a fine smock of silk, it shall be finer than thine. I will have a petticoat of silk, not of red, but of the best silk that is. . . . My lad, I will have a French fardingale ; I will have it low before and high behind, and broad on either side, that I may lay my arms upon it. . . . I will have my sleeves set out with wire, for sticks will break, and are not stiff enough. I will have my periwinkle so fine, finer than thine. I will have my cap of black velvet, with a feather in it, and my hairs shall be set with pearls," etc.

We can hardly imagine that More invented all this, though we may wonder how the long speech was recorded. At the end of it, the girl came to, exclaiming : " Jesus bless me ! "—the usual end to the others' trances also. She remembered nothing of what she had said.

Another point which More records is that some of the children, though they were unlearned and never went to school, " yet in their fits were able to answer in Latin questions propounded to them, so truly and readily as if they had soundly understood them." But we have heard in modern days of automatic writing in a foreign language by people not supposed to know that language. And there is the gift, if it is to be so esteemed, of " speaking with tongues," which Podmore in *Modern Spiritualism* compares with possession ; a still closer parallel. Podmore quotes the " Grandier possession case " of 1634–5, where there was an epidemic of ecstasy in an Ursuline convent, in which the inmates so spoke—resulting in the *curé*, Urbain Grandier, being burnt alive as a witch.[1] The phenomenon persists, or is alleged to persist, to very recent times.

[1] He quotes also the persecuted Cevennes peasants' case about beginning of the Eighteenth Century, where one infant of fourteen months spoke in French, not the natural language of its parents. I seem to remember, in Roman history, an infant who provided an omen (was it during the Carthaginian wars ?) by shouting " Victory ! " in the Forum. It is true that the language was Latin ; but this speaker had previously been really *infans*.

With regard to the two grown-up women at Cleworth,
we get fits similar to the children's, and a similar reluctance
to speak against Hartley, though complicated by the idea
of love-passages between them and him. We may surmise
that he was a person endowed with what Hollywood calls
" S. A." But, on the whole, what we have is a tale of
demoniacal possession, and of contagious hysteria, showing
most of the common features of such tales, yet more than
usually resistent to rational explanation. Only to the
demonic school of thought, clinging to the belief (respectable at any rate in its antiquity) in Satanic agency, is it
easy to explain. Darrell speaks scornfully of " Atheists
who think there are no devils." If, however, Hartley *was*
a servant of the Devil, what comes of that being's craft and
subtlety need cause no surprise.

Somehow, whatever skill in display the modern
exponents of the demonic school may have, this presenta-
tion of old wine in new bottles fails to make it attractive to
those who are not of the school. If the liquor in the jar
marked Faunus has lost its savour, can our palate be asked
to accept it as grateful ? Not when we suspect the trade-
mark.

It was natural for Hartley's judges to deal with him as
they dealt. They would no doubt have echoed the words
of the contemporary Henri Boguet, when he wrote to his
patron the Archbishop of Besançon : " If effect could be
given to my wish, the earth should immediately be cleared
of witches ; I would that they might all be united in one
single body, so that they might all be burned in one single
fire."

Yet one single rope did not suffice to hang Edmund
Hartley. We have heard the child's explanation of why
this was. Hartley himself merely confessed the truth of the
accusations against him, and died.

* * * * *

There is one other point to be noted in connection with
the dispossession of the bewitched at Cleworth, that all the
sufferers gave a description of what they " saw " as their
cure was being effected. Margaret Byrom, who was the
first to recover from her evil state, and who was also the

oldest, stated that her devil came out of her " in the likeness of a crow's head, round, which when it was out went and sat in a corner of the parlour, with darkness about it awhile, then went it out of the window with such a flash of lightning that all the parlour seemed to be on a light fire." It left with her a sort throat and " a most filthy smell, in so much that her meat was very unsavoury for a week after ! "

John Starkie said that " it went out like a man with a great bulch on his back, as big as a man ; very evil-favoured and ugly to behold."

The girls were not very original in their descriptions of their " lads." Anne Starkie's was " like a foul ugly man, with a white beard, and a great bulch on his breast, bigger than a man's head." Margaret Hardman's and Ellen Holland's were also black men. The little Elinor Hardman's, however, was " as an urchin or hedgehog, and crept, as she thought, out at a very little hole of the window."

The obstinate servant-maid, Jane Ashton, when she recovered on the day after the rest, saw her devil go out " in the likeness of a great breath [*sic*], ugly like a toad, and round like a ball."

Harsnett ridicules these visions, of which Master Dickoms seems to have been the first recorder, and is scornful of one of Margaret Byrom's unpleasant after-effect as a " popish stink." But if there was any outside inspiration it would have come from Puritan ministers. The malodorous association, moreover, is quite unsectarian.

PART IV
ODDMENTS

CHAPTER I

LADY WITCHES

FOR the most part, we have seen in the earlier pages of this book that the female witch is a person of low social status, very often an old, infirm woman, living partly by begging and partly by her reputation as a witch. Alice Nutter, who suffered death at Lancaster, is a rare exception ; and, as has been said, her fate was probably the result of nothing more than an inquisitive curiosity about the possibilities of sorcery. Among men the case is not the same. The he-witch is of a company far outnumbered by the she-witches. The wizard or warlock is on a higher plane. Often he is scientifically far in advance of his generation ; as we may suspect that Gilles de Laval, usually known as de Rais (or Retz) really was, though the Church made him out to be an inhuman, Devil-worshipping monster, and burnt him as such. The dangerous study of the occult, apart from mere charlatanry, attracted to it many men of exceptional intellect, while the proportion of women-students was small, and indeed became numerically negligible.

But it had not been always the case that only women of poor standing, and of little or no education, interested themselves in the forbidden subject. We may take now a few instances of the contrary, having to go back in one to the Fourteenth Century and in the others to the late Sixteenth. The one comes from Ireland, the others from Scotland. They all attained considerable notoriety, and doubtless, had the scene been England, would have attained much more. The Irish case, that of Dame Alice Kyteler, was rescued from oblivion by an ecclesiastical record of the trial and by the brief notice of the chronicler Holinshed ; the Scottish cases, occurring in a group, had an importance derived from the fact that involved in them was a plot against the man who afterwards became James I of England, so that they could not be ignored by the historians of the first of the Stuart kings in this country.

Alice Kyteler, whom Holinshed in his *Chronicles of Ireland* calls " the Lady Alice Kettle," came of a wealthy family in Kilkenny in the Thirteenth Century. Though there are references to the name in the history of the Pale, neither her parentage nor the date of her birth is established. She was a kinswoman, and may have been a daughter, of Robert le Kyteler, who did trade with Flanders. At the time of her trial she had been married thrice before, and had a fourth husband living. But for the trial, however, it is doubtful whether anything would be known of her, apart perhaps from her marriages.

By her first husband William Outlaw, or Utlagh, a rich banker and moneylender in Kilkenny, she had a son, also William Outlaw, who grew up to perpetuate the family. William senior was dead before 1302, in which year his widow married Adam le Blond. Then, in 1311, she became the wife of Richard de Valle, or Wall ; and finally, at some date unknown, Sir John le Poer. Two of her husbands had been widowers, with sons and daughters ; but she had no issue after William Outlaw. The fact of her affection for this son had considerable bearing upon the case, for she desired him to inherit her property, to which in his absence there would have been several other claimants.

There is nothing to show how the case started. Its record is preserved in a Latin manuscript in the Harleian collection,[1] edited for the Camden Society by Thomas Wright in 1843, under the title of *A Contemporary Narrative of the Proceedings against Dame Alice Kyteler, prosecuted for sorcery in* 1324. Though often quoted, this manuscript has never been translated, owing to the fact that its monkish author is much more interested in the treatment which befell the Bishop of Ossory, the prosecutor of Dame Alice, than in the lady herself, so that only six out of forty

---

[1] *Harl. Mss.* No. 641, which is subjoined to a continuation of the *Chronicle* of Martinus Polonus, attributed to a monk of Glastonbury who owned the volume in which it was contained.

pages in the Camden Society publication deal with her case. In reality the Bishop's wrongs are of very minor interest.

It may be gathered that an illness of Sir John le Poer had much to do with the definite formulation of a charge of sorcery against Dame Alice. The deaths of her three previous husbands were certainly unfortunate for her reputation, and there would not have been wanting people to suggest to Sir John that he was being poisoned by his wife. The distinction between poison and witchcraft was never clearly drawn ; as indeed it is not even in modern days, with this difference that alleged witchcraft tends to be reduced to actual poisoning.

When his suspicion had been aroused, Le Poer managed to get possession of his wife's keys ; and, according to Holinshed, the " rifeling the closet of the ladie " led to two discoveries, " a wafer of sacramentall bread, having the Divel's name stamped thereon instead of Jesus Christ," and " a pipe of oyntment wherewith she greased a staffe, upon which she ambled and gallopped through thicke and thin, when and in what manner she listed."

The evidence of witchcraft was sent to the Bishop of Ossory, Ricard de Ledrede, who had been a Franciscan friar in London before his consecration as bishop in 1318. Like the Pope who appointed him, John XXII, Ledrede was a bitter enemy of witches, and he at once instituted proceedings in his episcopal court, where he was assisted by John Darcy, Justiciar of Ireland, and others.

Not only Dame Alice was cited to appear. The existence was alleged of a whole pestiferous society of witches in the Kilkenny neighbourhood ; and an endeavour was made to round up as many as possible of its members.

Dame Alice, however, was the principal as well as the first object of attack. With regard to the poisoning charge, her former husbands' sons and daughters noisily besieged the Bishop with complaints that their fathers had been her victims. As to her general practice of sorcery, it was sought to prove that she had nightly conference with an evil spirit named *Robinus* (or *Robertus*) *Artis Filius*, Robin Artisson or Son of Art, to whom she used to sacrifice, on the highway, " nine red cocks and nine peacocks' eies "

(Holinshed). He was stated to appear to her variously in the shape of a dog, a cat, or a black man ; and she was accused of having carnal intercourse with him.

Another charge was of raking all the filth of the Kilkenny streets to the door of her son William Outlaw's house, with the incantation :

> To the house of William my sonne
> Hie all the wealth of Kilkennie towne !

The leading associates with her in her witchcraft were stated to be a mother and daughter, Petronilla and Basilia de Meath ; but the exact number of the accused does not appear. Miss Margaret Murray (*The Witch-Cult in Western Europe*, p. 285) gives thirteen names, including the mysterious Robin ; but she is anxious to establish the existence of a regular coven, for which thirteen is the proper number. (There were evidently more than thirteen, though this can, of course, be accounted for by supposing that there were a number of covens.) Conviction was secured, and the prisoners confessed their guilt.

Dame Alice was subjected to a fine and forced to abjure her heresy, though in her confession she had admitted all the charges and rather gloried in her guilt, attributing all her wealth to the evil spirit. Petronilla de Meath and possibly one other woman were condemned to be burnt. Petronilla, who was six times whipt in public, had endeavoured to shield herself by pleading that she was only a pupil of Dame Alice ; but before going to the stake she implicated William Outlaw in the witchcrafts. The Bishop of Ossory thereupon had him arrested and kept in custody for nine weeks, till through the intervention of Arnold le Poer, seneschal of Kilkenny, whom he is said to have bribed, he was set at liberty ; but not before an abjuration of heresy in church and a new profession of Christian faith. That he had considerable influence himself is shown by the fact that, as soon as he was free, he took revenge by having the Bishop imprisoned for three months—to the great indignation of the author of the Harleian manuscript.

Meanwhile, however, Dame Alice appears to have relapsed. She was cited to come before the Dean of St. Patrick's in Dublin. She obeyed and, on asking for a

DÉPART POUR LE SABAT

Gravé d'après le Tableau Original de D. Teniers du Cabinet de Monsieur le Comte de Vence

à Paris chez l'Auteur rue S'. Jacque au Temple du Goût

THE DEPARTURE FOR THE SABBAT

From an engraving by Aliamet, after the painting by Teniers

THE WITCHES

From the etching by Goya

day's grace to prepare her answer, was granted it on what was thought sufficient bail. On the advice of her son and other friends—" certaine of the nobilitie," says Holinshed—she escaped to England, and it could never be understood what became of her. Basilia, too, more lucky than her mother, disappeared with her.

The manuscript account ends by stating that " of the other heretics and sorcerers of the pestiferous society of *Robinus Artis Filius*, some were publicly burnt ; others, revealing their crimes, after abjuring their heresy were branded in front and behind with the Cross ; others were solemnly whipt through the township and the market-place ; others exiled outside the township and diocese ; others, escaping from the jurisdiction of the Church, were publicly excommunicated, and others, fleeing in fear and lying hid, have not yet been found. And so that most foul nest by the authority of Holy Church, the Lord helping by His special grace, was dissipated and destroyed."

The only person—if person is the right word—that did not appear in the whole of the proceedings is *Robinus Artis Filius*. The question remains who or what this was. To those living at the period it was the Devil. Even to some modern writers it was at least an evil spirit. To Miss Murray it is a human being, the Chief of the Coven, to whom he was generally known as their " Devil." Robin is one of the commonest names in this association ; but what are we to make of " Son of Art " ? It does not seem to have been remarked on that Art is no rare name in Irish history from early times[1] and that Robin, son of Art, is not therefore a very out-of-the-way appellation for an actual man, and especially for a man of mystery. That he (presuming that there *was* a man) kept away from the hands of the Bishop Ossory is most natural.

Whether we should go on from accepting a real Robin, son of Art, to accepting also a *societas pestifera* organised under him, with Dame Alice Kyteler as a woman official, mistress-witch, or " maiden," as in later times we find such called, is a difficult problem to solve. From what we hear

[1] I have no Gaelic ; but an Irish dictionary gives under " Art " the meanings " warrior, champion ; god ; (as adjective) noble, great ; and a personal name.

of the confessions, which is vague, and, like all confessions
in witchcraft trials, suspect, we might be tempted to make
the second acceptance. It is at least the easiest way out
of the difficulty.

It is extremely unlikely, however, probably impossible,
that we shall ever have any fresh light upon the subject.

The Scottish case is even more interesting than the Irish ;
for it has a political aspect, which is absent from nearly all
other affairs of sorcery, and it also helps to explain the great
hatred that James VI of Scotland and I of England bore
against witches. In it a plot is undoubtedly revealed to
compass the death of James and of his bride, Anne of
Denmark. The evidence is clearer than is usual, and,
though it includes much of the common fantastic accusations, presents some definite charges of criminal conspiracy.
From the point of view of the organisation of witches into
a society, it is the most important of all cases of the kind in
the British Isles.

The affair came to light at the end of the year 1590,
when a certain schoolmaster of Saltpans, Lothian, named
John Fian or Feane, *alias* Cunningham, was arraigned at
Edinburgh on December 26th, being accused of both
witchcraft and high treason. With regard to witchcraft,
it was proved to the satisfaction of the court that he had had
conference with the Devil ; and the charge of high treason
was linked up with this by its being shown, also to the
court's satisfaction, that he had sent a letter to a witch at
Leith, bidding her meet him and others at sea in five days'
time, for the purpose of raising winds when the King was
crossing to Denmark to fetch Anne ; that they had met at
sea, Satan being present and announcing to them : " Ye
shall sink the ship," which they thought they did[1] ; and
that he had again conferred with Satan, who promised to
raise a mist, whereby the King, on his return from
Denmark, should be cast ashore on the English coast.

Under torture Fian made a confession of his guilt, which
he signed in the presence of James himself. He was then
committed to a cell, where he acknowledged his most
ungodly life and his following the allurements of Satan,
by " conjuring, witchcraft, enchantment, sorcery and such

[1] There was actually a storm on James's voyage.

like," renounced the Devil and all his works, and vowed to lead the life of a Christian. The next day he stated that the Devil had appeared to him in the night, clad all in black, with a white wand in his hand, and had demanded of him whether he would continue his faithful service to him, according to his first oath. He had replied : " Avoid, Satan, avoid ! I have listened too much unto thee, and by the same thou hast undone me ; in respect whereof I utterly forsake thee." Thereupon, he continued, the Devil broke his white wand, and vanished from his sight.

All that day Fian seemed to show himself very penitent ; but the same night he found means of stealing the prison keys, and escaped to his home at Saltpans. But he was quickly pursued and captured. Brought before the King again, he now denied his previous confession, so that James, " perceiving his stubborn wilfulness, conceived and imagined that in the time of his absence he had entered into new conference and league with the Devil his master." A fresh torturing followed, with all the atrocious cruelty of which the Scottish law of the day was capable. But he could not now be induced to confess anything, " and would say nothing but this, that what he had done and said before was only done and said for fear of pains which he had endured."

Such was the account which Pitcairn gives from the contemporary *Newes from Scotland*.[1] Miss Murray, who devotes considerable space to the affair in her *Witch-Cult in Western Europe*, rejects the story of the stealing of the keys as absurd. She holds that Fian's confession (which disappeared from the Justiciary Records) may have implicated the head of the conspiracy, who either himself or through an emissary, contrived Fian's escape, and then met him after it at Saltpans, inducing him to retract his confession and endure all rather than give James ground on which to take action against higher people than him. So, she says, Fian, " like many a Christian martyr, atoned for the first betrayal by steadfast courage through cruel torment even to death."

[1] I only occasionally, here and elsewhere in this chapter, retain the Scottish spelling, and I have even substituted words where the original would be otherwise unintelligible to most modern readers.

The identity of the head of the conspiracy, whatever clue Fian's vanished confession may have given to it, was not plain until another of the accused had revealed it. Before the end of January, 1591, Fian was taken to Castle Hill, Edinburgh, and there was strangled at the stake before his body was burnt.

The second of the accused persons was Alice Sampson, whom *The Historie of King James the Sext* describes a " grace wyff, *alias* callit the wise wyff of Keith," and Bishop Spotswood in his *History of the Church and State of Scotland* as " a woman not of the base and ignorant sort of Witches, but matron-like, grave and settled in her answers, which were all to some purpose." She clearly had some practice as a midwife, and equally clearly was a professed witch, who was consulted by people of high degree.

The charges of witchcraft against her were exceedingly numerous, including many of a very trivial character. For instance, she had foreknowledge of " diseasit persounes " whether they would live or not ; she prophesied that So-and-so was " bot ane deid man " (and he died) ; and very many she healed of their sickness by her devilish arts. Another accusation was that " she, having done pleasure to the goodwife of Galashiels, for the which she did not satisfy her so soon as the said Agnes desired, therefore said to the goodwife that she should repent it, and within a few hours thereafter the said goodwife took a wodnes [madness], and her tongue shot out of her head and swelled like a pot ; wherefore she sent to her the thing that she desired and prayed her to come to her ; and she bade the servant go away home, for the goodwife was well."

More serious was the charge of personal dealings with the Devil ; and here she was convicted on her own admission. The first time she began to serve the Devil, she said, was after the death of her husband. Satan had appeared to her in the likeness of a man, and commanded her to acknowledge him as her master and to renounce Christ. To this she agreed, being moved by poverty and by his promises that she and her bairns should be made rich, while she should have power of revenge on her enemies. The Devil then appointed time and place for their meeting by night ; and, in sign that she was become his servant, he marked her on the right knee. But, she said, she believed this mark to have been a hurt received by her from one of her bairns lying in bed with her, which did not heal for half a year.

She also admitted to having a familiar spirit. When asked what she called this, she said " Holla, Master " ; for so he had told her to do.

She spoke of a quarrel with the Devil, at a convention between Cousland and Carberry, where she was present with a woman named Agnes Stratton and the Witch of Carberry. Here she complained against her master, saying she had never gotten good of him, and would renounce him. But she did not renounce him ; he promising her that nothing should go against her.

Still more circumstantial accounts of meetings with the Devil occur elsewhere, either in the records of the trial or in Sir James Melville's *Memoirs*, where they are probably taken from Alice Sampson's confession. In that confession she says that the Devil at North Berwick kirk attended the coming of the witches, in the habit of a man, and having made his ungodly exhortation, inveighing greatly against the King, received their oaths for good and true service to himself. When asked why he bore such hatred to the King, he replied that the King was the greatest enemy he had in the world.

Again, among the charges upon which conviction were secured was one of " sailing, with certain her complices, out of North Berwick in a boat like a chimney (the Devil passing before them like a rick of hay) to a ship called *The Grace of God*, in the which she entered, and the Devil caused her drink wine, and gave her other good cheer ; and at her being there she saw not the mariners, neither saw they her ; and when they came away the Devil raised an evil wind, he being under the ship, and caused the ship perish."

And now we get an actual mention of the name of the man supposed to be at the head of the conspiracy. Agnes Sampson, in the company of nine other witches, had been summoned to meet by night near Prestonpans, where the Devil was again present in their midst. There a body of wax, shapen and made by her and wrapt in a linen cloth, was first delivered to the Devil. He handed it back to her, and she to her next " marrow," and so every one handed it on in turn, saying : " This is King James the Sext, ordonit to be consumed at the instance of a noble man Francis Erle Bodowell."

This is the cat out of the bag ; Francis Stewart, Earl of Bothwell, sister's son and successor to the notorious Black Bothwell, and through his father, Lord John Stewart (a natural son of James V, but legitimised by the Pope), a claimant to the Scottish throne, should James VI die without an heir.

We have therefore the motive of the conspiracy, to accomplish King James's death and to raise Bothwell to the throne in his stead.

There are, however, further ramifications of the affair, as shown by two more of the charges upon which Alice Sampson was convicted. These run as follows :

" That when homeliness was contracted betwixt her and Barbara Napier . . . the said Barbara lamented unto her that a man called Archie had done her great wrong, and asked her counsel how to be avenged of him. Her answer was that she should make the help she could. And after puttioune [? conference] betwixt them the said Agnes prepared a bonny small picture of yellow wax, which she enchanted and conjured under the name of Archie, in the east end of the dowcatt of Craigmillar, in the Devil's name, and gave power to the said picture that, as it should melt away before the fire, so should that man whose picture it was consume and pine away till he were utterly consumed ; and she delivered the said picture unto the said Barbara, who said unto her, ' Take good tent that no thing be wrought to stay the purpose.'

" That she enchanted by her sorcery a little ring, with a stone in it, to the said Barbara Napier ; which ring she received from the said Barbara that she might allure Dame Jean Lyon's heart, then Lady Angus, to love and favour her ; which ring she sent again with her daughter, within ten days thereafter, to the said Barbara, to be used to the effect aforesaid."

Leaving Barbara Napier aside for the moment, we may conclude Alice Sampson's story. She confessed her guilt,

and indeed is said to have convinced King James of the
reality of her power as a witch by telling to his private
ear the exact words which had passed between him and
Anne of Denmark on the night of their wedding. She did
not save herself by this demonstration, for she was condemned for both witchcraft and high treason. The sentence
upon her was that she should be taken to the Castle of
Edinburgh and there bound to a stake and " wirreit "
(strangled) until she was dead, and thereafter her body
to be burnt to ashes ; and all her movable goods were to
be escheated to the King.

Agnes Sampson, like John Fian, had been tortured before
confession, but not to the same atrocious extent as the
unhappy schoolmaster. But then she had not like him
withdrawn her confession ; and she had given Bothwell's
name, though she had not escaped her doom by the revelation. Her extensive practice of sorcery weighed too heavily
against her.

It is perhaps worthy of note that she resembled many
other witches in the use, despite her admitted " Devil-
worship," of Christian charms. A specimen furnished by
herself begins—and we keep here the original spelling :

> All kindis of illis that ewir may be,
> In Cristis name I conjure ye ;
> I conjure ye, baith mair and les,
> With all ye vertewis of ye Mess.

As is usual, the language is older than the Reformation.
Barbara Napier's trial followed on May 8th. Her connection with Agnes Sampson in the matter already mentioned was not the most serious accusation against her,
though it showed her alliance with a witch. Nevertheless
it was this charge that nearly proved fatal to her.

The story has to be disentangled. Barbara Napier, as
she is called, was the wife of Archibald Douglas, an Edinburgh burgess. But the " Archie " of whom Agnes
Sampson had prepared the bonny small picture of yellow
wax was not Douglas, but Archibald, eighth Earl of Angus,
who had died in 1588, witchcraft being the suspected cause
of death. His wife, who had been Lady Jean Lyon,
daughter of the ninth Earl of Glamis, was not apparently

accused of having anything to do with it ; but Barbara had
been a friend of hers and, as we see, was anxious to become
so again. For her dealings in the matter of " Archie's "
picture she was convicted, and sentenced to the same fate as
Agnes Sampson. As, however, she was declared to be
" with barne " (bairn), the execution was delayed until
after the birth, and then, " nobody insisting in the persute
of her," she was released.

The other accusation was that Barbara Napier gave her
presence to " a most devilish and treasonable convention "
of witches held on Lammas Eve at a place between Mussel-
burgh and Prestonpans after King James had returned
from Denmark. There was a large gathering ; nine
" principals," who included Barbara herself, Agnes Sampson, John Fian, and Euphemia McCalyan, thirty " in-
feriors," and the Devil himself.[1] The last, in the likeness
of a black man, thought it meet to do the turn for which
they were convened (or, in other words, as chairman,
suggested that they should proceed to the business of the
meeting), whereon Agnes Sampson proposed the destruction of His Highness (the King), saying to the Devil :
" We have a turn to do, and we would fain be at it if we
could, and therefore help us to it." The Devil answered
that he would do what he could, but it would be long,
because it would be thwarted. He promised them a picture
of wax, but also ordered them to hang, roast, and " drop "
a toad, and lay the drops of the toad with other poisons
in His Highness's way, so that they might fall on his head
or body, " that another might have rule in his place and
the government might to the Devil."

Agnes Sampson was appointed to make the picture and
give it to the Devil to be enchanted ; and he promised to
give it to Barbara Napier and Effie McCalyan at the next
meeting, to be roasted. Another of the principals, Margaret

[1] Thirty-nine persons, *i.e.* three covens, Miss Murray points out,
in addition to the Devil. It may be remarked that at the next meeting,
at North Berwick kirk, the number present, seven score, is not a
multiple of thirteen.

Among the witches, it seems, the dames Napier and McCalyan
went by the names of "Naip" and "Cane," taken by some to have
been their witch-names. They are at least a sign of the sisterhood in
the association.

Thomson, was appointed to drop the toad, and yet another to seek some of His Highness's linen clothes to do the turn with.

Truly astonishing this business-meeting of witches must be acknowledged to be. Equally astonishing is the next meeting, at the kirk of North Berwick on All Hallows Eve, when seven score of witches assembled. Barbara Napier " dancit endlang the kirkyard," while some one played a trump, John Fian, muffled, led the ring, and Agnes Sampson and the rest all followed Barbara. The Devil then started up in the pulpit, like a mickle black man, with a black book in his hand, and called on them all, desiring them to be good servants to him and he would be a good master to them. But one Robert Grierson cried out, so that all might hear, that the promised picture of His Highness had not been given to them. " Have the turn done," he insisted.

The men only mentioned His Highness's name in Latin ; but the women called for the picture in plain terms. The Devil answered that it was not ready yet ; it should be gotten the next meeting, which should be held for that cause the sooner. " You promised twice and beguiled us," complained Grierson ; and four " honest-like " women were very earnest and instant to have it. Finally the Devil promised Barbara Napier and Effie McCalyan to give them the picture, " and that right soon."

Can this be all pure fantasy ? one is inclined to ask. Well, it is evidence given in a court of law, and was taken seriously as something upon which to decide whether a prisoner was to go to the stake or not. Barbara Napier, for some reason, was not sent thither, but was acquitted. Yet it is difficult to see why she escaped while others suffered. It is true that the assessors, or jury, were prosecuted the following month, as though they had given a false verdict ; but they too were acquitted.

The last trial recorded in connection with the North Berwick affair was the most sensational ; not because of fresh light being thrown, for there was none, but because of the higher social standing of the prisoner and the extra severity of her sentence. Euphemia McCalyan (whose name appears with many curious spellings) was daughter to Thomas McCalyan, Lord Cliftonhall, one of the senators of the Court of Justice. Her association with the witches was as fully proved as any others' in the series of trials. There is a strange point referring to her in one of the items against Agnes Sampson. The latter was convicted of having put " mwildis, or powder made of men's joints and members in Natoun kirk[1]," under Euphame McCalyan's bed ten days before her birth ; " which mwildis she conjured with her prayers, for staying and slaking of grinding the time of her birth." We do not know how the lady was able to explain a child-birth, since we do not hear of her being married.

Euphemia McCalyan was tried on June 9th, 1591, and charged with attendance at witch-coventicles at North Berwick and elsewhere, enquiring about the King's picture, helping to raise storms to wreck the royal ship, etc. Her dealings with the convicted and executed Alice Sampson allowed her no hope of acquittal. She was condemned to death, and on June 25th was taken to the Castle Hill and there burnt " quick," that is to say alive, without the favour allowed to John Fian and Agnes Sampson of being strangled before her body was given to the flames.

There is no reason stated why she should have been given this extra agony in death ; a barbarism usual in France, but not the rule in Scotland, where the burning of the witch's body after death was considered sufficient to prevent evil effects from its remaining upon earth. A scattering of the ashes followed, perhaps to prevent a chance of their being used in sorcery.

No records remain of the prosecution of other persons involved in the North Berwick conspiracy, though a fourth is said to have been executed in connection with it. Notably there is nothing about Bothwell himself. A supposed confession of guilt has disappeared. It is known that he was imprisoned but escaped, and that he did not obtain the King's pardon until two years later. He left Scotland, and retired to Naples, where he still had the reputation of a sorcerer. The end of his life found him in extreme want.

[1] One of the charges on which Alice Sampson was acquitted, by the way, was of passing to Natoun kirk with the Witch of Carberry, and " taking up the buriet people, junting (jointing) of them," to make enchanted powder for witchcraft.

De Lancre in his *L'Incredulité et Mescreance du Sortilege*, in 1622, quotes a letter which Bothwell in exile wrote to one who applied to him for guidance. " You Christians," said Bothwell, " are treacherous and obstinate. When you have any strong desire, you depart from your master and have recourse to me ; but when your desire is accomplished, you turn your back on me as on an enemy, and you go back to your God, who being benign and merciful pardons you and receives you willingly. But make me a promise, written and signed by your own hand, that you voluntarily renounce Christ and your baptism and promise me that you will adhere and be with me to the day of judgement, and after that you will rejoice yourself with me to suffer eternal pains ; and I will accomplish your desire."

Bothwell is still therefore the impenitent anti-Christian, such as might well have played the part of " Devil " among the North Berwick witches. What seems at first extraordinary is that he and his followers should so have mixed up his pretensions to the throne of Scotland with witchcraft. Yet it is not, perhaps, so extraordinary after all. Almost everybody at the time believed in the efficacy of witchcraft. Indeed, it was almost impious to deny it. The further assumption that witchcraft proceeded from the Devil was almost equally a matter of faith to Christians. Those who were not Christians were willing to accept the theory, interpreting " Devil," however, their own way. They allowed the use of the term to designate the human person whom they acknowledged as their master. That is to say, they used that term when forced to give evidence before their Christian accusers. What is not known is by what name they called him among themselves. That would necessarily be a secret.

It is true that very many names, other than Devil or Master, were given as those of the heads or the witches. But if the real names, they could only be revealed by renegades or by those who had not the fortitude to resist the tortures inflicted on them. John Fian was strong enough to suffer martyrdom rather than betray the name ; Alice Sampson was not.

We have strayed from the subject with which this

chapter began, the presence in witch-circles of women of
superior standing to the ordinary mass of the poor, unedu-
cated, and ignorant creatures who professed or were
accused of witchcraft. But, in truth, the two women who
have principally emerged as examples of the higher-class
female witch are rather shadowy apart from their witch-
hood. Neither Alice Kyteler nor Euphemia McCalyan
might ever have been heard of had she not had the imputation of sorcery brought against her.

Of a different kind was an English lady who, a considerable time after the North Berwick affair, was branded by
her enemies with the reputation of a witch. This was the
mother of the famous Sarah, Duchess of Marlborough ;
and it is more than likely that had the latter not had so
many bitter enemies her mother would never have been
branded with the name of witch.

Frances Thornhurst was born about 1625, the daughter
of Sir Gifford Thornhurst. At the age of eighteen she
married Richard Jennings ; and one of their children was
Sarah.

Among the Duchess's most venomous opponents was
Mary de la Rivière Manley, journalist, novelist, and
everything else with her pen. In *The New Atlantis* this
lady, not content with calling Mrs. Jennings " all that was
scandalous, impious, and detestable," also represents her,
under the name of Damareta, as a witch or sorceress, a
pupil of Timias—who is drawn from Sir Kenelm Digby,
writer, alchemist, and astrologer, and, according to John
Evelyn, " errant mountebank." Timias, says Mrs. Manley,
was left by his father a large inheritance and a little ambition. He was averse from the marriage-state, yet a votary
to Venus. Near St. Albans he was a neighbour to the newly
married Mrs. Jennings, and " her youth and gaiety put
her among the number of those who had the good fortune
to please him." He was, according to the same lady, the
real father of Sarah Jennings.

Further, Sir Kenelm taught his occult art to Mrs.
Jennings. It is certain that she had at one time a reputation for witchcraft, as the Tories in Queen Anne's reign
delighted to remember. The author, in 1712, of *The Story
of the St. Albans Ghost, or the Apparition of Mother Haggy*—

who is probably Swift, at his worst—makes her his Mother Haggy, " who held a correspondence with Old Nick, as was confirmed afterwards beyond the possibility of doubt." At the birth of her daughter Haggite (Sarah), the old woman's high-crowned hat leapt into the cradle, and, being caught by the nurse as it fell, was transformed into a coronet. " Such," cried Mother Haggy, " will be the fortune of my daughter and her fall."

We cannot, however, take these accusations of witchcraft very seriously. Political rancour welcomed all terms of abuse.

CHAPTER II

HOODOO

THOSE who may have had the fortune to come across a recent book, published originally in the United States of America, under the uninformative title of *Mules and Men*, will probably have made acquaintance with a subject of which they had but the slightest idea before—unless, of course, either travel in some parts of the world had brought it to their notice, or curiosity had led them to a literary investigation of it. To most people, it is safe to say, "Voodoo" (as it is commonly, but, it seems, incorrectly called) is but a vague name for a mysterious and repellent superstition, understood still to prevail among the negro races of mankind.

But Miss (or Mrs.) Zora Neale Hurston, the author of *Mules and Men*, is one of the blood of those whose very wide submission to the superstition she writes about ; and she returned from a college education to study it in the home of her childhood in Florida, and then in the still more enlightening neighbourhood of New Orleans. Largely her book is a collection of negro folk-lore tales and some songs, with their music. The most valuable part, however, is the section she devotes to her actual researches into the cult, in the course of which she did not fear to pass through the necessary and awe-inspiring initiations.

Readers of Lafcadio Hearn's earlier writings will be aware that New Orleans was in his time a city where strange negro beliefs flourished, and that he brought himself under suspicion, even into trouble, by his free venturing into the society of the coloured people. But they might not be prepared to hear that nowadays, when education of the descendants of forced immigrants from Africa into America has produced so many brilliant men and women, the old beliefs still flourish, hardly weakened in their power. Yet—

" New Orleans is now and ever has been the hoodoo capital of America. Great names in rites that vie with those of Haiti . . . keep alive the powers of Africa. Hoodoo is burning with a flame in America, with all the intensity of a suppressed religion. It has its thousands of secret adherents. It adapts itself, like Christianity, to its locale, reclaiming some of its borrowed characteristics to itself. Such as fire-worship, as signified in the Christian Church by the altar and the candles. And the belief in the power of water to sanctify, as in baptism."

We need not stay to dispute whether Miss Hurston's interpretation of the use of the altar and candles is correct. The most interesting part, to us, of what she writes is the similarity between hoodoo practices and those of the European witches we have been studying in the preceding pages. A few points may be noticed.

There is the same kind of necessarily secret society, with its sub-divisions under individual heads, answering roughly to the covens of witchcraft. (There appears no trace of the number thirteen, however.) The head man or woman is a " two-headed doctor " or " conjure-man," who is all· powerful among his immediate followers, and is equivalent to the " devil " of the witches' confessions—not the traditional Devil himself of Christianity, it is needless to insist.

The doctor is not always a man. One of the most celebrated was Marie Leveau, who was born at New Orleans in 1827, on the maternal side the descendant of two generations of female hoodoo doctors, while her father was a Frenchman of the name of Glapion. She lived in the Vieux Carré of New Orleans, the old French quarter, home of the illustrious chess-master, Paul Morphy. Indeed, she had two houses, being possessed somehow of ample means ; one in St. Anne Street, and the other in Bayou St. John's. At the latter she died, after having been carried with it and in it by a great storm into Lake Pontchartain and rescued, only to pass away the same night.

Miss Hurston could not meet Marie Leveau, who was dead long before she came to New Orleans. But she found her memory ever fresh, and people who claimed to be her disciples, and even kindred. A great tradition was her rattlesnake, which had dwelt by the altar at Bayou St. John's, and still survived as a skin. This may well be taken as an equivalent of the animal familiar in English witchcraft, though it would be rash to say that it was definitely such. The champion of ophiolatry might tell us that it was nothing of the kind. Nor had we better identify it with a totem. Merely, in a region that is so obscure and murk, may we venture to suggest analogies.

The main occupation of the hoodoo man or woman is harmful, though "bad work," that is the procuring of death, is only very occasional. The calling in of the expert to counteract evil wrought or attempted by others is very frequent. Miss Hurston notes a point whereon we are entitled to draw a close parallel with European witchcraft. It concerns the cases of people who believe that they have been "poisoned" and seek magical remedy. The actual instances of poisoning, she says, are rare. When the conjure-man tells the patient that he or she is poisoned, it usually means that "something has been put down" for him or her ; and then ordinary doctor's medicine is of no avail. "The hoodoo man does effect a cure where the physician fails, because he had faith working with him." This is precisely Boguet's view, except that he must put Satan at the back of the sorcerer,[1] and the hoodooist seems too polite to suggest that.

The "putting down of something" plays a large part in hoodoo. A favourite place is the doorstep of the person whom it is desired to harm. The grudge may be against a household, in which case "war-water" is potent to create strife in its midst ; oil of tar being put in a glass vessel, which is broken on the doorstep. The intended victims well know what it means when they see the broken glass— it is a case for the conjure-man. There is also the peace-making "water Notre-Dame," made from white rose oil, where we may suppose that there is no breaking of glass.

The charms are generally derived from plants, of which hoodoo has a large pharmacopeia, including "John the Conqueror," which must be gathered before September

[1] See p. 23, n. 1.

21st, and "Wonder-of-the-World root," which must be addressed with ceremony before being gathered, or the collector will suffer harm. There are supply-houses at which these herbs—from their names we should hardly call them simples—can be procured. But the "swamper," a root-and-conjure doctor, collects his own from the swamps; just as we hear of English witches going swamping.

A specially evil ingredient in the charms, used in nearly all of the ceremonies designed to produce death, is "goofer dust," dirt (as Americans call it) from a graveyard. Taken from sinners' graves, it is most potent. But some hoodoo doctors declare that there is great danger in its use, for the spirit of the dead may turn unruly and go on killing for the pleasure of killing. They take their goofer dust, therefore, only from infants' graves.

The use of candles in the enchantments is general; black for evil and death, white for peace, red for victory, pink for love, etc. Blue candles are ambiguous, since they sometimes are connected with success and sometimes with death.

A curious love-incantation, with an accompaniment of candles, is mentioned. A negress desiring to win a man's love is told by the hoodoo doctor to perform various rites, including the sticking of sixty pins into each of six red candles, while singing: "Tumba Walla, Bumba Walla, bring Gabe Staggers back to me!"

Miss Hurston assuredly suffered, to acquire her knowledge of hoodoo. She describes herself in one initiation as spending days in succession, lying naked on a snake-skin in a dark room, and fasting entirely except for a little water, until at last she awoke in a state of exaltation. This was not the end, however. To obtain the "crown of power," she had to be painted from right shoulder to left hip with the zigzag symbol of lightning in red and yellow paint, to give of blood from her finger to be drunk, to swallow blessed oil and eat spinach-cakes, and then proceed, in a decrepit motor-car, to the swamps, where a black sheep was sacrificed.

More horrible is the story of how she had once to throw a black cat, alive, into a cauldron of boiling water, and afterwards to take one of its bones in her mouth for some ceremony. Really, this is worse than the tale of Mary Smith's " great cat " on p. 37 above. Cats have indeed every reason to curse the name of witchcraft for the tortures that their poor slim bodies have undergone through it.[1]

After initiation the hoodoo doctor seems to be in a position to make a reasonably good income. Perhaps this was the source of Marie Leveau's wealth. The charge for " bad work " is about two hundred dollars. Naturally one asks, Suppose the victim does not die? But in Louisiana the victims are even more susceptible to suggestion than other victims of whom we have been reading. If there were a Holy Inquisition nowadays in New Orleans it would surely have a harvest among death-dealing witches, with evidence of deaths inexplicable upon ordinary grounds.

Even without the Inquisition, however, it may be enquired how hoodoo manages to " get away with it," how the avowed evildoers escape any penalty, even if it be only for pretending to exercise sorcery. Well, hoodoo is all underground. It is the suppressed religion, with its thousands of secret adherents, as Miss Hurston says. And it affects only the people of African descent, most of whom, through fear or otherwise, make no open complaint against it. We hardly ever hear of a case where a " white " person is alleged to have suffered from hoodoo. Therefore it is treated as negligible. Yet *Mules and Men* shows that hoodoo has an unholy grip on the Louisiana negro.

In a recent book on Brazil, *His Majesty the Emperor*, Mr. Ernest Hambloch comments on the prevalence of this same cult in that country, spreading its influence apparently beyond people of African descent. " Throughout all strata of Brazilian society," he writes, " there is a marked infiltration of voodoo superstitions, which a politically ambitious section of Roman Catholicism in Brazil found

[1] I have often wondered what, if any, reason for gratitude cat-kind has towards mankind for our now very long acquaintance and cohabitation. There are, I know, barbarians who look on cats as parasitic animals, and declare that they are destitute of affection. Well, possibly some people get the cats they deserve—but these barbarians do not deserve any cat, save (morally) that of the nine tails !

and still finds it more convenient to exploit for its own purposes than to eradicate. . . . The simple piety of the Christian chants became impregnated with the superstitious credulity of heathen incantations."

Those who have imagined that " voodoo " is limited to Africa itself and to Haiti, " where Black rules White," were very mistaken, it seems. This variety of witchcraft has a far wider field.

An effort has been made to connect the very word voodoo with a Fifteenth Century French term for one manifestation of witchcraft, *vauderie* (otherwise *vaulderie*), the practices of the Vaudois or Waldenses, spreading from the canton of Vaud originally. But in spite of the notoriety that the Vaudois obtained, it is more than doubtful whether there is any real connection between the two terms. Similarity of names is a deceptive trap, into which the Euhemerists are only too ready to fall.

Though there may be no connection between the names, however, there are many similarities between the sorcery of which the Vaudois were accused and the practices of the hoodooists.

In *The Times* of July 27th last there was a letter from Sir Hesketh Bell on the survival of anti-witchcraft legislation in the West Indies. In 1904, he pointed out, the " Obeah Act " was passed in the Leeward Islands, which provided that every person practising Obeah should be liable to be imprisoned for not exceeding twelve months, and, if a male, to whipping. The measure appears to have failed in its object, says the writer, for in 1932 the Obeah Act was amended, a term of imprisonment up to five years being made the penalty for practising Obeah. The Attorney-General of the Colony claimed that this was necessary, to combat the increase of superstition in the islands.

Obeah is another name for hoodoo or voodoo, and its instruments are the same, as for instance the use of herbs and drugs. If the Obeah-man, remarks Sir Hesketh Bell, restricted himself to the sale of charms and love-philtres, the harm would not be great. " But there is much reason to fear that many of the mysterious deaths which take place in the West Indies, and especially certain strange forms of lunacy, may be due to the effects of vegetable and other poisons, the knowledge of which was transplanted . . . by the slaves who came from West Africa."

With the harm done by mere suggestion the former Governor of the Leeward Islands does not deal.

CHAPTER III

NOT WITCHES

SOME students of witchcraft, struck by certain resemblances in the ways of the great beggar fraternities of the Middle Ages and those of the witches, have been tempted to link the two organisations up in a manner that is not warranted by such knowledge as we have of the two groups. It is true that there are resemblances ; but the practices are, so to speak, " in the common domain " of human behaviour, and the fact that they are found among the beggars and the witches is no justification for an attempt to establish a connection.

The main source of information concerning the beggars in England is a curious pamphlet by one Thomas Harman, *A Caveat for Common Cursetors*,[1] first published in 1566, and thrice republished in seven years, showing that it had a certain popularity. The author dedicates it to the Countess of Shrewsbury, though why she should be interested in what he calls " all these rowsey, ragged rabblement of rakehelles " we do not know. Harman took great pains to investigate his subject, and seems to have had the opportunity of examining a large number of the people of whom he wrote, giving even a list of names of notorious contemporary beggars and some quaint pictures.

There is no hint of magic in their proceedings. They live by begging, as of course many of the lowlier witches did ; by terrorism, again a weapon of the witches, but the terrorism of the beggars is physical, not moral ; and by sheer thieving, often brigandage. They are highly organised, with the two chief ranks among them " the rufflar " and " the upright man." It is the latter who appears to have attracted the attention of those who wish to find an

---

[1] *A Caveat or Warening for Common Cursetors, vulgarely called Vagabones*, by Thomas Harman Esquier (London, 1566). In the British Museum Library the catalogue-number of this is 188 b. 15.

analogy between cursetors and witches ; notably Mr.
G. B. Harrison, in the introduction to his *Trial of the
Lancaster Witches*. Both rufflars and upright men had great
authority over lesser beggars, and were in the habit of
appropriating or exacting a large share of their earnings.
The ruffler was a sort of swell mobsman ; but the upright
man was, if occasionally " swell " (Harman gives an illustration of the upright man Nicolas Blunt, in good attire
of the day), a man who traded much on women. He had
certain privileges, which were like those of the " Devils "
of witchcraft.

The beggars' jargon, " peddelers' French or canting," as
Harman calls it, had its special terms for women. Mort
was just woman ; a gentry mort, for example, a gentlewoman. The upright man's mort was more particularly
known as a doxy ; a term that has survived. But he was
not confined to one doxy. " The Doxes," says Harman,
" are broken and spoyled of their maydenhead by the
upright man, and then they have their name of doxes and
not before." Previously they are dells ; " a Dell is a young
wench, able for generation, but not yet broken by the
upright man."

There is really nothing of witchcraft in the promiscuity
of the upright man and the doxies. Nor is there anything
in the dances and feasts occasionally indulged in by the
beggars, when they had obtained anything to make merry
upon, to suggest the Sabbat. The beggars were not a
religious crowd. They might be, in the Elizabethan
phrase, " not idle neither well occupied " ; but their ill
occupations did not include, as far as we can tell, any
attention to the worship of strange gods.

To put the matter shortly, witches were often beggars ;
but the beggar-fraternity was not one of witches. It is the
expression " upright man " that has led students astray.
In the trial of a French witch, Silvain Nevillon, at Orleans,
in 1614,[1] a devil at the Sabbat is called *l'Orthon*. We cannot
infer from this any ceremonial orthophallicism among the
beggars. In canting there was little or no classical
phraseology.

[1] Miss Murray reproduces the full account in *Witch-Cult in Western
Europe*, pp. 246-8.

EPILOGUE

IT is difficult for its author to resist the conclusion that this book is ending where it ought to begin. But clearly there is no last word on witchcraft ; a *monstrum horrendum, informe, ingens*. As a field for theories it is alluring. As an exercise in definition its name has attracted countless writers, ecclesiastical, legal, and other. The divergences between the theories and the definitions are enormous. We have glanced at many theories, without finding any entirely satisfactory. As to definitions, we may now add one, not because it is the best, but because it does, with due allowance made for its framer's inevitable lack of foresight of the changes that were to come in the scientific conception of the universe, attempt to avoid the extreme and extravagant dogmatism of his own days. Reginald Scot writes :

"Witchcraft is in truth a cousening art, wherein the name of God is abused, prophaned, and blasphemed, and his power attributed to a vile creature. In the estimate of the vulgar people, it is a supernaturall worke, contrived betweene a corporall old woman and a spirituall divell. The manner thereof is so secret, mysticall, and strange that to this daie there hath never been any credible witnes thereof. It is incomprehensible to the wise, learned, or faithfull ; a probable matter to children, fooles, melan-cholike persons, and papists."

Scot could not resist the hit in the last word ; nor could he help his attitude towards the "vile creature" as con-trasted with Almightiness. He is very sound, however, in his representation of the difficulty of the subject to the wise compared with the not-wise ; though perhaps exces-sive in his employment of the word "incomprehensible." Not comprehended, witchcraft was ; but not beyond the power of comprehension.

The difficulty of comprehension may be ascribed largely

to a failure to recognise that there are several strains in witchcraft ; or, to vary the metaphor, that witchcraft is a large river fed by a number of tributary streams, of different character, some (shall we say ?) very muddy and impure.

Yet we must not press the metaphor unduly. We cannot separate the tributary streams entirely from one another. They do not flow entirely distinct, from sources definitely to be identified to the point at which they merge in the main river. Perhaps we might liken them rather to trickles through a marsh ; and that a marsh almost defying him who would map it out. So the tracing of the *fontes et origines* of the composite witchcraft can only be tentative.

One constituent of the whole is generally agreed to be the fertility-cult, the notion of ability to influence the powers of nature to reproduce, whether it be men, beasts, or crops.

The fertility-cult involves " sympathetic magic," since there seemed apparently to that elusive person, primitive man, no other means of influencing nature. But sympathetic magic in itself might be regarded as a separate constituent of witchcraft, being employed for other ends than the promoting of fertility. It may be desired by it to work not good but harm, notably injury to an enemy. From this we get the " blasting " power of the witches, exhibited either in the procuring of death, in crippling, or in the stopping of generation—the antithesis of fertility-promotion.

With the procuring of death is involved the use of poison for that object, so that *venefica*, poisoner, became almost a synonym for *malefica*, evildoer, itself a synonym for *striga*, witch. The poison being derived mainly from plants, we are brought to the herbalist-witch, the " swamper," etc.

But herbs are serviceable for medicine as well as for poison ; and there we have the doctor witch (not the witch-doctor), who cures patients, either by the virtue of herbs or by the faith they have in the herbs—and in the doctor ; a magic that may truly be called " sympathetic."

Reverting to the fertility-cult, we find that not only the old Inquisitors, but even many modern theorists (some, however, not devoid of the desire to burn or hang witches !) insist on its sexual, licentious character. By this means we

are introduced to the worship of an old, pre-Christian god—
Priapus to Payne Knight, the Horned God to Miss
Murray—whom we may be content to call simply the
Agnostos Theos, though the Inquisitors had no doubt of his
identity with Satan, Lucifer, Beelzebub, or the Devil whom
they cherished under so many an *alias*.

Now, admitting the fertility-cult, we have no reason for
not allowing the evolution of a god-idea in connection with
it, or even its evolution up to the stage of the god of the
Sabbats, represented at them by a man, appearing either
in human or in animal shape, *i.e.* disguised with a mask
and trappings. But we have, on the other hand, no
ground for the notion that this god was a blasphemous
parody of a predecessor. He was ante- not anti-Christian.
The worship of him was grossly distorted when he was
identified with Satan, and particularly when it was represented that the worshipper addressed prayers to that
bogey. In Stearne's *Confirmation and Discovery of Witchcraft*
the confession of Rebecca Weste is quoted, to the effect that
her mother " prayed constantly (and, as the world thought,
very seriously), but she said it was to the Devil, using these
words ' Oh my God, my God,' meaning him and not the
LORD." Ann Weste may not have been a pleasant old
lady, but we cannot therefore deny her sincerity. And how
shall we deny it to those who went to the stake as to true
martyrdom, and " as gaily as to a festival of pleasure and
of public rejoicing " ?

The element of Devil-worship, the silly folly of " Satanism," is not to be regarded as a real part of witchcraft.
This is not to say that Gilles de Rais and the fifth Earl of
Bothwell may not have been conscious Satanists ; but as
such (or if such) they did not represent genuine witchcraft.
Concerning the modern Satanists, as studied, for instance,
so painfully in some of the works of Mr. Arthur Waite,
theirs is not true Goetia, which is not for self-conscious
Satanists.

The whole question of whether witchcraft is evil must,
therefore, be answered apart from any importation of the
Devil into the matter. But can it be answered at all ?
If we start stripping off what we may consider accretions
to its original form, we shall probably find critics who

exclaim, " Oh, but you can't strip off that ; it's certainly original ! " And yet is it not possible to conceive of the Idea laid up in Heaven, of which the shadow on earth is that thing known as witchcraft ? The element of mysticism in the art cannot be denied. The old hags, whom we have met in such profusion in preceding chapters, were, no doubt, the reverse of mystical. But Dr. John Dee was a mystic, if often a fool. He held, with his master, Cornelius Agrippa, that the practice of magic was one of the lawful ways to the divine knowledge. He did not like, indeed was extremely pained, to be called a witch. But witch he was, nevertheless, and an ornament to witchcraft.

We have said something about the fairy element in the craft ; not concerning the fairies of pretty fantasy or quaint fable, but those of tradition based on facts that have become attenuated until they can scarce be recognised as fact. It is not necessary to do more than repeat the suggestion, by whomsoever it was first made, that the idea of the connection between witches and the fairies was not a mere dream ; that the witches inherited their cult, and possibly even some of their blood, from a remote prehistoric race, the little dark people whom their conquerors had driven from their homes into the wilds, and then in superstitious dread called their Good Neighbours.

We shall do no more than mention two words that cannot be entirely omitted in any discussion of the origins of witchcraft ; animal-worship, and totemism. It would be rash, especially where totemism is concerned, to venture a foot upon ground so consecrated to the steps of the specialist. Besides, the shadow of Primitive Man is over it ; and that ghostliness it is not well to disturb.

*   *   *   *   *

In witchcraft and its history we have a truly curious blend of the mysterious, grotesque, obscene, cruel, pitiable, and venerable, the revolting and the fascinating. We cannot read of it without being forced to admit that " there is something in it," though what that something is no man can tell another so as to convince him.

That it is primitive stands out clearly ; so, too, that it is universal. That it is sempiternal—was, is now, and ever shall be—well, it is reasonable to conjecture from the past and the present as to the future, unless we are convinced by the babble about Progress, deducing a millennium that we certainly are not agreed in wanting.

It has the qualities, then, of a Catholic Church. A Catholic Church, it may be objected, of malignity. But how shall we say that in its essence it is malign? The blood of the witches, of those who died glorifying their faith, cries out against this.

What faith is his, who dieth for his faith?

INDEX